THE BATTLE FOR
SICILY'S SOUL

THE BATTLE FOR SICILY'S SOUL

THE RISE OF THE MAFIA AND THE FIGHT TO FREE SICILY FROM ITS EVIL TYRANNY

CLAUDINE CASSAR

First published in Malta by Alert Publishing 2022
© 2022 Claudine Cassar
www.claudinecassar.com

ISBN 978-9918-615-00-1 (paperback)
ISBN 978-9918-615-02-5 (.mobi ebook)
ISBN 978-9918-615-01-8 (.epub ebook)

For Andrew

*and in memory of the brave men and women who fought the Mafia
and lost their lives in the battle for Sicily's soul*

CONTENTS

Map of Sicily with Key Locations

Introduction 1

Section I
A Primordial Soup 5

Chapter 1
A History of Exploitation and Oppression.............................7

Chapter 2
The Genesis of Cosa Nostra 20

Section II
The Culture Heist... 55

Chapter 3
Mythology of Cosa Nostra... 57

Chapter 4
Sacred Symbols and Rituals 87

Chapter 5
The Social Priests vs Cosa Nostra 113

Chapter 6
The Fascists vs Cosa Nostra...119

Section IV
Picking up the pieces after World War II.......................................125

Chapter 7
The Winds of Change...127

Chapter 8
The Fight against the Communists..136

Chapter 9
The Resurgence of Cosa Nostra..153

Chapter 10
The End of the Entente Cordiale...161

Section V
The Palermo Renaissance...191

Chapter 11
The Tipping Point..193

Chapter 12
The Risorgimento..217

Chapter 13
The Holy See joins the Battle...230

Section VI
The Twenty-First Century..245

Chapter 14
The Swinging Pendulum...247

Bibliography 261

Acknowledgements 266

Notes 267

MAP OF SICILY WITH KEY LOCATIONS

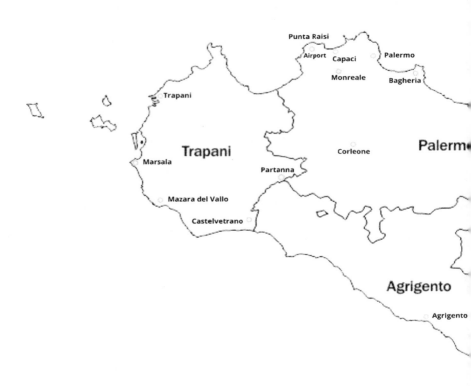

Messina

Milazzo

Messina

Enna

Catania

Catania

Caltanissetta

Siracusa

Syracuse

Ragusa

Ragusa

INTRODUCTION

The Italian Republic has been plagued by organised crime since its very inception, with the oldest and most powerful criminal societies originating in the southern part of the country. These are Cosa Nostra in Sicily, the 'Ndrangheta in Calabria and the Camorra in Naples. In the twentieth century new mafias came into being - the Stidda in Sicily, the Sacra Corona Unita in Brindisi, Lecce, and Taranto, and Società Foggiana in the Province of Foggia.

This book focuses on the Sicilian Mafia, which is the archetype of mafia organisations worldwide. It examines how social conditions, politics and international forces coalesced in Sicily during the nineteenth century to form a toxic primordial soup, out of which rose Cosa Nostra.

The Mafia, which was made up of a network of *cosche* (clans) controlling different territories on the island, appropriated Sicily's cultural norms and the sacred symbols and rituals of the Catholic Church, manipulating and corrupting them to suit its criminal purposes. In this way it created a façade of respectability and *convivenza* (co-existence) with the Sicilian people, camouflaging its true nature as a bloodthirsty and vicious criminal organisation, killing and maiming people for profit.

In the 1970s, the Corleone *cosca* (clan), led by Luciano Leggio, started manoeuvring to take over control of the Mafia and the highly lucrative narcotics trade. When Leggio was captured and imprisoned, he was replaced by his second-in-command, Totò Riina, also known as *la belva* (the beast). Riina was hell-bent on controlling Cosa Nostra, launching a vicious war on the other clans and massacring hundreds of *mafiosi* and their family members in what became known as the Great Mafia War. At the same time, he orchestrated the assassinations of journalists, police officers and other justice officials who had become an inconvenience. In the end, the Corleonesi succeeded in taking over control of Cosa Nostra, with Riina becoming the boss of bosses of the Sicilian Mafia.

What Totò Riina and his allies had not considered, however, was the backlash from the defeated *mafiosi* who feared for their lives and the lives of their loved ones. They had also not anticipated the reaction of the Sicilian public, the Catholic Church, or the Italian State, who could no longer ignore the ravages wrought on the island by mafia activity.

The massacre thus led to the breaking of *omertà* (the vow of silence) by various *pentiti* (repented *mafiosi* who turned state's evidence). The first high profile *mafioso* to defect was Tommaso Buscetta, who sat with Judge Giovanni Falcone for forty-five days, describing the inner workings of Cosa Nostra. Based on this information, and further testimony from the flood of *pentiti* that followed, a Maxi Trial commenced on the 10th of February 1986, indicting 475 *mafiosi*, of which 333 were found guilty and imprisoned.

The Maxi Trial and the subsequent high-profile assassinations of Magistrate Rosario Angelo Livatino in 1990, Judge Giovanni Falcone and his friend and colleague Judge Paolo Borsellino in 1992, and the mafia terrorist attacks on the Italian mainland along with the murder of Fr Pino Puglisi in 1993 outraged the Italian public and led to a massive crackdown by the authorities to eradicate Cosa Nostra. The Catholic Church was no longer able to sit on the fence, and finally the ecclesiastical authorities took a firm stand against the Mafia. This further weakened the criminal organisation, which had already been decimated because of the mafia war and the Maxi Trial.

This book looks at how Cosa Nostra manipulated Sicilian society and the Catholic Church for decades, disappearing into the background while hiding in plain sight. The roots of the Mafia in the island's religious superstition, bigotry and legends were so strong that it took over one hundred years and a massacre for the vows of secrecy to be broken, revealing the true face of the criminal association.

Civil society, the Italian State, and the Catholic Church are now engaged in a relentless and ongoing battle with the Mafia for Sicily's soul.

SECTION I

A PRIMORDIAL SOUP

"It is often said that all the conditions for the first production of a living organism are now present, which could ever have been present. But if (and oh what a big if) we could conceive in some warm little pond with all sorts of ammonia & phosphoric salts — light, heat, electricity present, that a protein compound was chemically formed, ready to undergo still more complex changes, at the present such matter would be instantly devoured, or absorbed, which would not have been the case before living creatures were formed..."
Charles Darwin, 1871

CHAPTER I
A HISTORY OF EXPLOITATION AND OPPRESSION

"*If by mafia they mean having such a strong sense of honour that it is sometimes taken to the extreme; if they mean being steadfastly intolerant of bullying and injustice, showing the generosity of spirit to stand up to the strong while supporting the weak; if they mean being so loyal to your friends that your loyalty is stronger than anything, even than death; if by mafia they mean feelings like these, even though they might sometimes be exaggerated, then what they are talking about are the distinguishing traits of the Sicilian soul, so I too am a mafioso and I am proud to be one.*"
Vittorio Emanuele Orlando, from a speech in 1925.[1]

The Sicilian Mafia is a centrally controlled criminal organisation with its own history, mythology, rituals, and laws, insidiously rooted in the culture and traditions of Sicily, which it has misappropriated and corrupted for its own ends. In fact, to truly understand the nature of Cosa Nostra, we cannot look solely at the criminal society itself, because it does not exist within a vacuum. One must also consider the history, economic realities and power hierarchies which moulded Sicilian culture, since only then can we appreciate how the Mafia was able to seize control while operating in the shadows.

This chapter gives a brief overview of the history of the island and the sequence of events that created a market niche which was subsequently seized by ruthless, entrepreneurially minded men who formed the genus of the social and criminal phenomenon that is the Sicilian Mafia.

It will also show how the harsh realities faced by generations of Sicilian peasants created mental frameworks of meaning that became embedded in the local culture, unconsciously and powerfully influencing the way the population of the island understood what was happening around them, as well as their long-enduring lack of a sense of agency when it came to countering the wave of violence and criminality unleashed by Cosa Nostra.

1.1 First Inhabitants and Colonisers

The first inhabitants of Sicily arrived more than ten thousand years ago, during megalithic times. Cave drawings in the Grotta dell'Addaura, near Palermo, have been dated by archaeologists to 7000 BCE. Over the following millennia various peoples made Sicily their home.

From 1500 to 800 BCE the Sicanians inhabited the centre of the island, while the Sicels (from whom the name Sicily originated) lived in the eastern part and the Elymians in the west. The three indigenous peoples co-existed in relative harmony with the Phoenicians, who had also settled in parts of the island.

In 800 BCE the Greeks occupied the eastern part of the island. While the Phoenicians were primarily interested in trade, the Greeks were focused on growing their empire. Over time, the Greeks subjugated the indigenous inhabitants of Sicily, with the process of colonisation gaining traction around 733 BCE. The Greeks turned Sicily into a bustling hub of trade and built beautiful temples and towns, with Syracuse, on Sicily's south-eastern coast, becoming the epicentre of the western world. However, their lust for war and obsession with conquest and riches led to them stripping the island bare. They felled entire forests to build ships for their military campaigns, not considering the impact this would have on the ecosystem of the island. Mudslides destroyed arable land and polluted the sea, destroying the livelihood of peasants and fishermen, who were catapulted from poverty into destitution.

In 264 BCE the Romans and Carthaginians became embroiled in the First Punic War, fighting for control of the island. After twenty-three years of battles on land and sea, the Romans finally defeated Carthage and in 241 BCE Sicily became the first foreign province of Rome. Once again, the colonisers bled the island dry. Large swathes of land were gifted to important and influential Romans, creating the first generation of absentee landlords who had no connection to the land they owned. They controlled their vast estates in Sicily from the comfort of Rome and prioritised the maximisation of yields, with no consideration given to sustainability. Sicily became the breadbasket of the Roman empire. The islanders were merely a source of slave labour for the estates, working their hands to the bone eking out a meagre living while the absentee landlords enriched themselves from the fruit of their hard labour.

As empires waxed and waned, Sicily changed hands many times – the Vandals, the Visigoths, the Byzantines and the Saracens, who arrived in 827 CE. For over two hundred years Sicily thrived under Arab rule. The emirs broke up the large estates established by the Romans and poured investment into the land. They built irrigation systems for the fields and modernised farming techniques. In addition, they introduced new crops such as citrus, pistachio, date palms, cotton, silk and sugar cane.

The oranges and lemons brought to Sicily by the Arabs would come to play an important part in the story of the Mafia centuries later.

1.2 The Normans and the Introduction of Feudalism

In 1071, after ten years of battles and military expeditions against the Emirate of Sicily, the Normans, descendants of the Vikings who had settled in northern France and founded the duchy of Normandy, succeeded in seizing control of part of the island. The first Norman Count of Sicily was Count Roger, who ruled from 1071 to 1101. He continued fighting the Saracens until they were fully defeated, and by 1090 he was lord of all of Sicily, with his male descendants ruling the island until 1194.

Count Roger I and his son, Count Roger II, were enlightened rulers under whose reign Sicily became a multi-ethnic melting pot, bringing together the very best intellectuals, philosophers, artists and craftsmen from all over the Mediterranean. Palermo became a cosmopolitan, pluralistic town where different peoples of different religions rubbed shoulders and co-existed harmoniously. There were Arabs with their mosques, Jews worshipping in synagogues, and Orthodox Greeks and Catholics praying in their respective churches. This created a breath-taking legacy of art and architecture which can still be enjoyed to this day. The most notable examples are the Norman Palace, the Palatine Chapel and Royal Palace in Palermo, and the Cathedral of Monreale.

Away from the city, however, it was a different story. The Normans introduced a feudal system, granting land as fiefs to noblemen in return for their allegiance and military support. The main reason for the decision to rule Sicily in this manner was that it was practically impossible for them to police the entire island, especially the remote and mountainous interior. By splitting it up into *stati* (states), they were able to delegate this responsibility to their vassals.

The feudal barons wielded total control over their fiefdoms, maintaining their own armies, laws, and taxation systems. The Norman rulers had effectively given up centralised control of Sicily in a bid to secure the loyalty of their barons and their military support in times of war. Just as in the case of the citrus fruit introduced by the Saracens, the feudal system instituted by the Normans was also an important development that created the social conditions and environment that enabled the emergence of the Mafia hundreds of years later.

In 1194, when Count Roger's bloodline died out, control of Sicily passed into the hands of the Hohenstaufens, a German dynasty that at the time ruled the Holy Roman Empire. The German kings were locked in a power struggle with the papacy, so Pope Clement IV formed an alliance with Charles of Anjou, the younger brother of King Louis IX of France, who invaded Naples and Sicily, ousting the Hohenstaufen King Manfred of Sicily. In return, the Pope made Charles the king of Naples and Sicily in 1266. The coming of the French heralded the beginning of a harsh occupation. On the 30th of March 1282, during evening Vespers, the Sicilians revolted against the French, ousting Charles of Anjou. This created an opportunity for King Peter III of Aragon, who was married to Constance, the daughter of King Manfred. He invaded the island and was proclaimed king at Palermo.

The Kingdom of Aragon, with its centre of power in Barcelona, consisted of most of the territory of what is nowadays Spain, and it controlled most of the islands and ports in the Mediterranean. Towards the end of the fifteenth century, King Ferdinand II of Aragon and his wife Queen Isabella I of Castile, founded the *Tribunal del Santo Oficio de la Inquisición* (Tribunal of the Holy Office of the Inquisition), commonly known as the Spanish Inquisition, in a move designed to impose *"un rey, una fé, una ley"* (one king, one faith, one law) throughout their empire.

The Spanish Inquisition first arrived in Sicily in 1487, with the purported mission of combatting heresy and defending the integrity of the Catholic faith. For over three hundred years, until it was abolished in 1782, the Inquisition was used to control the Sicilian nobility and terrorise everyone on the island, annihilating the open-minded multi-ethnic culture that had been encouraged and cultivated by the Normans. Anyone who had different ideas or tried to push for progress was seen as a threat, tried for heresy, and if found guilty, forced to participate in an *auto da fé* (act of faith), a procession through the streets of Palermo wearing penitential garments and holding a palm frond and a candle to make public amends and reconcile with the true Catholic faith. If the accused refused to repent, they were sentenced to death and burnt at the stake. It is important to highlight that those found guilty usually had their property confiscated and were stripped of any public office, so the proceedings were ripe for abuse and were sometimes used for financial gain or to silence political rivals or enemies.

The Spanish Inquisition killed freedom of thought and expression, enforced conformity and stifled social progress. It also created a culture of mistrust, both between Sicilians and those who ruled them, and between the islanders themselves, because nobody could be sure that their neighbour would not betray them in a bid to save themselves.

During these years of tyranny, rumours abounded of secret sects founded to fight against injustice. Tales of a confraternity of knights became popular legends passed down from generation to generation. These knights, called the *Beati Paoli,* were said to live in the tunnels and catacombs under Palermo and emerged at night in dark cloaks to execute those they judged corrupt. Historians agree there is a basis of truth to these folkloristic tales, and that such a sect did exist, although it is likely its members were more interested in settling their own scores and furthering their own interests than fighting for the poor.

This destruction of trust and the proliferation of myths about Sicilians taking justice into their own hands because their rulers were corrupt and unjust, were important contributions made by the Spanish towards the genesis of Cosa Nostra.

While all this was happening, other major forces were pushing for change on the island. Feudal barons struggled to find sufficient workers for their estates, while Palermo was overcrowded and full of beggars and petty criminals. Laws were introduced to encourage the creation of new villages on the feudal estates and people were persuaded to move from the towns and the coastal areas to these new settlements in the Sicilian interior. In addition to Sicilians, several nationalities of immigrants displaced by wars in foreign lands settled in these communities to work the land, along with people from countries such as Greece, imported by the barons who paid for their passage on the understanding they would work on their estates. The landlords also recruited small armies of strongmen, commonly known as *bravi*, to protect their properties and act as enforcers, keeping the peasants and workers in check.

A charter issued in 1520 by a feudal lord dictated the terms on which the settlers were allowed to move onto his lands.[2] The main stipulations of the contract were that the settlers were to build their own houses in the area designated by the feudal lord for the hamlet, and that an expanse of land was to be made available for them to cultivate and use for grazing. However, the settlers did not have any title to the land they lived on, cultivated, or used as pasture for their cattle, and they were to pay their landlord one tenth of their crop and an annual fixed fee for every head of cattle.

As the settlements grew and the workforce expanded, the balance of supply and demand shifted. Workers were no longer in short supply, so landlords started to change the terms in the charters in their favour. One of the most important changes was that instead of paying a tenth of their crop, the peasants had to pay a fixed ground rent. This was a much more advantageous proposition for the feudal lord, since it secured his income even in times when harvests failed, essentially passing the risk onto the peasant cultivating the land. It was also an important move because it tied the peasant to a plot in the estate, creating an incentive for him to invest in the land. By creating this tie between the peasant and the land, the landlord was effectively securing the future supply of labour on his estate. In addition to these arrangements, the landlords also converted more virgin land, distributing it between the peasants based on sharecropping contracts, creating a second source of income both for the peasants and for themselves.

A very important aspect of the feudal agreement was the grant to the peasants of *usi civici* (common use rights) on pasture and forest. This gave them the right to glean the fields after the harvest to gather any leftover grain or crops, collect wood and stones, and hunt and forage for wild fruit and herbs. They could also allow their cattle to roam and graze. The *usi civici* were very important to the peasants since when harvests were poor those rights were their main means of subsistence.

Most of the feudal barons had multiple estates which were sometimes geographically distant from each other. This made it impractical for them to manage, so in most cases they used a different system to monetise these properties. Instead of dealing with multiple small leaseholders and sharecroppers, they leased large tracts of land to one leaseholder, based on a contract called the *gabella* (from the Arabic word for tax). These leaseholders came to be known as *gabellotti*.

The different revenue streams created by these contractual arrangements enabled the feudal lords to accumulate considerable wealth, and as their coffers filled many barons built luxurious villas in Palermo, making the town their permanent base and breaking contact with their land and the people who worked for them. The absentee landlords wanted to secure their income while committing the least amount of time and effort possible to their estates, so they gradually converted more of their estates to the *gabella* contract, creating a passive income stream that supported their idle life of luxury in the town.

This was the final ingredient required for the toxic primordial soup. All the elements required for the emergence of Cosa Nostra were in place – what was needed was the spark to set genesis in motion.

1.3 The Bourbons and the Shift to Latifundia

In 1716, after the War of the Spanish Succession, the Crown of Aragon was abolished and its territory was combined with Castile to form the Kingdom of Spain. The kingdom was ruled by the Bourbon dynasty, which was descended from the Capetian Dynasty, also known as the Royal House of France.

Prince Charles of Bourbon, heir to the Spanish throne, claimed the kingdoms of Sicily and Naples in 1734, after they had been lost during the years of unrest in Spain. By now the great majority of the large estates had been put in the hand of *gabellotti*, who split the estates into smaller plots and sublet them to peasants, subsequently collecting rent and produce from them. This system benefitted both the nobles, who only had to deal with one tenant, and the *gabellotti*, who were able to pass on their costs to their sub-tenants. The peasants at the end of the chain, on the other hand, bore all the risk and were left with very little after settling all their dues.

In 1799 Napoleon conquered Naples and King Ferdinand I requested the help of the English, who had just defeated the French in the Battle of the Nile. Lord Nelson went to the Bourbon King's aid, taking Ferdinand and his family to safety in Sicily, where British troops were stationed with a force of more than 15,000 men. Within months Nelson recaptured Naples and Ferdinand was restored to the throne. However, in 1806, the Napoleonic army returned, and Ferdinand was once again obliged to escape to Sicily. The French took control of Naples and Napoleon declared it an independent kingdom, appointing his brother Joseph Bonaparte as king. Two years later Joseph was transferred to Spain and replaced with Napoleon's brother-in-law, Joachim Murat. Murat abolished feudalism and modernised the legal system, making him very popular with the great majority of his subjects.

Unlike Naples, Sicily did not fall to the French because it was protected by the British. At this time the island had a population of circa 1.6

million, two thirds of whom lived on feudal estates under the control of the nobility and their agents. In the 800 years that had passed since the feudal system had been introduced on the island, the barons had grown in power and succeeded in converting the temporary nature of the estates they had been granted to permanent ownership that could be passed on from generation to generation based on agnatic primogeniture, meaning that the entire estate was inherited by the firstborn son. The system of *quasi-allod* (almost full ownership) meant that they could not sell any of the land without the permission of the sovereign. It also meant that the land could not be seized by creditors.

In 1812 Lord William Bentinck, the commander of the British forces in Sicily, pressured King Ferdinand to draw up a constitution for the island that ended the feudal system and created a two-chamber Sicilian parliament in Palermo that was independent of the one in Naples. The new constitution abolished the system of *quasi-allod*. Feudal landlords obtained full and unencumbered ownership of their land (full *allod*) in exchange for agreeing that the Bourbon sovereign would now have sole control over the administration of law, justice and taxation on the island. The main results of the reform were that feudal landlords became allodium landowners, free to sell their lands, and that Sicilians who had so far never owned land but who had accumulated wealth could now purchase tracts of land and become landowners. In the process the feudal rights previously enjoyed by peasants, namely the *usi civici* of gleaning and pasturage, were lost.

When Napoleon was defeated in 1815, King Ferdinand was restored to the throne of the kingdom, which was now known as the Two Sicilies. Seeing as he no longer required the protection of the British, he rescinded the new constitution and repealed all parliamentary reforms. That said, he pressed ahead with the reform of the feudal system, aiming to centralise control of the island under his rule. A few years later, in 1824, the Bourbons passed a law empowering creditors to seize lands in payment for debts. The ramifications of this law were considerable and far-reaching. Over the previous century feudal landlords had never had to worry about losing their estates because of the rules of *quasi-allod*, so some of them had borrowed considerable sums of money from *gabellotti* or other tradesmen. Now these creditors were able to seize their land in payment for their debts.

The land reform laws passed by the Bourbons also dictated that peasants on the *latifundia* should be given one fifth of the *feudi* they had worked on, in compensation for the loss of their common use rights. However, this did not translate into reality. The new landowning class and the nobility took over all the land available and the peasants ended up totally disenfranchised, not having the means or the knowledge required to fight for what was theirs by right.

Unfortunately, the Bourbon rulers had made a critical mistake. They seized control of Sicily on paper, but not in practice. They did not have the manpower and bureaucratic setup required to properly govern the island, so although landowners were supposedly subject to the rules and laws set in Naples, they now held all the cards and were determined to prevent any form of land transfer to the peasants.

The loss of common rights pushed peasants into destitution, forcing some of them to resort to banditry to survive. Their main targets were, of course, the wealthy, who became increasingly concerned about the resulting surge in criminality and violence. The Bourbons were in no position to enforce the laws and administer justice in Sicily, so it became necessary for the rich to engage security to protect themselves. The Bourbon administration thus lost the opportunity to take and retain control of the *"monopoly on the use of violence."* The result was the creation of *"entrepreneurs in violence,"* establishing the genus of the mafia.[3]

1.4 The Protection Racket

Earlier we spoke about the *bravi* –thugs employed by the feudal barons to protect their *feudi* and their property and families in Palermo. When feudalism ended and the large estates broke up, several *bravi*, who were well-versed in the tactics of intimidation and coercion, lost their employment and began looking for other ways to use their specialised skillset and experience. Emerging as they did into a total lacuna of control by the State, they were able to take over the region around Palermo in a vicious stranglehold.

"Indeed, if on the one hand those who were previously in almost exclusive control of the use of violence now needed it less, on the other hand, now freed from all constraints and privileges, the industry of violence gained an independent existence and organisation. This had the effect of multiplying and infinitely diversifying the aims for which violence was committed. In fact, now it is no longer just about crimes committed to favour the designs of this or the other grandee. The evildoers, while always ready to serve others, also work for themselves, and their industry is a new source of far more crimes than those that the bravi of the ancient barons and the brigands of the past could commit in their own interest. Moreover, the organisation of violence has become more democratic and is now accessible to many small interests that did not before have access to it before. So the suppression of the armed forces and baronial privileges in general has made violence an institution accessible to almost each and every class." Leopoldo Franchettti, 1876[4]

These entrepreneurs in violence were the first generation of *mafiosi*, offering their services to those able and willing to pay for them. This included several cartels and unions who needed strongmen to collect money and enforce the rules of membership. Members of these societies paid an annual membership fee, a part of which was used to pay the *mafioso* who was overseeing the administration of the societies. *La Societa dei Mulini*, for example, was made up of millers who colluded to sustain the price of flour. Their appointed *mafioso* made sure that all the millers honoured the terms of the agreement, cutting production when it was required to reduce supply and protect the price, and contributing financially to make good on the losses of those whose turn it was to under-produce. *La Societa della Posa*, on the other hand, was a union of cart drivers and apprentice millers who paid the *mafioso* (often in kind, in the form of spying or enforcing for the mafia boss) to ensure that they would be prioritised by members of *La Societa dei Mulini* when it came to the recruitment of workers.[5] The bartering of services between *mafiosi* and unions of this type is one of the reasons for the confusion that often arises when trying to differentiate between *mafiosi* and their clients.[6]

This could explain why so many different societies and professions were accused of being *mafiosi* – the Fratellanza (brotherhood) of Favara, for example, was made up of sulphur miners, but they are also often described as a mafia *cosca*. The truth could lie somewhere in the intersection between the mafia, the sulphur mine owners, and the union of sulphur miners, in the same way as it did in the case of the Mulini and the Posa in the example described above. A *mafioso* would be offering protection to the sulphur mine owners against payment, while also protecting the interests of the workers in return for services rendered. Thus, Fratellanza members would indeed be enforcing or intimidating people who were not under the *mafioso's* protection, but they would not in fact necessarily be *mafiosi*.

To become trusted protection agents, *mafiosi* needed to ensure that they commanded *rispetto* (respect), which translated into the fear they were able to invoke in others. Obviously, this was a competitive business and only the most ruthless and wily were able to stay on top, in what was effectively a dog-eat-dog business model. To maintain their position they often had to resort to violence, but their modus operandi also included spying on people and understanding what their weak points were, so they could coerce or threaten them effectively should the situation require it. So *mafiosi* needed armies of spies and informants to make sure they knew exactly what was happening in their territory. It makes sense to surmise that they had the same kind of arrangement described above with many of the other societies that thrived in Sicily at the time, with protection services sometimes being repaid in kind. Tradesmen such as barbers could listen to their customers' gossip. Coachmen could keep tabs on the houses of ill repute frequented by well-to-do citizens. Market brokers could report on which orchards had the best harvests. This theory is borne out by the fact that the prefect of Trapani, in 1874, wrote a report where he described "*la maffia*" as consisting of "*market middlemen, barbers, shepherds, bakers, millers, pasta makers, coachmen, and carters.*"

Each gang, or *cosca*, was led by a *capomafia* who presented himself as an arbiter of truth and justice, often stepping in to make the peace and settle scores between clients, while simultaneously manoeuvring to inject fear into potential customers by directing his underlings to wreak havoc and mayhem. This dichotomy is how the myth of the honourable *mafioso* came into being.

The *mafiosi* were able to act with impunity because they enjoyed the protection of the rich and well-connected people who had recruited them to safeguard their interests. Acting totally outside the limits of the law, while still enjoying the protection of the powerful, *mafiosi* were able to sell protection from the violence and terror that they were oftentimes unleashing themselves.

In 1838 a Bourbon official called Pietro Calà Ulloa wrote a report where he mentioned the existence of brotherhoods in many Sicilian villages.

"... (In Sicily) there is not a single official who does not prostrate himself before the local men of influence and power, and who does not intend to corruptly benefit from his position and office... The general corruption has induced the population to turn to solutions which are strange and dangerous beyond measure. In many towns and villages there are fraternities, sort of sects that are called parties, without political aim, without colours, without meetings, without any other link but the dependence on a leader, who may be here a landowner or there an archpriest. Common funds serve to meet certain mutual needs, for example, to release a criminal or to accuse an innocent person... The population colludes with and protects convicts. When thefts take place, mediators emerge and offer their services to make up for the stolen goods... Many high-placed magistrates protect these fraternities ... it is impossible to induce the guards to patrol their area... At the centre of this state of dissolution is the capital (Palermo) with her luxury and corruption... a city in which live 40,000 proletarians whose subsistence depends on the pomp and caprices of the rich and powerful." Pietro Calà Ulloa, 1838

By abdicating the responsibility for the policing of Sicily and the enforcement of laws, including those that protected both the landlords and the peasants, the Bourbons had paved the way for the Sicilian Mafia to rise from the ashes of its failed land reform.

CHAPTER 2
THE GENESIS OF COSA NOSTRA

"*We should not delude ourselves any longer. In Sicily there is a sect of thieves that has ties across the whole island... The sect protects and is protected by everyone who lives in the countryside, like the lease-holding farmers and herdsmen. It protects and colludes with traders. The sect is not afraid of the police, because its members are confident that they will have no trouble evading capture. They are also not afraid of the courts, because evidence for the prosecution is rarely produced because of the pressure the sect puts on witnesses.*"
Baron Turrisi Colonna, 1864[7]

In 1864, Baron Turrisi Colonna wrote a report called Public Security in Sicily where he referred to interconnected sects that had proliferated all over Sicily over the previous twenty years. These brotherhoods came into being during the waning years of the Bourbon regime and were now gaining traction after the unification of the Kingdom of Italy in 1861.

2.1 The Unification of Italy
On the 21st of July 1858, the Prime Minister of Piedmont-Sardinia, Camillo Benso Count of Cavour, secretly met Napoleon III. This led to the signing of a military alliance with the French to expel Austria from northern Italy, with the Sardinians committing to cede Savoy and Nice to the French in return for their support.

In March of the following year the Piedmontese mobilised their army, provoking Vienna by conducting military manoeuvres close to the border. The Austrians retaliated by invading Sardinia, but the tables turned when the French army joined the fight. The Austrians finally conceded defeat in July 1859. The terms of the Armistice ceded Lombardy to France, who in turn handed it over to Sardinia.

Cavour then turned his attention towards central Italy, where the Pope was the sovereign ruler of a large expanse of territory known as the State of the Church, or the papal states. This meant that the Holy See, which at the time was led by Pope Pius IX, was not only a spiritual but also a secular power, wielding political control over several Italian regions. In 1848 the papal states consisted of 19 apostolic delegations which were then grouped into four regions called legations and a district which surrounded Rome.

The first legation was Romagna, which included Bologna, Ferrara, Forli and Ravenna. The second was Marche, which included Urbino, Pesaro, Macerata, Ancona, Fermo, Ascoli and Camerino. The third was Umbria, which included Perugia, Spoleto and Rieti. The fourth was Marittima and Campagna, which included Velletri, Frosinone and Benevento. And finally, the District of Rome, which included Rome, Viterbo, Civitavecchia and Orvieto.

Now that the Austrian hold on Italy had been weakened, and with the support of the French and the British, the Kingdom of Piedmont-Sardinia proceeded to annex Parma, Tuscany, and the Papal State of Romagna after their citizens revolted and requested annexation with Piedmont. The loss of Romagna was a major blow for Pius IX, particularly because of the active involvement of his subjects who had revolted against him. He reacted by issuing an excommunication of all those who were involved in the rebellion in his papal states.

At this point the Pope still controlled three legations and the District of Rome, a span of territory that cut right across the Italian Peninsula and ran all the way from the Adriatic Sea on one side to the Tyrrhenian Sea on the other. This meant that the Piedmontese were sandwiched between

Austrian lands in the north and the papal states in the south, making them vulnerable to a concerted attack by the papal army and the Austrians. It was also problematic for the Italian unification project because the peninsula was effectively split in two, with a separate kingdom between the northern and southern parts of the kingdom.

2.2 Garibaldi and the Expedition of the Thousand

Giuseppe Garibaldi was born in Nice on the 27th of July 1807. His father was a ship owner and trader who had been granted French citizenship by Napoleon Bonaparte when his hometown of Nice became part of France because of the Treaty of Campo Formio in 1797. Garibaldi's mother, Domenica, was a devoutly religious woman. The family was poor, but Domenica saved enough money to send Giuseppe to school. However, when his father died of tuberculosis in 1823, Giuseppe quit school and became a merchant sailor.

Garibaldi was both an idealist and fearless. He took part in several armed clashes, including the so-called revolution of 1831 which sought to establish a republic in Naples. It soon became clear that he was a talented military strategist and an astute leader of men, making him an excellent general and a dangerous foe. A committed nationalist, dedicated to freeing Italy from foreign rule, Garibaldi was convinced that the many Italian states could be unified into one country.

On the 11th of May 1860, Giuseppe Garibaldi landed in Sicily with a rag-tag army of around one thousand volunteers, in what came to be known as the Expedition of the Thousand. His reputation as a popular hero preceded him and was further burnished when he defeated the much larger Bourbon army at Calatafimi, in the province of Trapani in southern Sicily, on the 15th of May. This victory became a clarion call to Sicilian peasants and labourers who still lived in conditions that were feudal in everything but name. The peasants rose up and supported him, believing that once the Bourbons were driven out they would finally be saved from their lives of misery. Garibaldi marched on Palermo, which he took over by the 6th of June, and he then made his way across the island, capturing Milazzo in July. Having conquered Sicily, he crossed the Strait of Messina, arriving in Naples on the 7th of September 1860.

Count Cavour used the rapid advance of the revolutionary army to convince Napoleon of the wisdom of taking over the Papal State of Umbria in central Italy to create a corridor right through the papal states, connecting the northern and southern parts of the peninsula.

The papal territory was protected by an army made up of Austrian soldiers and a mix of other nationalities. Pope Pius IX had appointed General Lamoricière as his Commander, entrusting him with the defence of his kingdom. On the 7th of September Cavour issued an ultimatum to the Pope, threatening attack if he did not dismiss his foreign troops. Four days later the Piedmontese invaded Umbria and rapidly advanced to Castelfidardo, a town in the province of Ancona, right in the middle of the Italian peninsula, where they defeated the papal army in a fierce battle on the 18th of September.

What remained of the papal army retreated to the Papal State of Marche, with the Piedmontese in hot pursuit. The soldiers who made it to Loreto surrendered, leaving General Lamoricière to defend the capital of the Marche, Ancona, with a contingent of only 45 men. After a short siege, the city surrendered on the 29th of September 1860. The Pope's territory had been decimated and now consisted only of Lazio. The Piedmontese had succeeded in taking over a large part of the papal states just in time to unite with southern Italy, which had been taken over by Garibaldi.

The following month, on the 21st of October 1861, Garibaldi organised plebiscites in Sicily and Naples about the annexation of the Kingdom of the Two Sicilies to the Kingdom of Sardinia. Voting was restricted to men of a certain age and financial standing, so peasants had no say in the matter. In Sicily a total of 432,053 men voted in favour of annexation, while 667 men voted against. The plebiscite in Naples also passed with a strong majority, enabling Garibaldi to hand over southern Italy to King Vittorio Emanuele II. On the 26th of October 1860, Garibaldi met Vittorio Emanuele II in Naples and greeted him as the King of Italy.

Garibaldi did not ask for riches or titles as a reward for the service rendered to the King – what he requested was to govern Naples and Sicily as viceroy during the transitional period until the new king could put in place a proper administration. His request was denied, in what was possibly the death blow for any hope of establishing law and order in southern Italy and taking over the monopoly of protection. It also spelled doom for any hope of proper reform. It is now impossible to say how things would have turned out had Vittorio Emanuele acceded to his request. However, given Garibaldi's reputation as a champion of social reform, as well as the sense of obligation that he probably felt towards the people who had supported his cause, there was indeed a chance that he would have done something to improve the lot of the poor and disenfranchised in the region.

The Kingdom of Italy was officially proclaimed on the 17th of March 1861, by a parliament assembled in Turin. However, the area around Rome was protected by French troops and not included in the kingdom. This, of course, created great animosity because the Italians thought of Rome as their capital, and yet it was ruled by a different king.

The government of the fledgling Kingdom of Italy required the support of the landowning class on the island, who had supported annexation to put a halt to Bourbon reforms that threatened to destabilise the status quo in Sicily. Only literate men aged 25 and over who paid more than a specified amount of tax had the vote, so the illiterate peasants barely eking out a living were of no use to the Piedmontese. This made it possible for the upper classes on the island to block any meaningful reform and prevent expropriation of their land. Thus, the peasants' hopes of any form of land reform were nothing more than a pipe dream and were soon dashed.

The centre of power of the new Kingdom of Italy was in the northern part of the peninsula. The Piedmontese administration had little to no understanding of what had happened and was still happening in the south. Seen from their perspective, the illiterate peasants and labourers were people who had not emerged from the dark ages, so they arrived at the facile conclusion that the criminality and violence on the island was to be attributed to the lower classes.

"But with the abolition of feudalism and the feudal rights of the gentry, the law changed and the old way of doing things was no longer legal. On

24

the one hand, the law no longer allowed bullying or violence, defining such behaviour in all cases as criminal. This change was accomplished by the legislation brought by the Kingdom of Italy in 1860. On the other hand, the de facto conditions remained unchanged, allowing free reign to those who used tactics of intimidation and violence, due to the absolute powerlessness of the State to impose its laws by force. This led to the distinction between legal and illegal acts disappearing in the mind of the entire population ... The result was that having lost any means of distinguishing between licit and unlawful violence and the continued reality that violence remained the foundation of social relations, this was indiscriminately accepted as the status quo by the entire population." Leopoldo Franchetti, 1876[8]

2.3 The Expropriation of Ecclesiastical Lands

As can be imagined, there was not much love lost between Pope Pius IX and the administration in Piedmont. The anticlerical government, which had been so careful not to offend secular *latifundia* landowners in Sicily, had no reason to pander to the Church. So in the 1860s they expropriated massive tracts of Church land, purportedly to break them up into small lots to sell to peasants, who would then be able to settle and improve their quality of life. This was a major event in Sicily since the Church owned around 10 percent of the arable land on the island. However, once again, the new administration left matters in the hands of the landowning class, who proceeded to corrupt the process and purchase most of the land itself.

The Piedmontese made exactly the same mistake the Bourbons had made when they attempted to enact land reform. Instead of taking control of the process and ensuring that the laws were followed and the land was transferred to those for whom it was intended, they delegated the entire process and did not police what was actually happening. Unfortunately, this opportunity to regenerate and reinvigorate the economy of Sicily through the redistribution of land was squandered. Corruption and rigged auctions were rife, and landowners and the Mafia colluded to obtain the lion's share of the windfall.

Thus, the government lost the opportunity to finally force through a semblance of justice on the island. In a report about Sicily that Baron Sonnino published in 1877, he eloquently bemoaned the missed opportunity of the *"eversione dell'asse ecclesiastico"* (destruction of the ecclesiastical patrimony) – *"we relinquished the only effective means of producing a social and economic revolution in half of Italy, without political change, disorder, hatred, or injustice, to the advantage of all, winning the great blessings of thousands and thousands of families... nowhere else might that wealth have been better employed as an instrument for the nation's regeneration, without causing the State any loss or irking the sensibilities of the touchiest of Smithian economists."*[9]

The result was a tragedy for Sicilian peasants, who not only lost the opportunity to finally own their own land, but also lost the *usi civici* on Church estates. They could no longer hunt or forage or graze cattle on these lands, so they suddenly became totally and completely dependent on the good will of the landlords and the *gabellotti*.

Relations between Piedmont and the Holy See came to a head on the 20th of September 1870 when the Italian army marched into Rome, which surrendered after offering a token resistance. Pope Pius IX declared that he had become a prisoner in the Vatican and excommunicated King Vittorio Emmanuele and the Prime Minister of Italy, Giovanni Lanza. He announced that the Italian State was not legitimate and issued a decree of *non expedit*, which meant that Catholics could not run or vote in national elections. This dispute between the Church and the Italian State was to last for almost seventy years and came to be known as *la questione romana* (the roman question).[10]

The decree of *non expedit* only applied to national elections and not to local elections. Churchmen all over Italy shifted their focus to building strong relationships with local administrations in their parishes, attempting to influence politics at the grassroots level. In Sicily, working with the local administration meant working with the Mafia, which had infiltrated local politics through a combination of bribery, intimidation, and extortion. The ecclesiastical authorities thus formed an *entente cordiale* with mafia bosses, weaving a web of complicity that would take much bloodshed and over one hundred years to be shattered.

There are also some reports of priests who moonlighted as *mafiosi*, but this was the exception, not the rule. What was a lot more common was a priest using the pulpit to fulminate against the government in Piedmont, while reserving the front pew in the church for the *capomafia* and his family, and organising processions and other religious events where *mafiosi* were given prominent positions that burnished their credentials in the eyes of the faithful. Most Sicilians were devout and followed the dictates of the Church, so this situation further eroded their trust in the government in Piedmont and fed the narrative that it was only the Mafia that could act as guarantor and protector on the island.

In the final decades of the nineteenth century, the living and working conditions of Sicilian peasants went from bad to worse. The *latifundia* covered 80 percent of the island, the same area that had been covered by its previous incarnation, the feudal estates. Over the preceding forty years, ever since the Bourbons had made land marketable and enabled creditors to seize land in payment for debts, ownership of the estates had changed hands. Whereas in 1812 there were around 2,000 landowning families, by the 1860s, the number had increased to 20,000.[11]

The transformation in ownership of the land did not result in much change in the interior of the island. The large estates were originally made up of several *feudi* that operated largely as standalone ecosystems. When the estates were split, they simply broke them down into separate *feudi*. So from the perspective of the peasants the only change was that suddenly a new owner, who they probably never got to see let alone speak to, took over the *feudo* and terminated their *usi civici*.

The new class of landowners that arose after the feudal system was abolished fostered the mythology of *Sicilianismo*, presenting themselves as proud and honourable Sicilians, oppressed by nobles for centuries and now fighting for the rights to which they had been denied for so long. This narrative became an important part of the rationale used by the new elites when they launched political and legal fights to obtain more land, ostensibly to be re-distributed amongst landless peasants, although of course once the land was acquired, they kept it for themselves.[12] It also became a very convenient camouflage for the true nature of *mafiosi* and an excuse regularly cited by their powerful protectors to justify their collaboration with them.

The landowning families were upwardly mobile, intermarrying with the nobility and in many ways copying their way of life. Many of them moved to Palermo, signed *gabella* contracts with a new generation of *gabellotti*, and washed their hands of responsibility for the living conditions of peasants on their estates. These contracts were usually signed for a period of six years, granting the *gabellotto* a lease against payment of a fixed yearly rent paid annually in advance. In cases where they did not lease out their estate, the landowners employed an *amministratore* (administrator) who ran the estate in much the same way as the *gabellotto*, but in this case, he was paid a salary. The main difference between the two setups is that in the case of the *gabellotto,* any share of the crops or payments made by the peasants were retained, whereas in the case of the *amministratore,* these were passed on to the landowner.

The system worked as follows. Each tract of land was split into plots of around five hectares, which were rented out to peasants on sharecropper contracts for periods of a year. The *gabellotto* (which will now be used to mean *gabellotto* or *amministratore*) also provided the seed required for cultivation, imposing a high rate of interest by using different measures when giving out the loan and collecting the payment.[13]

The sharecroppers provided their own ploughs, mules and equipment required to work the land. When the harvest was brought in, the first concern was the return of the seed provided by the *gabellotti*, who took a large measure of seed from the crop for each small measure of seed they had initially provided– the difference between the quantity of seed loaned and the quantity of seed repaid was known as the *addito* (addition). Once the debt was repaid, the remaining harvest was split into three parts – with the *gabellotto* taking two and the peasant retaining one.

However, it did not end there. On every estate the *gabellotto* employed a *soprastante* (overseer), a *uomo di fiducia* (trusted man) who oversaw the day-to-day management of the estate. Each estate also had *campieri* (field guards) who were armed and patrolled the estate on horseback. These men were chosen for their toughness and readiness to resort to violence when protecting the interests of the estate manager. In fact, one could say they had to exhibit constant ruthlessness and violence since it was a cut-throat business. Furthermore, to maintain *rispetto* in the eyes of the peasants they had to ensure that there could be no doubt that they were the top dogs of the pack.

The *soprastante* and the *campieri* had the power of life or death over the peasants. They decided who got which plots of land and they acted as arbiters in any issues that arose. They also assigned additional jobs to the people they favoured – this included working as herdsmen, day labourers or watchmen. In a sense, they were the administration, police and the judiciary all rolled into one, with the law of the estate consisting solely of what was in their best interest and that of their employer, the *gabellotto.*

Peasants therefore had to curry favour with these people to increase their chances of being given a sharecropper contract or some other means of employment. This meant that after the harvest, peasants felt obligated to give gifts to the *soprastante* and *campieri* to remain in their good books. They also had to pay them for protection because the plot of land assigned to them was often quite a distance away from where they lived, so as they travelled from one plot to the next, or from one job to the next, they were at risk of being attacked by brigands. These protection payments were commonly referred to as *cuccia.*

By the time all the levies and payments were deducted from the harvest, the peasant ended up with a scant 20 percent of the produce in a good year.[14] When the harvest was poor, he ended up with even less. This meant he had to take out loans from the *gabellotto* at usurious rates of interest ranging from 25 to 100 percent to replace damaged equipment or animals required to work the land. The loss of the *usi civici* made a bad situation even worse because there was no alternative way for them to feed their families, so they often ended up borrowing money simply to make ends meet.

The situation amounted to bonded labour. The peasants were trapped, each year owing the *gabellotto* more and more money and becoming increasingly beholden to the *campieri* who both terrorised and protected them in turn. As in the case of the *bravi*, the *gabellotto*, *amministratore*, *soprastante* and *campieri* were experts in the arts of intimidation and coercion, so they too had the requisites to become *mafiosi*, or to cooperate with *mafiosi*, when the right opportunities arose.

In conclusion, the ending of the *quasi-allod*, the breaking up of the large estates and the disbanding of the companies of *bravi* employed by the barons, the schism between Church and State which exacerbated the lack of trust in the authorities, and the rapidly growing demand for protection services by the expanding wealthy class, together created the perfect environment for Cosa Nostra to grow and take over the island.

2.4 La Questione Meridionale

In the years following the unification of Italy there was much debate about the social, cultural and economic gaps between northern and southern Italy, in what came to be called the *questione meridionale* (the southern question).[15]

The situation in Sicily was by far the worst in all of Italy, including the southern part of the peninsula that had also been under the control of the Bourbons. Little to no investment had been made in developing the infrastructure on the island. In 1862, Sicily had an average of 222 metres of road per thousand inhabitants, versus the 580 metres of road for Italy as a whole. It had an average 5 metres of railway tracks laid per thousand inhabitants, versus the 127 metres average for the whole country. Even more worrying was the situation in the education sector. Sicily boasted 0.35 primary school teachers per thousand inhabitants, as opposed to the one teacher per thousand inhabitants in Italy as a whole.[16]

In 1875 Pasquale Villari wrote a series of letters to the editor of the publication *L'Opinione*, attributing the predominance of brigandage and criminality in southern Italy to the mismanagement of the region by its previous rulers – the Bourbons. The collection of letters, known as *Le Lettere Meridionali* (The Southern Letters) are considered the first expression of the *meridionalismo* (meridionalist movement) which strove to find ways to bridge the great divide between north and south.

Villari described the south in less than glowing terms, linking what he referred to as the insubordination and backwardness of the inhabitants of the region to the poverty and underdevelopment resulting from decades of misrule. Southern Italy, he claimed, was a problem that needed to be addressed by the new Italian State. He also made proposals as to how the southern question could be resolved.

In a letter that focused on the situation in Sicily and the phenomenon of the Mafia, Villari starts by acknowledging that he knew very little about Sicily.

"In this letter I will begin to discuss the evils that afflict Sicily. The thing is much more difficult for me since I know very little about the country. And it is even more difficult, in that opinions on this subject vary, even among those who were born and who lived on the island. I will therefore be cautious in my approach."[17]

He goes on to discuss the terrible suffering of the poor in Sicily, initially focusing on the atrocious working conditions in the sulphur mines and the plight of children forced to work underground in inhumane conditions.

"It is now known that Sicily is troubled by those social wounds, of which so much is said now, mainly in its western part. Here precisely, not for the time being dealing with Palermo which gives rise to other considerations, is the centre of the sulphur mines, which, after agriculture is the largest and richest industry on that island. An industry that employs many tens of thousands of workers of all sexes and ages. And it is known that the workers in the sulphur mines are treated unfairly. Not only do they not take all necessary measures to save the lives of the workers, who sometimes are suffocated by the gases that emanate from them, or burnt alive when sparks ignite the gas, or buried alive because of the poor construction of the shafts: but worse still follows. The human being is subjected to work which, from what I hear, appears to be most cruel and almost impossible. Hundreds and hundreds of boys and girls descend steep and dangerous stairs, dug out of thick soil and mud. When they arrive at the bottom of the mine, they are

THE BATTLE FOR SICILY'S SOUL

loaded with sulphur, which they carry on their backs as they climb up the steep, slippery stairs where they are constantly in danger of falling and losing their lives."[18]

One would think that having started his letter by admitting that he knew little to nothing about Sicily, he would have held back from expressing any strong opinions. However, notwithstanding his admitted lack of knowledge about the island, and even while acknowledged the miserable living conditions experienced by peasants and mine workers in Sicily, Villari concluded that it was this abused class of workers that was the source of the evil that plagued the island.

"In the Congress of Milan, the Honourable Di Cesarò, the Honourable Luzzalti and others generously protested and expressed their pain at the enormous tragedy unfolding in Sicily, which is all the more serious when one considers that it is not only the health of these people that is destroyed, but also the morality of the whole population. The weak are destroyed, while the strong survive to rule, tyrannise, and oppress children in those dark tunnels where anything can happen. Man loses hope and becomes a beast in such circumstances, becoming an enemy of the society that treats him so ruthlessly.

Here, then, we have a first source of evil. One can see and feel first-hand how the morality of certain social classes is destroyed. In Sicily we are seeing the same phenomenon as has been seen in all mining countries, with some distinct differences. Elsewhere it was immediately thought of remedying the situation with laws which protect the worker and especially the child, defining the number of hours they should work and forbidding children from being assigned tasks that could kill them or cause them to lose hope. The life and morality of the worker were effectively protected; evil was stopped in its path."[19]

These two paragraphs require some analysis and thought. While Villari is admitting that the workers in the mines – men, women, and children – worked in inhumane conditions that should be illegal, his rationale is not based on human rights and dignity. He is instead saying that laws governing their working conditions should be put in place to stop these workers from becoming evil and a danger to civilised Italians.

Interestingly, and one could say, somewhat illogically, he goes on to point out that the epicentre of the evil is in Palermo, even though according to him the evil purportedly comes into being in the mines and *latifundia* in the centre of the island.

"The Sicilian problem presents itself in all its frightening severity in the province of Palermo, where a social reality which we still do not fully understand produces not the Camorra but the Mafia. This phenomenon has been studied and described in great depth, first by Baron Turrisi-Colonna, then by the honourable Tommasi-Crudeli and then by others who looked at the various historical elements that helped generate and increase this evil."[20]

He then asks an interesting question - *"The Mafia increases in power, takes revenge, kills, even manages to provoke popular uprisings. Who commands and who obeys, who are the oppressed and who are the oppressors?"*[21]

When considering the answer to this important query, he returns to the conundrum of Palermo. The following quote makes it clear that Villari is aware of the flaw in his argument. If the Mafia originated in the *latifundia*, why was it that mafia style criminality was focused in areas that were as different to *latifundia* as night was to day?

"To this was added a very singular piece of news, the truth of which I have been able to ascertain in many ways. The greatest number of crimes are committed by inhabitants of the surroundings of Palermo, who are mostly not poor but have some form of title to the land on which they cultivate their oranges. In the Conca D'Oro agriculture thrives; large estates do not exist; the peasant is wealthy, mafioso, and commits many crimes. Initially I could not believe this news, which seemed to subvert all the principles of political economy and of social science; but this fact came up a thousand times and was a thousand times reconfirmed."[22]

In the end Villari brushes over this conundrum, returning to his initial premise about the origins of the evil of the Mafia, propping up his argument with anecdotes collected from landowners based in Palermo and a letter he claims he received from a man who had formed part of Garibaldi's army.

"To my surprise, when I questioned some well-informed and competent Sicilians about the situation in Palermo and the terrible conditions in the latifundia, they started laughing. In all of this, they said, there is not a single word of truth. You say that we are the oppressors of the peasants! The truth is that we are the ones who are oppressed by the peasants! It is the Mafia that prevents us from visiting our estates. One of the men declared that he had not been able to visit his lands for 10 years, because they were administered and guarded by the Mafia, and his life would be in danger if he tried to replace them."[23]

What was even more worrying than the claims about the purported evil lurking within the hearts and minds of peasants and mine workers, were the recommendations made about how to resolve the issue. Villari proposed the establishment of a despotic government which would not flinch from using violence to eradicate the problem and gain full control over the island and all those who inhabited it.

"It is therefore clear that the remedies are of two kinds: repressive and preventative. There is no doubt that it is necessary to severely punish the crimes with prompt and exemplary justice; but imprisonment is useless if you do not isolate the guilty far from the island.

To succeed, however, with only repressive means, we should bring repression to the point of extermination. If the state uses tactics of terror the crimes would cease, except of course if the condition that produced the evil remains. But extermination requires an immense show of force which would never be allowed by a liberal government. What is needed is despotism."[24]

Villari had no way of knowing it, but years later Italy did, indeed, have a despotic government that, as he suggested, attempted to exterminate the Mafia with the type of tactics he recommended. However, it only succeeded in cowing the Mafia temporarily. In the aftermath, Cosa Nostra returned, stronger and more ruthless than ever before.

In a subsequent letter focusing on brigandage, Pasquale Villari summarises his position and the problem that faced the Piedmontese government as follows:

"I assume that by now the reader is already convinced that the Mafia has its roots in the countryside, and that to destroy it one must improve the conditions of the thousands of farmers who work on 77% of the arable land in the interior of the Sicily. I am also sure that this will be a cause of great concern. On the one hand some will say: These are evils which will take time to resolve. On the other hand, others will say, perhaps more insistently: Why do you want to raise such a difficult social issue in Italy? Don't we already have enough problems to solve – this is the last thing we need. We have finally gained some peace on the peninsula, and you would now like to unleash such a terrible calamity upon us. It would be a great crime against the country to fuel hopes in the peasantry that can never be fulfilled. They are by far the largest and least civilised class in the country; if they were to rise against us, who could stop them?"[25]

"I do not know if the will and the strength of the Municipal and Provincial authorities is enough to correct this evil. But I firmly believe that the government of a civilised country should, in these cases, either force others to sort it out, or sort it out itself. ... We need some kind soul to go to those places, describe in detail and portray the life and the moral state of those people, and denounce it to the civil world as an Italian crime." [26]

Pasquale Villari met Leopoldo Franchetti and Sydney Sonnino in Florence in a group of conservative intellectuals opposing the left-wing government. The two men heeded Villari's call for someone to look into what was happening in Sicily, so they travelled to the island in 1876 to conduct an investigation into the state of Sicilian society.

The result was a report called *Inchiesta in Sicilia* (Inquiry in Sicily). The section titled *Political and Administrative Conditions in Sicily* specifically mentions organised groups exercising social control through violence.

"It would be difficult to exaggerate the importance of the part played by the mayhem, the shootings and above all the fear of shootings in all kinds of relationships between people in Palermo and the area surrounding it ... This

is how friends and allies are protected and defended. This is how the most energetic and the most skilful secure for themselves absolute domination in all things both public and private, with no limit other than the violence of other powerful men. It is also true that sometimes it is not violence that is at play in interactions between a powerful man and the people he is imposing upon. Such a man does not doubt that he is powerful and would perhaps be scandalised to hear that what he requires is contrary to law and that he only obtained it by means of intimidation. But the truth is that it is not only violence that is used to intimidate and coerce. In Palermo, as in any other country, social codes are often an excellent tool for this purpose; as in any other country and even more, the use of tricks and deceptions is not outlawed. Nonetheless, if we go to seek the first foundation of the influence of those who have real power, it is almost inevitably found in the fact or fame that such a person has possibility, directly or through third parties, to use violence." [27]

The *Lettere Meridionali* and the *Inchiesta in Sicilia* were fiercely rebutted by the rich and the powerful in the south. They insisted that outsiders could not understand the reality of Sicilian life, and that a lot of what the northerners were calling evil, or criminal, was nothing but *Sicilianismo*. In other words, according to them, it was just the locals taking matters into their own hands and resolving their issues without outside interference.

2.5 The Lemon Groves of Palermo
"After hearing many such stories, the scent of orange and lemon blossom starts to smell of corpses." Leopoldo Franchetti [28]

2.5.1 The cure for scurvy
When the Arabs took control of Sicily in 827 CE they planted citrus trees on the island. The trees thrived in the area surrounding Palermo known as the *Conca d'Oro* (Golden Shell), since it was blessed with both the right climactic conditions and fertile soil containing above average quantities of limestone needed to create the perfect environment for such orchards. The fruit was a crop like any other, until a Scottish navy surgeon called James Lind made it his mission to find a cure for scurvy, a disease that was decimating sailors at sea.

Lind started researching naval logs, trying to find a clue as to why some crews were spared while others were not. After reaching the conclusion that the issue was related to diet, he came upon the findings of John Woodall, surgeon general of the East India Company, who had written about the curative power of lemons on men afflicted with scurvy.

In 1747, James Lind joined the crew of the Royal Navy ship *Salisbury* and set off on a long sea voyage. As expected, after two months at sea, some of the sailors started to exhibit symptoms of scurvy, which included muscular pain, sunken eyes, pale skin, diarrhoea, weight loss and fever. Lind waited until he had 12 clear cases, and he then split them into pairs, in what appears to be the first recorded case of randomised medical trials. The six pairs of men were given the same care and ate the same food, but each pair was given a different daily supplement. The first pair was given vinegar, the second was given cider, the third was given diluted sulfuric acid, the fourth was given seawater, the fifth was given a paste of plant extracts and the sixth was given two oranges and a lemon. Of the twelve men only two recovered – the pair that had been given citrus fruit.[29]

Lind's discovery slowly percolated through the navy, but there were many sceptics and naysayers who prevented the discovery and related cure from going mainstream. However, in 1779, any claims to the contrary were put to rest by another Scottish navy surgeon called Gilbert Blane, who was the physician for the fleet led by Admiral George Brydges. Blane discovered that adding distilled ethyl alcohol to lemon juice preserved it for long periods of time. He then took several barrels of juice on a sea voyage to the Caribbean. When the sailors started to get ill with scurvy, he immediately cured them by giving them the preserved lemon juice. The results were irrefutable, so upon their return to Britain the Admiral lobbied to have Blane appointed as Commissioner of the Sick and Hurt Board, an important platform that enabled the physician to institute new regulations in 1795 that imposed the provision of a daily supplement of lemon juice, mixed in grog, for all the sailors. This move eliminated scurvy in the Royal Navy and led to a massive surge in demand for lemons from Sicily, as it was already well established as an exporter of citrus fruit.[30]

It is thus that one thousand years after the Arabs first planted the trees in Sicily, the citrus groves growing in the area around Palermo became the source of great riches for the island and became the catalyst required for the formation and growth of the Sicilian Mafia.

When the Napoleonic Wars ended in 1815, demand for lemon juice and lemon essences grew exponentially, with orders coming in from far and wide, especially the United States. This coincided with the changes in land tenure implemented by the Bourbons, which meant that more people could now acquire land, both in the centre of the island, but more importantly, in the *Conca d'Oro*.

To get an idea of the magnitude of the trade in Sicilian lemons, one should consider that between 1795 and 1814 the British Navy ordered 1.6 million gallons of lemon juice.[31] By 1834, Sicily was exporting more than 400,000 crates of lemons per year. This grew to circa 750,000 crates annually in the 1880s. Furthermore, the profit on the export of lemons was more than 60 times the profit yielded by other crops grown on the island.[32]

Citrus fruit is easily portable, so the orchards rapidly became the target of thieves and brigands. Initially, the orchard owners tried to protect their investments by building high walls and unleashing packs of guard dogs, but this was not enough to keep the thieves at bay.[33] Unfortunately, the weak rule of law on the island meant that the landowners did not have anyone to turn to for protection, so they had to resort to paying the men of honour to guarantee protection for the precious fruit throughout the supply chain – from tree to ship.

The orchards in the *Conca d'Oro* were very different from the *latifundia* – instead of large tracts of land which justified the employment of guards on a retainer, the citrus groves were much smaller. It was thus possible for one man, or a group of men working together, to guard more than one allotment – giving rise to the "*industry of protection.*"[34]

Studies using data of lower court judgements of seventy towns in western Sicily, as listed in a report presented to the Italian Parliament by A. Damiani in 1886, have shown a clear link between the fragmentation of landholdings and the rise of the Mafia. When one of the orchard owners purchased protection from the men of honour, theft was redirected to other orchards whose owners were then obliged to do the same. This created a shift in the dynamic between landlords and protectors. Unlike the case of the *latifundia* where groups of men protecting large estates usually had one client and thus were dependent on him, in the case of the orchards in the *Conca d'Oro*, the protectors could dictate terms because they had the upper hand.[35]

However, when researchers expanded the scope of the study to include the whole dataset of court judgements collected by Damiani, which included 143 towns all over the island, it emerged that while fragmentation did have an impact on mafia presence, the strongest determinant of Mafia activity was in fact the cultivation of citrus.

2.5.2 Terror in the Conca d'Oro

Antonino Giammona was born in 1820 in a village called Passo di Rigano in the province of Palermo. His family was extremely poor. Initially Giammona worked as a manual labourer, but the Sicilian revolution for independence of 1848 gave him an opportunity to make a name for himself. In 1860 he joined Garibaldi's army in the fight to liberate Sicily from the Bourbons.[36] At face value one could say that he exemplified *Sicilianismo*, fighting for freedom for himself and the landless poor.

The hopes for a Sicilian *risorgimento* (renewal), however, were short-lived. Instead of helping the poor and landless in Sicily, the new government introduced heavy taxation and imposed conscription. Young men, who were needed to work in the fields, were instead forced into military service. Many of them sought to avoid conscription by fleeing to the mountains and resorting to banditry to survive, while others gave up on Sicily and emigrated.

On the 16th of September 1866, thousands of infuriated villagers joined bandits who had come down from their hideouts in the mountains in open revolt against the Piedmontese government, in what came to be known as the Rivolta del Sette e Mezzo (Seven and a Half Days Revolt). The mob attacked the Palazzo Reale (Royal Palace), which was the seat of the Mayor and Prefect of Palermo. The new police force, known as the Carabinieri, attempted to protect the palace, but they were greatly outnumbered and they suffered heavy losses.

By now *mafiosi* such as Giammona had built a strong network of influence and patronage with the new landowning class, so they did not want to upset the status quo. As a result, the *mafiosi* took up arms to violently repress the revolt, unequivocally dispelling any claim that the Mafia was the protector of the weak and the poor, fighting against injustice and the rich.

Antonino Giammona became the leader of the Uditore mafia clan, taking on the persona of a man of honour and a paladin of Sicilian pride, while in truth possessing none of those values or honourable motives. It did not take long until he cast covetous eyes on the citrus groves clustered around Palermo, which in the 1870s were yielding extraordinary returns.

In 1872 a doctor called Gaspare Galati took over the management of a lemon grove that his daughters and their aunt had inherited after the premature death of his brother-in-law, brought about by a heart attack after receiving several threats from the Uditore Mafia. Dr Galati discovered that the caretaker of the grove, Benedetto Carollo, was stealing fruit and running the business into the ground, so he fired him and employed another peasant to replace him.

What Dr Galati did not know was that Carollo was one of Giammona's men, and that the actions of the caretaker were designed to enable Giammona to step in and purchase the property at the lowest price possible. Within days the Uditore Mafia executed the new caretaker, shooting him in the back multiple times as he walked through the lemon groves.

Once again, Dr Galati employed a new caretaker, but he too was shot and barely survived the attack. Clearly, Giammona had no compunction about killing or maiming peasants to send Galati a message. The *mafioso* might have styled himself as a hero of the people, but he was no Robin Hood. In his eyes the peasants were expendable, collateral casualties in his campaign of terror and enrichment.

After rebuffing Giammona for three years and receiving countless threats, Dr Galati abandoned his medical practice and escaped with his family to Naples. In a last-ditch attempt to try to thwart the *mafiosi*, he sent a report to the Minister of the Interior in Rome describing what was happening in Sicily and how the local police were turning a blind eye to the surge in criminality.

Upon receiving the memorandum, the Minister of the Interior ordered the Palermo Chief of Police to investigate the claims made by the doctor. At this stage what happened is astounding, and clearly illustrates how *mafiosi* were working hand in hand with landowners, local officials, and administrators. Instead of supporting Dr Galati and denouncing Giammona and the Mafia, several lawyers, judges, landowners, priests, and politicians signed a statement in Giammona's favour, claiming that his actions were nothing but *Sicilianismo*, motivated by a desire to stand up to bullies and defend the weak.

None of them made any mention of the fact that Giammona and his clan terrorised all the peasants living in Uditore, a small village with only 800 inhabitants. In 1874 alone, Giammona's clan was responsible for the murders of twenty-three peasants, which included several women and children, and the maiming of a further ten. Antonino Giammona was wielding violence in a very strategic manner, building a reputation by killing peasants to terrorise anyone who was brave, or reckless, enough to challenge him.

In a book called *The Rulers of the South* published in 1900, the author Francis Marion Crawford wrote thus of the Mafia:

"Its tyranny is more outwardly visible in the country, and particularly in the rich lands that surround Palermo, than in Palermo itself, or in the other cities most infected by it. One reason of this is the great development in the cultivation of oranges and lemons during this century. The crops are relatively very valuable and are especially tempting to thieves because they are immediately marketable and easily carried off; the lands are cut up into innumerable small holdings, and, without patrolling every orange grove with soldiers, which is impossible, the authorities could not possibly prevent

the depredations of the fruit-stealers. The Mafia affords all who appeal to it the most thorough protection, and its despotism over the orange-growing regions is absolute; for, in return for such great advantages, landholders, whether owners or tenants, are only too glad to serve it at need and to abstain from all recourse to law."[37]

This description of the situation on the island at the end of the nineteenth century sheds light on why supposedly upstanding members of society were colluding with the so-called men of honour. Under the circumstances, this was the only way they could protect themselves and their property from the wave of criminality washing over the island. By paying a *mafioso* for protection they were effectively purchasing insurance against pilferage at every stage of the supply chain from the planting of the tree, to the process of cultivation, harvesting and packing of the fruit, to storage, and then ultimately, transportation to the docks.

"This seems to be the cause of that infinite tangle of violence in every direction, which at first can confuse those who, through an almost instinctive intellectual process, try to distinguish between the oppressors and the oppressed. Because he who is powerful today can be a victim tomorrow, and to one no more powerful than he. And the most peaceful man can find himself in need of using violence, or at least to make an alliance with those who use violence, even if only for legitimate self-defence." Leopoldo Franchetti[38]

In addition to protection from theft, the *mafioso* also cultivated a network of relationships that enabled him to act as guarantor in negotiations between producers and *sensali* (brokers), providing assurances to the broker regarding the quality of the fruit, and to the producer regarding the financial aspects of the transaction.

"… every landholder is obliged to maintain a 'guardiano' or watchman, in addition to the men he employs upon his land. There are, therefore, several thousands of these watchmen in the orange groves of the Golden Shell alone, and they are without exception Mafiusi since they have the monopoly of their business and can altogether prevent the employment of strangers in their occupation. The landholder who attempts to oppose the monopoly will

lose his whole crop in a night, and, if he persists, his life is not worth a year's purchase." Francis Marion Crawford [39]

When one considers the above, it becomes clear that far from being opposed to law and order, the new mafia *cosche* that emerged in the years after the unification of Italy were in fact part of law and order. They came into being in a society where the police and judiciary had given up on controlling criminality on the island and were instead using politically aligned criminals to maintain a semblance of control. This can to a certain extent explain the perplexing defence of Giammona by many police officials, judges, and landowners – as far as they were concerned, he was essential to guarantee the smooth running of business and society.

2.6 The Sulphur Mines

While the *mafiosi* of Palermo were taking over the citrus groves in the region, other clans in the centre of the island were focusing on another source of wealth – sulphur. This mineral was in high demand because it was used in the production of a wide variety of products ranging from fertilisers to explosives. Conditions in the mines were atrocious, as alluded to in the *Lettere Meridionali* written by Villari.

In 1900 a police inspector called Antonino Cutrera used data obtained from local police forces to create a map showing the towns that had been infiltrated by the Mafia, and how strong their impact was on local communities. Seeing as not all crimes in Sicily were committed by *mafiosi*, he did not base his study on criminality statistics alone. The resulting map shows mafia infiltration based on the estimates and input of police officers in the various localities, supported by statistics, court documents and newspaper reports.[40]

His findings are interesting because they make it possible to trace the expansion of the Mafia over the twenty years or so after the Damiani report. Researchers have found that at the beginning of the twentieth century, sulphur production came into the mix as a determinant of mafia presence.[41] Clearly, the entrepreneurs of protection had expanded the scope of their operations to service new industries, and by the early 1900s they had taken on the role of protectors and guarantors of the various stages of the sulphur mining, transportation and selling process.

Police and court records relating to criminal activity in Favara in 1885 include a mention of brotherhoods with an organisational structure, statute, rules and initiation rituals similar to those of the criminal clans in the Palermo district. No parallels were drawn between the *cosche* at the time, but in retrospect it is evident that the Mafia had spread in the Sulphur territories.

It is easy to see why the possible link was missed at the time. Favara and Palermo are over one hundred kilometres apart, separated by regions of almost impenetrable mountains. It is thought that the connection occurred in prison when criminals were brought together to serve their sentences on islands such as Ustica prior to 1879. It is likely that the prisons were used to recruit *mafiosi*, initiating them while incarcerated and then sending them out to colonise new territories and increase the reach of Cosa Nostra.[42]

In 1898, Ermanno Sangiorgi, the new *Questore* (head) of the Palermo police, started compiling detailed reports for the Ministry of the Interior that described the network of criminal clans that had proliferated in the area. He authored thirty-one reports, written between November 1898 and February 1900. Totalling 485 pages, the combined reports give a comprehensive description of the setup of the Mafia at the time.

Sangiorgi described Cosa Nostra as consisting of eight *cosche* that controlled the territory around Palermo, each of which had a boss and underboss. These were identified as follows – Piana dei Colli, Acquasanta, Falde, Malaspina, Uditore, Passo di Rigano, Perpignano and Olivuzza. These cosche did not operate independently – they were part and parcel of one criminal organisation, with the bosses coming together as a centralised board of governance, controlling the organisation's business strategy, administering a welfare system to support the families of members who were in prison, and dispensing justice based on their own internal laws.

The *Questore* also detailed the pyramidical hierarchy of these mafia *cosche*, including the overall leader known as the *capo* (head or leader), who delegated control of different localities to various *sottocapi* (deputies), who in turn had assistants, known as the *consiglio direttivo*.[43] The *capo* and *sottocapi* ensured that all members of the clan followed the rules of the society, and that any men who broke the rules were severely punished. Members of the *cosca* were initiated in a ritual that incorporated fire, blood, and a holy picture.

These reports were drafted as part of an ongoing investigation into the racketeering and trading in influence predominant in the region. Sangiorgi wanted to prove in court that the Mafia was a unified organisation, thus enabling the judiciary to use the laws that punished criminal association. Unfortunately, however, by the time the *mafiosi* were brought to trial the government had changed, and Sangiorgi had lost his political support. The star witness in the proceedings recanted, and several witnesses vouched for the accused. All the hard work of Sangiorgi and his team ended up wasted.

The Sangiorgi report was filed away and forgotten, and the authorities continued operating on the understanding that the Mafia was a loose network of independent criminal groups operating in different territories and occasionally collaborating when it was in their interest to do so. It would take another eighty-five years for the brave judges of the Palermo Antimafia Pool to finally shine a bright light on the murky inner workings of Cosa Nostra, exposing its true nature for all the world to see.

2.7 The Fasci Siciliani

You may recall that the meridionalist letters penned by Pasquale Villari in 1875 concluded that the suffering and deprivation endured by Sicilian peasants and labourers had warped their morality and made them evil. This was, according to him, the reason for the emergence and growth of the Mafia on the island.

The truth, of course, was very different. While there is no doubt that originally the Mafia emerged from the lower social classes, the growth of the criminal phenomenon on the island was nurtured by the actions of the rich and powerful, and not the poor. By 1866 *mafiosi* such as Giammona were aligned with the landowners and politicians. Far from being the champions of the poor, they became the stick that the rich used to beat up the poor and keep them subjugated.

The peasants, manual labourers and sulphur miners did in fact fight back, but they did not do so through the Mafia. Cosa Nostra was their enemy, wielded by the rich to kill any demands for better working conditions or calls for agricultural land reform.

Nowhere was this more evident than in the case of the Fasci.

By the 1880s it was amply clear that the unification of Italy had not resulted in better conditions for most Sicilians. A wave of socialist fervour swept over the island, fanned in no small part by Giuseppe de Felice Giuffrida, a committed socialist who founded the first official Fascio movement in Catania in 1891. The word Fascio means bundle in Italian and alludes to the coming together of labourers to jointly advocate for workers' rights. Several similar movements were set up all over the island, collectively known as the Fasci dei Lavoratori (Workers' Leagues) or the Fasci Siciliani (Sicilian Leagues).

The Fasci was a movement that brought together farm labourers, peasants, sharecroppers, artisans, and sulphur mine workers. Their main aim was to pressure owners to improve working conditions. The miners wanted a reduction in work hours and better wages, while peasants called for a reduction in the rent and taxes collected by landowners and the *gabellotti*. In addition, they called for agrarian land reform to ensure an equitable redistribution of misappropriated agricultural land.

In January 1893 a group of peasants in Caltavuturo protested because common land had been illegally taken over by a local administrator. The Mafia attacked the protestors and started shooting into the crowd with machine guns. In the subsequent mayhem several soldiers joined the rampage and shot at the protestors. In total, eleven peasants were killed and forty were injured. A few months later, at another protest in a village called Giardinello, *mafiosi* started firing at the peasants from the mayor's house. Once again, soldiers joined the fray. In total, seven demonstrators were killed. These are but two of many such episodes in different towns and villages all over Sicily, including Lercara, Gibellina, and Belmonte

THE BATTLE FOR SICILY'S SOUL

Mezzagno, where labourers and peasants made their voice heard, calling for fair payment and social justice.[44]

That year a severe drought hit Sicily and the living conditions of the poor deteriorated to unprecedented levels of misery, giving the Fasci movement added momentum.

"The state of the countryside is disheartening: the olives fall, dry and shrivelled, from the trees. Lemon and orange trees are slowly dying, pasture has become almost non-existent, and the poor peasants are suffering more than anyone else the effect of such calamity. Misery is immense here, as all over the island." Giornale di Sicilia, October 1893[45]

To quell the protests, the Mafia spread to parts of Sicily where they previously had no presence, but where miserable living conditions had strengthened the local Fasci movements.[46] This deployment of the Mafia against the Fasci by the landowning class was in fact a primary factor in the expansion of the territory controlled by Cosa Nostra in the last decade of the nineteenth century. Once the *mafiosi* set themselves up in a new town or village they not only subdued the peasant protestors, but they also colonised the locality, using corruption and coercion to infiltrate local politics, gaining considerable power in the process.

The violence did not deter the Fasci, and on the 21st of May 1893 they organised a regional conference, bringing together ninety Sicilian Fasci groups. The conference was attended by around 500 participants who agreed on the main aims of the movement and to formally affiliate with the Socialist Party.

In October 1893, Bishop Guttadauro of Caltanissetta issued a strongly worded pastoral letter taking a stand in favour of the poor - *"The discontent that has spread across the island is understandable and we cannot ignore it. The rich exploit and abuse the poor, who are made to live a life of hardship and disillusionment."*[47] The Bishop urged parish priests, who he called the *"protectors of the poor"* to intercede on behalf of their parishioners with the landowners and the *gabellotti "to establish a fair balance between the value of the work of the peasants and the investment provided by the gabellotti, in such a way that the harvest is fairly divided between them...*

parish priests should remind the rich of the teachings of the Church, through the words of the Pope, not to treat the workers as slaves, but to respect their human dignity, to act in line with the teachings of Christ, and to distribute work in such a manner as takes into consideration the strength and abilities of the workers, as well as their age and sex. It is their duty is to treat each worker fairly and not to take advantage of their desperation."[48]

Emboldened by the popular commitment to the cause, the Fasci presented several proposals to landowners and mine owners, who rejected them out of hand. This infuriated the Fasci, many of whom resorted to strikes, which in some cases spiralled into violence. The public unrest escalated to such an extent that the landowners requested help from the State. Prime Minister Francesco Crispi declared a state of emergency in Sicily on the 3rd of January 1894, declaring that the Fasci movement was illegal and calling for the arrest of the leaders of the movement.

Tens of thousands of soldiers were sent to Sicily, adding their might to that of the Mafia to suppress the protests, resorting to extreme violence and even killing to destroy the movement. Thousands of demonstrators were imprisoned or sent to penal colonies.

In the aftermath of the bloodbath, in which 108 Fasci lost their lives, the leaders of the Catholic Church closed ranks and aligned with the army and the government, denouncing the activists as agents of Socialism, acting to destabilise the new Italian State. The Bishop of Noto Blandini called the Fasci *"an evil sect which has been designed by Satan"* and proclaimed that socialists should be locked up in mental asylums for foolishly aspiring to an equitable distribution of goods. The Bishop of Nisseno issued a pastoral letter denouncing the protesting peasants as *"fatally deluded by evil troublemakers,"* while the Archbishop of Palermo issued a condemnation of the *"socialist rabble-rousers"* and invited General Morra di Lavriano to his palace to thank him in person for quelling the riots and restoring order on the island.

Demoralised and hopeless, thousands of peasants emigrated to countries where they hoped to be able to earn a decent living, in what came to be known as the Great Emigration.

Timeline of events mentioned in this section

1500 BCE	Three indigenous peoples inhabit Sicily - the Sicanians in the centre, the Sicels (from whom the name Sicily originated) in the east and the Elymians in the west.
800 BCE	The Greeks arrive in Sicily in 800 BCE, and the colonisation of Sicily begins in earnest circa 735 BCE.
264 to 241 BCE	The First Punic War. After twenty-three years of fighting on land and sea, the Romans finally defeat the Carthaginians and in 241 BCE Sicily becomes the first foreign province of Rome.
827	Sicily falls to the Saracens, kicking off a long period of wealth and investment on the island, including the introduction of citrus trees.
1071	The Normans defeat the Arabs and seize the island. This heralds over one hundred years of peace and prosperity. During this time a feudal system is introduced in Sicily.
1194	The Norman bloodline dies out and Sicily passes into the hands of the Hohenstaufens.
1266	Charles I of Anjou invades the island.
1282	On the 30th of March 1282, during evening Vespers, the people of Sicily revolt against the French, ousting Charles of Anjou.
1282	Peter of Aragon becomes the new ruler of Sicily.
1487	The Spanish Inquisition arrives in Sicily, establishing an office in Palermo.
1734	In 1734, Prince Charles of Bourbon, heir to the Spanish throne, claims the kingdoms of Sicily and Naples.
1747	Dr James Lind discovers that giving sailors citrus fruit cures scurvy.

1779	Dr Gilbert Blane finds a way to preserve lemon juice, making it a viable solution for the prevention of scurvy on long sea voyages.
1795	The British Royal Navy institutes a regulation imposing the provision of a daily dose of lemon juice for all sailors, leading to a massive surge in the demand for lemons.
1799	Napoleon conquers Naples and King Ferdinand I flees to Sicily, under the protection of British troops stationed on the island. Within months Lord Nelson recaptures Naples and Ferdinand is restored to the throne.
1806	The Napoleonic army returns to Naples and King Ferdinand once again flees to Sicily.
1812	Lord William Bentinck, the commander of the British forces in Sicily, pressures King Ferdinand to draw up a new constitution for the island to end the feudal system and create a two-chamber Sicilian parliament in Palermo that would be independent of the one in Naples.
1815	Napoleon is defeated and King Ferdinand returns to power in Naples. He immediately rescinds the new Sicilian Constitution but continues with the land reforms. The end of the Napoleonic wars leads to a massive increase in demand for lemon juice and lemon essence, particularly from the United States.
1824	The Bourbons pass a law empowering creditors to seize land in payment for debts.
1838	Pietro Calà Ulloa, a Bourbon official, writes a report mentioning the existence of "brotherhoods" in many Sicilian villages.
1848	Sicilian revolution for independence
1858	On the 21st of July the Prime Minister of Sardinia, Camillo Benso, Count of Cavour, secretly meets Napoleon III to discuss a military alliance.

1859	In March the Sardinians mobilise their army, leading to retaliation by the Austrians, who invade Sardinia. The French join the battle and the Austrians are defeated.
1860	On the 11th of May Giuseppe Garibaldi lands in Sicily with an army of around one thousand volunteers. By June he has taken over most of the island, including Palermo, and by September conquers Naples.
	On the 18th of September the Piedmontese-Sardinians defeat the papal army at the Battle of Castelfilardo, and within weeks they take over all the papal states except Latium, the region surrounding Rome.
	On the 26th of October Vittorio Emanuele II meets Garibaldi in Naples, who greets him as the King of Italy.
1861	The Kingdom of Italy is officially proclaimed on the 17th of March by a parliament assembled in Turin.
1861 onwards	The Italian government expropriates large tracts of land owned by the Church, ostensibly for a programme of land reform.
1862	The Piedmontese government passes a law imposing military conscription for young men.
1864	Baron Turrisi Colonna writes a report called Public Security in Italy, describing a "sect" that he estimates as being around twenty years old.
1866	The Rivolta del Sette e Mezzo. Bandits and Sicilians attack the Palazzo Reale. The carabinieri are unable to control the riot.
1872	Dr Gaspare Galati takes over the management of a lemon grove in Palermo. The Uditore Mafia led by Antonino Giammona attempts to scare him into submission.
1874	Terror in Uditore, a village of 800 inhabitants. Twenty-three peasants, including women and children, are murdered and an additional ten peasants seriously injured over a twelve-month period.

| 1875 | Dr Galati escapes from Sicily and sends a report to the Minister of the Interior in Rome detailing the situation in Palermo and the apparent unwillingness of the police to do anything about it. |

The Minister of the Interior orders the Palermo Chief of Police to investigate the claims made by Dr Galati.

1875 — In 1875 Pasquale Villari publishes *Le Lettere Meridionali*, which focused on the social, cultural, and economic gaps between north and south Italy.

1876 — Publication of *Inchiesta in Sicilia* by Leopoldo Franchetti and Sydney Sonnino. Specific mention is made of organised groups exercising social control through violence.

1889 — Socialist winds start to blow over Sicily, and peasants and labourers come together to protest their miserable working and living conditions.

1891 — Giuseppe de Felice Giuffrida founds the first official Fascio movement in Catania, bringing together farm labourers, peasants, and sulphur mine workers in a call for better wages, a reduction in the rent collected by landowners and the *gabellotti*, and a more equitable redistribution of agricultural land.

Politicians and owners deploy the Mafia to quell the peasant and labourer protests.

1893 — Severe drought exacerbates the misery of the poor, energising the Fasci. A regional conference is organised on the 21st of May, bringing together the ninety Fasci groups in Sicily. It is attended by approximately 500 members who agree to formally affiliate with the Socialist Party.

In October Bishop Guttadauro of Caltanissetta issues a pastoral letter in support of the poor, urging parish priests to help parishioners negotiate with the owners and *gabellotti*, to improve the terms of land rental contracts and ensure that workers were paid fairly and freed from the tyranny of usury.

1894   Prime Minister Francesco Crispi declares a state of emergency on the island and sends 40,000 soldiers to Sicily to quell the unrest. The Fasci movement is decimated by the violence unleashed by both the Mafia and the army.

The leaders of the Catholic Church denounce the Fasci as agents of Socialism, acting to destabilise the new Italian State.
Mass emigration ensues.

1898 to   The Palermo Police Commissioner, Ermanno Sangiorgi,
1900   sends 31 reports to the Ministry of the Interior, written between November 1898 and February 1900. Totalling 485 pages, the combined reports give a comprehensive description of the setup of the Sicilian Mafia.

SECTION II

THE CULTURE HEIST

"*The Mafia wasn't born today: it comes from the past. Before, there were the Beati Paoli who fought with the poor against the rich, then there were the Carbonari: we have the same oath, the same duties.*" Tommaso Buscetta[49]

CHAPTER 3
MYTHOLOGY OF COSA NOSTRA

"*The Mafia is oppression, arrogance, greed, self-enrichment, power and hegemony above and against all others. It is not an abstract concept, or a state of mind, or a literary term... It is a criminal organisation regulated by unwritten but iron and inexorable rules... The myth of a courageous and generous man of honour must be eradicated, because a mafioso is just the opposite.*" Judge Cesare Terranova

Mafiosi describe themselves as men of honour. Their identity is built upon a mythology steeped in the traditional values, culture, and politics of Sicily, which they have misappropriated and corrupted for their own ends.

The process of colonisation of Sicilian popular culture started in the early 1860s, and initially it was not masterminded by the Mafia itself. However, once the process was under way and *mafiosi* realised how useful it was to inhabit the realm of popular culture, they took up the narrative, making it their own, and over a period of a few decades they created a whole mythology about the origins of the Mafia, the nature of the organisation and the values and motivations of the men who were a part of it.

3.1 The origin of the word *Mafioso*
"*Before Buscetta, we did not even know the Mafia's real name.*"
Judge Antonino Caponetto

In the Sicilian dialect the word *mafiusu* or *maffiusu* when applied to a man meant he was proud, bold, or full of swagger. The female equivalent *mafiusa* or *maffiusa* meant the woman in question was beautiful.

In Tuscany, in the 1400s, the word *malfusso* meant a crook, while the Florentines used the word *mafia* or *maffia* to refer to extreme poverty, and the Piedmontese used *mafi*, *mafio*, or *mafium* to describe someone who was disfigured or antisocial.

Some historians claim that *mafiusu* was derived from the word *mahjas* in Arabic, which means braggart or arrogant. Others propose the words *mu'afa* which means safety or protection or *marfud*, which means to reject or to refuse.

There has been much debate amongst scholars about the origin of the word, but there is now some form of consensus that the most likely etymologies are the ones that trace the root back to Arabic. This makes sense given the fact that Sicily was under Arab rule for 234 years, followed by another 134 years of Norman rule during which Arab Muslims rubbed shoulders with Jews and Christians in cosmopolitan Palermo.

It is unlikely that we will ever be able to pin down the exact origin of the word, but what is certain is that in nineteenth century Sicily a *mafiusu* was someone who was self-confident and in control of his own destiny. The members of the *cosche* did not call themselves *mafiusi* or think of themselves as *mafiusi* – the use of the word in their regard was the brainchild of Giuseppe Rizzotto and Gaspare Mosca who incorporated the word in a title of a theatrical production called *I mafiusi di la Vicaria* (The *mafiosi* of the Vicaria), which was first performed in 1863.

The play was about a prison gang in Palermo that prioritised honour above all else. The gang had a vitally important code of *omertà*, a word derived from the Latin root *homo* which means manliness and was understood to refer to the practice of a man resolving his own problems and defending his honour. The gang members collected *pizzu* (beak-full) from other prison inmates, just like the mafia *cosche* collected protection payments from anyone in their territory who required their services. The story of the play was firmly anchored in the mythology of the good mafia

– a mafia made up of honourable Sicilians who protected the weak and fought for justice. In one scene in the play the *capomafia* falls onto his knees and begs God for forgiveness when he finds out his men killed a prison inmate who had collaborated with the police. He is so affected by this unjust murder that he resigns as boss.

The theatrical production was a rip-roaring success, with fifty-five performances in 1863 alone. It then toured all over Italy and was staged over two thousand times over a period of twenty-one years. The play appealed to a wide swathe of Italians, irrespective of class. In the audience were nobles and workers, and even King Umberto I watched the production.[50] The message about the noble *mafiusi* spread far and wide, and the parallels with the *cosche* in Sicily were so obvious that the term became synonymous with the Sicilian clans, entering the collective imagination and soon percolating into official reports. In 1865 the newly appointed prefect of Palermo, the Marquis Filippo Antonio Gualterio, penned a report where he referred to the criminal organisations in the city as "*the so-called Maffia or criminal association.*" This document is significant, because it is the first time the criminal organisation is referred to in such a manner formally by the State.

Also in 1865, an article appeared in a French travel magazine, written by a French anarchist in exile called Elisée Reclus. In the article he claimed that there existed in Sicily a secret criminal organisation with around 5000 members who "*live on the proceeds of all kinds of deception and fraud.*" He described *il pizzo*, explaining that all tradesmen had to pay it in order to be safe - "*it may be said that the whole city obeys two powers: Italy and the maffia*" – and spoke of the criminal organisation having "*simple signs, furtive gestures and enigmatic code words: the anonymity of the group enables it to deploy many methods designed to strike terror, and the occasional stabbing shows that it possesses its own judges and tribunals.*"

Ten years later the name Mafia had become entrenched in the public's consciousness and had been purloined by the "entrepreneurs of protection". In 1876, in the report *Inchiesta in Sicilia*, Leopoldo Franchetti describes the process of appropriation as follows –

"The Sicilian use [of the word mafia] ... is precisely expressed with the adjective mafioso, which does not mean a man committed to crime, but rather a man who knows how to enforce his rights, whatever the means he uses to achieve this end. And since in this society we have tried to describe, violence is often the better means that one has to engender respect, so it followed naturally that the word came to mean a man committed to blood. Hence the noun mafia found a class of violent men and troublemakers who needed a name to define them. Given their special character and importance in Sicilian society, they had the right to a different name from that defining vulgar criminals in other countries."[51]

The *mafiosi* were thus endowed with an aura of glamour and danger that they cultivated with pride, with Francis Marion Crawford[52] describing the typical *mafioso* at the beginning of the twentieth century as follows - *"...He wears his hat upon the left side, his hair smoothed with plentiful pomatum and one lock brushed down upon his forehead, he walks with a swinging motion of the hips, a cigar in his mouth, a heavy knotted stick in his hand, and he is frequently armed with a long knife or a revolver. He stares disdainfully at every man he meets with the air of challenging each comer to speak to him if he dare."*

This was the start of a heated debate about the word *mafia* that took over one hundred years to resolve – with one side associating the word with criminal activities and the other declaring that it referred to nothing more than Sicilian pride and a tendency to resolve any issues privately, without turning to the authorities.

I mafiusi di la Vicaria was just the first of many theatrical productions that influenced public opinion regarding the nature of the Mafia and the significance of what was happening in Sicily. In 1880 Giovanni Carmelo Verga published a collection of stories called *Vita Dei Campi* (Life in the Fields), including *Cavalleria Rusticana* (Rustic Chivalry). The story was later adapted for the theatre and ten years later it was used as an opera libretto by Pietro Mascagni for his eponymous opera.

The one-act opera premiered on the 17th of May 1890 at the Teatro Costanzi in Rome, with Queen Margherita and several music critics in the audience. It portrayed the so-called traditional Sicilian values of honour and courage, with the two male protagonists taking the law into their own hands to resolve a private matter. The opera thus reinforced and disseminated the viewpoint that any mafia activity was in truth a form of Sicilian self-sufficiency, inculcated in Sicilians over hundreds of years of exploitative foreign rule. A resounding success, in the vein of *I mafiusi di la Vicaria*, the opera was produced in various locations around Italy, and its message spread nationwide.

The character of the *mafioso* was now well established in public opinion. The following description is from Giuseppe Pitrè, an Italian folklorist, medical doctor and senator for Sicily -

"The mafioso wants to be respected and almost always respects others. If he has been offended, he doesn't turn to justice, or the law; if he did so this would be proof of weakness, and would offend omertà, which regards as schifiusu (disgusting) or 'nfam (vile) those who for whatever motive turn to the magistrates." [53]

Later in the book we shall be talking about the testimony of a *pentito* called Tommaso Buscetta[1]. However, at this stage it is interesting to note that one of the very first things the *pentito* clarified related to the name of the criminal organisation.

"The word 'mafia' is a literary creation. ... the real 'mafiosi' call themselves simply 'men of honour' ... and the organisation is called 'Cosa Nostra' as in the United States." Tommaso Buscetta[54]

---

1 Tommaso Buscetta was born in 1928 in Palermo, in a very large poverty-stricken family. By the age of seventeen he was already a foot soldier in the Mafia. For several years he was involved in cigarette smuggling, but he then became instrumental in setting up Cosa Nostra's international drug trafficking network. In the 1980s Buscetta collaborated with Giovanni Falcone in Sicily and with prosecutors in the US. His testimony in the Pizza Connection trial led to him being awarded American citizenship and a place in the witness protection program. He died of cancer aged 71 in 2000 and is buried under a false name.

Buscetta's statement was confirmed by Antonino Calderone[2], another *pentito*.

"This is Cosa Nostra. Cosa Nostra! Do you understand? And Cosa Nostra is not Mafia. The police, the journalists call it Mafia ..."[55]

3.2 The Psychology of Victimisation

To understand how Cosa Nostra managed to hide in plain sight for so long, it is essential to put ourselves in the shoes of a people who had been subjugated and victimised for centuries.

When foreign powers colonise a region with the aim of extracting as much wealth from it as possible, the local culture slowly morphs until it becomes not only acceptable, but also admirable and desirable to fight back against the authorities. In such situations banditry and violence are justified as a necessary means to an end.

It is also important to keep in mind that generation after generation of islanders had lived in a society where justice was always out of reach. Their rulers did not intervene to ensure their safety, and many were left at the mercy of despotic feudal lords with no checks and balances to ensure any true justice. This created a massive deficit of trust, not only in the authorities but also between Sicilians, because if one Sicilian cheated another, there was no sure way of obtaining redress. The situation was exacerbated in the feudal estates where the landlord was only interested in maximising his profit, and the *bravi* and *gabellotti* had total and absolute power over the peasants and other labourers on the estate. The only way to have food on the table and a semblance of protection was to curry favour and pay homage in whatever currency these ruthless individuals requested.

---

2 Antonino Calderone was born in 1935. He was the grandson of Antonio Saitta, who had founded the first Mafia *cosca* in Catania. Calderone was initiated into Cosa Nostra in 1962. He rose through the ranks until he became the second in command to his brother, Giuseppe Calderone, who was the boss of the Catania mafia. In 1978 Giuseppe Calderone was killed and a few years later Antonino Calderone fled Sicily with his family to escape from the terror unleashed by the Corleonesi.

This collective frame of mind was the foundation upon which the Sicilian Mafia built itself. It had taken centuries of shared trauma for Sicilians to internalise this world view, and by the time Cosa Nostra came into being this perspective was inexorably entrenched in local culture. Nowadays we take out insurance to safeguard our health, lives, homes, and investments, and that is exactly how Sicilians perceived their cooperation with *mafiosi* – they were paying a premium to the entrepreneurs who had the monopoly of protection in Sicily.

3.2.1 Learned Helplessness

The phrase *learned helplessness* was coined by Martin Seligman, an American psychologist. In 1967, Seligman and his colleagues at the University of Pennsylvania were conducting experiments to understand depression, when to their surprise they realised that some of the dogs in their experiment were acting in totally unexpected ways.

In the first phase of the experiment Seligman assessed how dogs would react to irritating electric shocks. These were not very strong and did not injure the dogs, but they were unpleasant. The first group of dogs were put in a cage where they could stop the shocks by pressing on a button. They quickly discovered this and started pawing the button regularly to stop the shocks. After that a second group of dogs were put in the cage, but the button was deactivated. The poor dogs ran around the cage trying to get away from the irritating shocks, but they soon learned there was no means of escape.

In the second phase, Seligman moved the dogs to a different type of enclosure. The dogs were put on one side where they got the small shocks. Dogs from the first group, whose button had stopped the shocks, immediately ran off and discovered that the other half of the enclosure was safe. Dogs from the second group, however, sat down and were shocked repeatedly, but they did not make any attempt to escape. They just accepted the electric shocks passively. This response is what led Seligman to develop his theory of learned helplessness.

This type of learned behaviour can be seen in many other situations. One well-known example relates to circus elephants. When elephants are little, their trainers tie them to a stake in the ground. Initially the baby elephant tries to pull the stake out of the ground but quickly learns that it is not strong enough to do so. As the elephant grows, it becomes strong enough to free itself. However, by then it is totally conditioned to believe that escape is not possible, so it does not even try.

The same principle applies to people. When someone is in a highly stressful and abusive situation, they rapidly learn that their situation is hopeless, that change is not possible, and that their only option is to accept their lot in life. This is what happened to generation after generation of Sicilians who lived under the yoke of abusive colonisers, despotic feudal lords, ruthless *bravi*, greedy unethical *gabellotti* and finally, the Mafia.

3.2.2 Maslow's Hierarchy of Needs

Abraham Maslow was another American psychologist, and the founder of Humanistic Psychology. He developed a theory to explain what motivated people to behave in certain ways, in what came to be known as the *Hierarchy of Needs*. This psychological theory is based on five tiers of human needs that are often depicted as a pyramid, with the most fundamental needs of human beings at the bottom and the less pressing needs on top.

At the very bottom of the pyramid is the most basic need of all – physiological, meaning the provision of the basics required for survival, such as food and shelter. The next level of needs relates to safety, after which come love and belonging, moving on to esteem and finally the pinnacle of the pyramid, self-actualisation.

The hierarchy of needs has been used in many fields to explain what motivates people. It is of particular interest in education, where teachers use it to understand how to motivate their students. It is also used by businesses to understand what drives their customers' behaviour and how to influence them to buy their products or services. And I believe it can also be applied to a swathe of Sicilians to understand their motivations and behaviour when it came to dealing with *mafiosi*.

According to Maslow, although human beings have multiple needs, they will only be motivated to act on those needs that are most pressing.

If someone is hungry, they will focus on their physiological needs and focus all their efforts on getting food. It is only when they have food, water, and shelter that they will turn their attention to next level, safety. Once they are safe, they will then look for love, friendship, and a sense of community. As each level of need is satisfied, the person moves up a level in their path towards self-actualisation.

When people are born in families and societies where their fundamental needs (food, water, shelter, safety) are met, they take this for granted and focus on the next level of need – love and belonging and a sense of community. However, if people exist in a situation where they are constantly struggling to have food on the table and a roof over their heads, their main priority will always be the satisfaction of these basic needs, and they will not have the time or energy to dedicate any effort to building relationships and trust within their community. Each person becomes isolated in their battle for survival.

When one thinks of the peasants and other labourers in Sicily, it is easy to see how the hierarchy of needs impacted their behaviour. In the *Lettere Meridionali*, Paolo Villari claimed that evil had infected peasants, manual labourers, and sulphur miners in Sicily who were willing to sacrifice their children's safety to earn money.

"From 1859 until today we have lacked the courage, the social solidarity necessary to make the law that so many [other countries] have already made. It is now discussed in the administration, and naturally everyone agrees that it must be done. However, will there be time to approve and discuss it in Parliament during this session, or will the House be too busy, too tired, too overwhelmed with other priorities? AND once this law is approved, will the government enforce it? The miners will undoubtedly protest, claiming that their freedom and their rights are being restricted. The pickaxe workers will protest and say that by prohibiting the work of the children then the earnings of adults will decrease. Mothers will raise their voices and cry out that their children are being prevented from earning their daily bread, and that thus they will starve."[56]

Villari is obviously critical of mothers who chose to allow their children to work in the mines – but he does not address the truth of their claims. If families did not have any food, then sending their children into the mines to earn a pittance with which they could buy something to eat was in fact their only reasonable option. Their safety needs were a luxury they could not afford to think about when faced with the real and present danger of starving to death.

It is this basic misunderstanding about human psychology that made it impossible for the wealthy northerners to understand their impoverished compatriots in the south. It also resulted in many scholars describing the behaviour of the downtrodden as complicity and widespread *omertà*, when in truth it was simply a case of people doing what needed to be done to survive.

The theory also holds for Sicilians who were not on the poverty line. The newly formed bourgeoisie were no longer motivated by their physiological needs, so they progressed to concern about their safety. To use an earlier analogy, they perceived their cooperation with *mafiosi* as equivalent to paying for insurance to safeguard not only their assets but also their lives.

At the next level of the social and motivational hierarchy, those who had their physiological and safety needs met were motivated by a need for belonging and the building of interpersonal relationships they could depend on for support. This explains the phenomenon of the *fratellanze* (brotherhoods) which operated as cartels, as well as actual membership in a *cosca*, where men became a part of a new family that became central to how they identified themselves and their network of relations.

The truly wealthy, on the other hand, in many cases were looking for power because they were motivated by their esteem needs. They wanted to be perceived as successful, rich, and well-connected, and if that meant consorting with *mafiosi*, then so be it.

Cosa Nostra did not create the Sicilian value-system and the way the islanders viewed and understood the world around them. The local culture and folklore were formed and rooted in the harsh realities of the region and centuries of oppression on one side (peasants and labourers) and privilege (landlords) on the other. What *mafiosi* did was misappropriate the Sicilian worldview and the underpinning popular folklore and mould them to suit their nefarious purposes.

Nowhere is this more obvious than in the way *mafiosi* appropriated the legends of the Sicilian Vespers, the Carbonari, and the Beati Paoli.

3.3 The Sicilian Vespers

On the 30th of March 1282, native Sicilians revolted against the French ruler Charles I of Anjou, whose reign was steeped in brutality. Over a period of six weeks they killed thousands of French men, women, and children.

There are various accounts about what sparked the insurrection, but the common theme is that a congregation of Sicilians came together to celebrate the evening prayers (Vespers) on Easter Monday at the Church of the Holy Spirit on the outskirts of Palermo. At this point a Frenchman harassed a Sicilian woman, but there is no consensus as to the exact details of the attack. In one telling a helpless Sicilian girl is raped by a French soldier who leaves her for dead, and her mother runs through the streets of Palermo screaming in despair "Ma fia! Ma fia!" which meant "my daughter" in medieval Sicilian dialect. The story goes that the attack on the girl sparked a revolt, just as the church bells started ringing to announce Vespers. News of the rebellion quickly spread, and rioters took to the streets, killing the French wherever they came across them. Within weeks the entire island was under the control of the rebels, who also burned the French ships in the harbour.

One of the claims made by the men of honour is that Cosa Nostra is descended from the rebels who succeeded in ousting Charles of Anjou from Sicily. The screams of the despairing mother have also been appropriated, with some professing that this is where the Mafia got its name. Scholars have dismissed these claims as fanciful notions with no basis in fact, however this does not deter *mafiosi* from including these credentials in their pedigree, and in fact in the 1980s several *pentiti* mentioned the Sicilian Vespers as part of the origin story of Cosa Nostra.

3.4 The Carbonari

The Carbonari (charcoal burners) was a secret society that came into being in Naples during the Napoleonic wars. It is believed to have been an offshoot of freemasonry, with similar initiation rituals and membership rules.

The secret organisation was made up of a network of cells focused on fomenting armed revolt to defend the rights of the common man. Initially they opposed Joachim Murat, the brother-in-law of Napoleon, who had installed him as the new King of Naples when the Bourbon Ferdinand escaped to Sicily. However, when Ferdinand returned to his court in Naples in 1815, they rapidly rallied against him, demanding a constitution.

The Carbonari were involved in uprisings in 1820, 1821, 1830 and 1831. However, in February 1931, when they marched on Rome, they were decimated by the Austrian troops, and it became clear that their dreams of launching a revolution would never materialise. Membership in the Carbonari slowly dwindled down to nothing, with some of the members going on to form a new movement called Giovane Italia (Young Italy).

3.5 The Beati Paoli

The Sicilian Vespers and the Carbonari were both often mentioned by *pentiti*. However, the legend that truly captured people's imagination and influenced their views about Cosa Nostra was the story of the *Beati Paoli*, rumoured to be a secret order of knights who defended poor Sicilians from the excesses of the feudal landlords and the Holy Inquisition. These Sicilian Robin Hoods purportedly hid in the tunnels and catacombs under Palermo, emerging at night in black hooded capes to avenge those who had suffered injustice at the hands of the church or the State.

It is believed that the Beati Paoli had their headquarters in a cave that is nowadays known as the *Grotta dei Beati Paoli* (Cave of the Beati Paoli) under the *Capo* district of Palermo. It can be accessed through a door in the Alley of the Orphans, alongside a church dedicated to St Maruzza. The door leads to a flight of steps that goes straight down to what was originally a natural cave eroded over centuries by the River Papireto.

Extensive works were conducted in the cave by Arab and Norman engineers, as well as by subsequent users of the place, as is evidenced from the cobbled floor and smooth walls and, somewhat more ominously, by staples for iron fetters embedded in the walls, where victims of the sect were said to have been tethered with iron chains around their ankles. The cave is connected to a labyrinth of tunnels running under the city where extensive Christian catacombs are located.

The myth is that the Beati Paoli met in the cave at night and set up a tribunal, mirroring the modus operandi of the Inquisition. The sect considered all accusations of injustice presented to it, deciding how to avenge the wrongdoing. If the accused was found guilty, the sentence was usually death. The knights then roamed through the streets of Palermo at night, seeking out the guilty to administer their version of justice.

There is general agreement amongst historians that the secretive sect did, in fact, exist. It most likely originated as a peaceful confraternity of monks dedicated to St Francis di Paola, who focused on prayer and good works, which is why they came to be known as the *Beati Paoli*. The monks wore dark habits, explaining the black hooded capes described in the legend. When the Inquisition started wreaking havoc on Sicilian society, the monks rebelled and fought back. That said, there is no evidence that they were committed to avenging the oppressed or fighting for the poor. In fact, the likelihood is that they were noblemen using violence to settle their own personal vendettas and to accumulate more wealth and power.

The first written record of the legend of the Beati Paoli was authored by Francesco Maria Emanuele Gaetani, the Marquis of Villabianca, an Italian historian who was born in Palermo in 1720. He was well-connected and held many prestigious posts, including senator of Palermo, general commissioner in the Kingdom of Sicily, governor of the noble Company of Charity and governor of the Monte di Pietà. However, what is most important for our purposes is the fact that he was intensely interested in the history of Sicily and over his lifetime published many books about the island, including the *Opuscoli Palermitani* (Palermo Pamphlets). In vol. XVI, *Opuscolo sui Beati Paoli* (Pamphlet about the Beati Paoli), he wrote about the legend he had heard when he was a little boy.

According to his writings, the Beati Paoli was a cult made up of wicked men who terrorised the upper classes of Sicily, acting as vigilantes on behalf of the lower classes and torturing and killing all those who stood in their way. One must of course remember that as a child in a noble family, he would have heard the story told from the perspective of the upper classes, and not that of the peasants who the Beati Paoli were supposedly avenging.

Interestingly, he dates the existence of the cult to the sixteenth and seventeenth centuries, which aligns with the activities of the Spanish Inquisition on the island. What is also clear is that at the time he heard the story the Beati Paoli were already in the realm of legend, with the activities described having happened over one hundred years earlier. The Beati Paoli thus might very well have existed in the sixteenth and seventeenth centuries, but they were extinct by the eighteenth century, which is a very important point to highlight given the claims later made by *mafiosi*.

In 1836 a Sicilian writer called Vincenzo Linares also reconstructed the story of the Beati Paoli, which he called a "vengeful sect." The tale was initially serialised in a Palermitan newspaper called *Il Vapore* and subsequently formed part of a book of stories published in 1840. The following is an extract from Linares' story about the Beati Paoli.

"He entered through a small door just three palms high, which soon closed behind him, sending a shiver down his spine; the space he had just entered resembled a grave. He descended a stone staircase, until he reached a damp and dark grotto. There stood an altar with a crucifix, lit by a lamp. An altar in a cave!

Was this a place where sacrifices were made by followers of the occult? What was the reason for the presence of the Cross in such a mysterious place?

They then made their way down a long corridor, the walls of which were decorated with daggers, arquebuses, pistols, and weapons of all kinds: on the right hand he saw a room with piles of paper; on the left another room full of old cabinets, with water trickling down cracks in the rocks; they followed the passageway, winding this way and that, until they reached a large grotto which seemed to be their ultimate destination.

The room was carved out of the bare rock, with black drapes that gave the place a grim and frightening atmosphere. The elliptical shape of the room included several niches all around, at a short interval from each other. In these were positioned men armed from head to toe, in the same pose as that of the corpses buried in the underground catacombs. The guards were dressed in black habits, in the manner of ministry officials, and a black hood covered their heads.

In the middle of the cave was a stone table on which there was a statuette carved out of stone. The figure was wrapped in a cloak, carrying a scale in the left hand and a sword in the right. Clearly it represented justice, signifying that justice saw everything and was sure of her decisions.

A big lamp illuminated the dark vault, and that light, reflected on their proud faces, gave the scene the appearance of a mystical painting, on the lines of the macabre paintings by Rosa.

The scene echoed the descriptions in local legends of the occult and the mysterious covens of witches which met on the Sabbath, when possessed by the spirit of Satan they conspire to the detriment of men.

At the bottom of the grotto were piles of weapons, knives, pistols, daggers. The leader of the sect, easily identifiable by his large hat, sat down near the table. He seemed to be the oldest man in the room; nevertheless, his eyes sparkled like fire and the tanned skin and wrinkles of his face revealed a soul not tamed by the passage of time but strong in purpose and experience. At his side sat a secretary or chancellor, who wore the same black habit, unfolding many cards placed on the table. When everyone took their seats, a profound silence ensued."

In 1848, Carmelo Piola wrote a poem in Sicilian dialect about *Li Beati Pauli Ligenna Popolare* (The Beati Paoli of Traditional Legend). In the poem the Beati Paoli meet in a large cave with an altar on which two candles illuminate a missal flanked on each side by a dagger. The members of the sect are described as honourable men, guided by their strong faith as they discussed how to avenge injustice.

The story was then taken up by Benedetto Naselli who wrote a play called *I Beati Paoli o La Famiglia del Giustiziato* (The Beati Paoli or The Family of the Executed Man) which was first performed on the 21st of December 1863 in Palermo. The plot is based on a leader of the sect who abuses his power and orders a murder for his own personal interest. The corrupt state judiciary then attempt to pin the crime on an innocent man to give the impression that justice had been served. A painter called Andrea Valenti is arrested, and after being subjected to torture he finally confesses to the crime and is sentenced to death, becoming yet another victim of the villainous leader of the Beati Paoli. Valenti's wife, Maria, who is blind, and their two children are left destitute. However, she fights back, determined to clear her husband's name. Thus, we see that in Naselli's version of the legend the motivations of the Beati Paoli were anything but pure.

Five years later, in 1868, a Catholic-Regionalist bloc won a decisive victory in local elections. The new mayor, Domenico Peranni, was determined to defend Sicilian culture against those who were attempting to defame it, so he set out to reinforce the traditions and folklore that he felt were strongly representative of the true nature of the inhabitants of the island. The feast of Santa Rosalia, the patron saint of Palermo, was re-launched, while the legend of the Beati Paoli was given a more convenient political slant. The sect became the vanguard of the revolt of the Sicilians against foreign (in which many people also read Piedmontese) oppressors. So important was the reinterpretation of the legend in the political reality of the time that the new council of administration of Palermo officially sanctioned it by renaming the street and the square in front of the entrance to the cave that was said to have been used by the sect in honour of the Beati Paoli.[57]

A few years later, in 1873, Giuseppe Bruno Arcaro published an essay entitled *A page of Sicilian history* in which he described the Beati Paoli as leaders in an ongoing revolt against the injustices perpetuated by foreign governments that attempted to destroy Sicilian traditions and tried to turn them into Spaniards, Piedmontese, or Germans. The Beati Paoli were thus cast as heroes, yearning for Sicily's independence and freedom, while fighting against the privilege of the nobility.

This, therefore, was the spirit of the time in 1875 when Giuseppe Pitrè recorded the oral folkloristic tales about the Beati Paoli, which he described as a secret society made up of brave men from the lower classes who defended the weak and took revenge on those who exploited and tormented them.

The political rehabilitation of the legend was now complete. From rich nobles who murdered people who stood in their way and framed innocent poverty-stricken people for their crimes, the Beati Paoli had become members of the lower classes protecting Sicilians from the infamy and arrogance of the administration in the north. This interpretation would have been particularly powerful at the time, given the strong animosity between the Holy See and the anticlerical government in Piedmont, as described in chapter 2.

Thirty-four years later, in 1909, a Sicilian journalist and writer called Luigi Natoli wrote a serialised novel about the Beati Paoli for the national newspaper *Giornale di Sicilia*, using the pseudonym William Galt. Spread over two hundred and thirty-nine episodes, appearing in the newspaper between May 1909 and January 1910, the novel told a tale of courageous men coming together as a secret society, operating under the cover of night in Palermo between 1698 and 1719, fighting against the oppressors of the people.

The novel was loosely based on the oral tradition and the written accounts of the Beati Paoli, but it was a work of fiction, not a historical account. The story is a saga at the centre of which is the noble La Motta family, who in 1698 receive the terrible news that the head of the family, Duke Emanuele della Motta, had been killed at war, just as his wife Donna Aloisia gives birth to their son. Unfortunately, the late Duke's brother, Don Raimondo Albamonte della Motta, was an evil man who saw his brother's death as an opportunity to steal the title and the family riches, so he conspired with his manservant and a witch to kill Donna Aloisia and the child. However, the lady escaped and before dying she entrusted her child to three strangers who came to her aid.

Several years later, a young man called Blasco da Castiglione, the illegitimate son of Don Emanuele, arrives in Palermo. A friar helps him find employment with Don Raimondo. In the meantime, one of the servants who had saved Donna Aloisia hides in a church after trying to assassinate Don Raimondo. Here he meets Don Girolamo, the man who had come to Donna Aloisia's aid and subsequently raised her son, who is now known as his nephew, Emanuele. After talking to the manservant, Don Girolamo realises that Emanuele is the legitimate son of Duke Emanuele della Motta, and that Don Raimondo was the one who was responsible for Donna Aloisia's death, subsequently usurping the title that should have gone to her son.

Don Girolamo was a member of a secret sect, the Beati Paoli, who met regularly in an underground room under the church of San Matteo. Upon learning of Don Raimondo's treachery, the knights agree to avenge Donna Aloisia. The situation escalates when Matteo Lo Vecchio, a corrupt police officer employed by Don Raimondo, breaks into Don Girolamo's home and discovers detailed minutes taken during the secret tribunal, including all the accusations made against Don Raimondo and the fact that Emanuele is in truth the legitimate heir of the late Duke.

While travelling to Messina, Matteo is attacked by robbers who steal all his belongings, including the documents he had himself stolen from Don Girolamo's house. Blasco witnesses the robbery and chases the bandits, recovering the stolen items. He reads the minutes of the Beati Paoli tribunal and discovers that Emanuele is his half-brother.

Don Raimondo arranges for Don Girolamo's wife and his nephew Emanuele to be arrested on trumped up charges. In retribution, the Beati Paoli kidnap his daughter, Violante, and his wife, Gabriella. Blasco opposes this, since the women were not responsible for Raimondo's sins. However, the head of the Beati Paoli rejects his argument, explaining that the sect was committed to avenging the countless abuses and injustices inflicted by the rich upon the poor and the powerless. The rich used the corrupt police and state officials to thwart justice, but the Beati Paoli were incorruptible and uncompromising, and would stop at nothing to ensure that such crimes would be avenged.

"The lords of the state were the nobles and the clergy because they possessed all the wealth; all official positions went to them; the most

important and influential offices could only be conceded to the nobles who helped, supported, and protected each other. Whatever violence or crime they committed, they were certain of their impunity; the heaviest penalties were limited to exile in some fine royal palace where they were housed and served with comfort and enjoyed the greatest freedom. But the lower and middle classes knew only misery and servitude, and the law struck them with the most ferocious punishments possible"[58]

When Don Raimondo finds out that his wife and daughter were kidnapped, he is frantic with worry. Blasco visits him, reassuring him that the ladies are safe, and proposes an exchange. The Beati Paoli would release Gabriella and Violante as soon as Don Raimondo arranged for the release of Don Girolamo's wife and Emanuele, as well as giving to Emanuele what was rightfully his. Don Raimondo agrees and is finally reunited with his beloved daughter.

The Beati Paoli then kidnap Don Raimondo and formally accuse him of all his crimes during a tribunal held in their cave, forcing him to sign a statement giving up his title as Duke and recognising Emanuele as the true heir to the title. Don Emanuele's faithful manservant then stabs him. He dies a few days later and Emanuele is acknowledged as the true heir of the Dukedom.

Four years later, the new Duke is already corrupted by his position and power. Attracted to Gabriella, who spurns him, and engaged to Violante, who loves Blasco, he loses his mind and in a fit of rage and jealousy he tries to rape the two women. Gabriella saves herself and her stepdaughter by killing Emanuele, after which she kills herself. In the end, the incorruptible Blasco becomes Duke and he marries Violante, and as these stories always end, they lived happily ever after.

The Beati Paoli, however, were not satisfied. Don Raimondo had been punished, but the time had come to act against the corrupt police officer, Matteo Lo Vecchio. The man is assassinated, and at his funeral the good people of Palermo thronged the streets celebrating his death, preventing him from getting a decent burial and instead throwing his corpse ignominiously into a well.

The novel ends with Don Girolamo becoming the head of the Beati Paoli and with justice fully served, both in the case of the evil Don Raimondo and in that of the corrupt state official who had protected him.

"They were a reactionary, moderate force: they rose up to defend and protect the weak, stop injustice and violence: they were a state within the state, formidable because secretive, feared because they judged without possibility of appeal, punished without mercy and struck without failing. And nobody knew the identity of the judges or the executioners. They seemed to belong more to myth than reality. They were everywhere, heard and knew everything, but nobody knew where they were or where they met."[59]

The serialised novel was so popular that it was published in a single volume by the publishers Gutenberg of Palermo in 1921. It became a best seller and firmly established the *Beati Paoli* as honourable vigilantes in the public's imagination. In 1947 the novel was turned into a film called *I Cavalieri dalle Maschere Nere* (The Black Masked Knights), produced by the *Organizzazione Filmistica Siciliana* (Sicilian Film Society) and directed by Pino Mercanti. The film created a new wave of demand for the book, which was re-printed in 1949 and once again in 1955 by the publishers La Madonnina di Milano.

Natoli also wrote a sequel called *Coriolano della Floresta*, which takes place fifty years after the end of the previous book. In this story the Beati Paoli are still operating in the tunnels under Palermo and Blasco di Castiglione and Coriolano della Floresta are re-united in the battle between good and evil, coming to the aid of a young couple who fall in love.

3.6 The Creation of a Pedigree

"The Mafia wasn't born today: it comes from the past. Before, there were the Beati Paoli who fought with the poor against the rich, then there were the Carbonari: we have the same oath, the same duties." Tommaso Buscetta[60]

On the 12th of March 1909, an Italian American policeman called Joseph Petrosino was killed as he waited to meet two informants in a square in Palermo. He was well-known in the US for battling organised crime in New York, and he had come to Sicily to find proof of crimes committed by *mafiosi* in Sicily before emigrating to the US, with the goal of deporting as many of them back to Italy as possible.

One month later, in April 1909, a witness came forward to testify that Don Vito Cascio Ferro, a *mafioso* who was suspected to be the mastermind of the assassination of Petrosino, had asked him *"...to take a letter to a house next to a church near the Monte di Pietà in Palermo. The entrance to the house was through a small door next to the church where a young deaf-mute woman would take the letter."*[61]

The witness claimed he had gone to the small door as instructed, and the deaf-mute woman led him down the stairs, where he entered a room full of mysterious looking men who he had never seen before. The atmosphere in the room, he claimed, convinced him that this was an important meeting place where weighty decisions and agreements were made in secret.

In the margin of the report is a note written by the Commissioner of Police himself – *"... the church mentioned by the witness is the Beati Paoli church in the square of that name and the house which is indicated is next to the church."*

The timing could not have been better. In a fortuitous stroke of luck for Cosa Nostra, the following month, in May, the first Beati Pauli episodes appeared in the *Giornale di Sicilia*. The depiction of honourable vigilantes in the novel proved to be a golden opportunity for the criminal organisation, capturing as it did the public's imagination. It catapulted the Beati Paoli from the past and the legendary into the public consciousness in the present, enabling the *mafiosi* to appropriate the legend and made it their own.

Cosa Nostra positioned itself as the descendant of the Beati Paoli as portrayed in the novel, carrying forward the torch of protectors of the poor and the weak. With each new rumour coming out of the investigation into the killing of Petrosino, and the publication of episode after episode of Natoli's saga, the two became more and more intertwined in the minds of the public. It was no longer clear where legend ended and reality began.

From that point onwards the Beati Paoli and the Sicilian Mafia became inextricably connected, creating an important clarion call to young men to join Cosa Nostra, ostensibly in a drive to ensure justice for the weak.

The idea of a state within a state, or a group of people operating in the shadows righting the wrongs of the rich and undoing the cover-ups of the state, was a very convenient smokescreen for an organisation that was collecting a security tax in the form of *pizzi* from all those who had something that needed to be protected. Natoli's novel thus became a blueprint for the public persona of Cosa Nostra; an attractive camouflage behind which they could continue killing and looting rich and poor alike.

The success of the Mafia's appropriation of the legend became amply apparent in a play called *La Mafia* written ten years later by Giovanni Alfredo Cesareo, and first performed in the Eliseo Theatre in Rome in 1921. Consider the following passage from the play, where Rasconà, a lawyer who is the head of the *mafiosi* of the region, explains the main purpose of the Mafia, in terms that echo the mission of the Beati Paoli from Natoli's novel -

"You make me laugh, you know! Justice exists ... You, for example, are on the side of justice, are you not? Your daughter gave herself to the man she loves. The young man can't wait to make her happy by marrying her. But the despotic baron, out of jealousy and spite, opposes the match. Justice here would mean forcing that man to do the right thing. But who can do that? You? The law? No. Only I can do that. Because I am not the law which is justice for the powerful few; but I am strength which is the law for all. When the weak, the betrayed, and the oppressed realised that justice was nothing but trickery and violence, they said – let's exchange parts, so let trickery and violence be our justice. This is what you call mafia; basically, it is social revolt!"[62]

When challenged about the violence and terror wreaked by the *mafiosi*, Rasconà justifies it using the same argument made by Coriolano, the head of the Beati Paoli, when challenged by Blasco in Natoli's novel - *"I am Rasconà, a faithful friend and bitter enemy. What do I do? I do what I like.*

What methods do I use? Methods which make your carabinieri look like men of straw. And the proof is that you, Sir Prefect, come here the first time that something serious crops up."[63]

It is important to note that unlike Natoli's novel, which was set more than a hundred years earlier, spanning 1698 to 1718, Cesareo's play was set in 1910. This meant that the actions and words of the *mafiosi* were not presented as part of some long-lost legend. They were instead set in contemporary times, and the themes of abuse and injustice by the rich, and the corruption of state officials, as well as the political realities described, rang very close to home to all those who watched the production.

An important theme in the play is the relationship between Rasconà and the politician Terrasini, who at first appears to be the Mafia's protector, but is soon exposed as being under the thumb of the Mafia boss. The *mafiosi* were presented as a solution to a real and present problem, influencing public opinion and encouraging them to turn a blind eye to the criminal reality of the Mafia, focusing instead on the chimera of the noble bandits, protecting the poor like an army of Robin Hoods, where the end always justified the means.

One could say that Cesareo's play concluded the arc that the assassination of Petrosino and Natoli's novel had begun. The Mafia had successfully managed to colonise Sicilian folklore and appropriate the legend of the Beati Paoli as their own.

What is interesting, however, is the fact that the origin story of the Mafia was not only imprinted in the mind of the public, but also became part of the identity that *mafiosi* internalised when they were initiated. They themselves came to believe that they were the descendants of the Beati Paoli, and that like them, they were the protectors of the weak, originally protecting the locals from foreign rulers, but then evolving to safeguard their interest from the bureaucrats and politicians in Rome.

In the minds of many *mafiosi*, this became an important part of how they rationalised the discrepancy between the reality of what they were doing, meaning the killings and injustice that they themselves were perpetuating, with the fantasy of being arbiters of justice. Just as Coriolano had justified the actions of the Beati Paoli to Blasco, the *mafiosi* told themselves that any method is justifiable if the circumstances warranted it.

However, in some cases the cognitive dissonance arising between the mental image of honourable *mafiosi* and the reality of their behaviour became too difficult to ignore. In the 1970s, Leonardo Vitale, a member of the Altarello di Baida clan, turned himself in to the police after suffering a crisis of faith and recognising the evil of the organisation he had joined. He claimed he had been tricked into joining the Mafia because he was told it was the modern incarnation of the Beati Paoli.

"They pricked my middle finger with a bitter orange thorn and set fire to a sacred holy picture asking me to repeat the sacred oath of the Beati Paoli. After that, I kissed all the men of honour attending the ceremony on the lips, without the tongue however, and I officially entered into the Altarello Family."[64]

Initially Vitale was committed to his *cosca*, but he was soon sickened by the crimes and the violence. His mother was a devout Catholic and she encouraged him to turn away from his fellow *mafiosi* and try to make up for the wrong choices he had made. One could say he was, in fact, the only true *pentito* because he turned state's evidence out of his own free will and not as part of a deal after being arrested for a crime.

Vitale was released ten years later, only to be assassinated by Cosa Nostra as he returned home from mass as vengeance for having broken *omertà*. However, by then the Great Mafia War unleashed by Totò Riina[3] was under way. The massacre of hundreds of *mafiosi* and their family members led to several *mafiosi* breaking *omertà* in return for state protection for themselves and their loved ones.

"The winning and losing clans don't exist because the losers are dead. They, the Corleonesi, killed them all." Salvatore Contorno[65]

---

3 Salvatore Riina was born on the 16th of November 1930 in Corleone. By the age of 19 he had already been found guilty of murder and imprisoned until 1956. Two years later he was involved in the assassination of the Corleone Mafia boss Michele Navarra, which paved the way for Luciano Leggio to take over the *cosca*. In 1969 Riina went into hiding, and when Leggio was arrested in 1974, Riina became the new boss of the Corleonesi.

The first high profile *mafioso* to defect was Tommaso Buscetta, whose family had been decimated by the Corleonesi. He turned to the state after two of his sons disappeared, probably victims of *lupara bianca*, meaning a mafia killing where the corpse is unlikely to be found, either because it is dissolved in acid or because it is buried in concrete in a construction site. In 1984 he met Judge Giovanni Falcone[4] and gave detailed testimony about the workings of Cosa Nostra. He also spoke about the Beati Paoli, emphasising the noble and honourable origins of Cosa Nostra.

"Cosa Nostra ... also developed as a force which wanted to defend ... and protect Sicily. Because we Sicilians felt neglected, abandoned by foreign governments and also the one in Rome. This is why Cosa Nostra made the laws on the island instead of the state. It did this in various periods of history, even when it wasn't called Cosa Nostra. I know it was once called the Carbonari, then the Beati Paoli and only then did it become Cosa Nostra." Tommaso Buscetta[66]

Buscetta was not the only senior *mafioso* to turn state's witness and become a *pentito*. Another high-profile witness was Antonino Calderone, who had been the *sottocapo* (second in command) to his brother Giuseppe, the boss of the Catania mafia, who had been assassinated by order of the Corleonesi. Calderone and his family left Sicily in 1983 to escape the carnage of the second mafia war and settled in France. He was arrested three years later in Nice, and he asked to speak to Giovanni Falcone in 1987.

---

4 Giovanni Falcone was born in Palermo on the 18th of May 1939 to Arturo Falcone and Luisa Bentivegna. He had two older sisters – Anna and Maria. He graduated with a law degree in 1961 and three years later he became a magistrate and joined the Prosecution Office in Trapani, where he worked for twelve years. In 1978 he returned to Palermo, initially working in the bankruptcy court but then joining the investigative branch of the Public Prosecutor's Office, a few months after the assassination of its head, Judge Cesare Terranova. The man who replaced him, Judge Rocco Chinnici, assigned Falcone to investigate the heroin-trafficking network formed by the Inzerillos in Sicily and the Gambinos in New York. Falcone was a pioneer in the use of financial information during investigations. He used skills he had learned in bankruptcy court to examine suspect financial transactions identified from reports he requisitioned from all the banks in Palermo. He also built a strong relationship and collaboration with investigators in other countries, which proved fundamental when it came to tracing the international reach of the Mafia.

"I know a lot about the Mafia, because I am a member of it." Antonino Calderone[67]

Giovanni Falcone flew to France and on the 9th of April 1987 he met Calderone in a prison in Marseille. For a whole year the antimafia prosecutor flew to Marseille weekly. He collected over one thousand pages of testimony from Calderone. The *pentito*'s claims were painstakingly cross-referenced and checked, leading to the issuing of one hundred and sixty arrest warrants.

Antonino Calderone emphasised the so-called pedigree of Cosa Nostra – *"I'll tell you how Cosa Nostra was born. It was born during the Sicilian Vespers. When the people rebelled, and the Beati Paoli were born too. They all derive from what happened at Palermo. ... I knew these things. But the others, I think, didn't know anything. They had absolutely no idea of who these Beati Paoli were. I don't want to give myself airs, but I had read these books. Also the ones about 'Coriolano della Floresta', 'Talvano the bastard' and such like. I had done my research."*[68]

This is therefore the background to all the talk of honour and protection by *mafiosi* and the spiel they used when they approached business owners to ask for monthly payments, presenting *il pizzo* using the same terminology of a tax charged by the state for the provision of security services. The power and hold of Cosa Nostra had become so ingrained in the Sicilian psyche that this behaviour became normalised, and the Mafia was able to exert control over the community without needing to resort to overt threats or violence.

"When I show up here, you must covertly feel my weight. I will never threaten you explicitly, I will always be smiling, but you will always know that behind my smile there is a threat looming over your head. I won't tell you. I'll do something to you. If you get what I'm saying, that's fine. If not, you'll suffer the consequences." Tommaso Buscetta[69]

3.7 The Godfather
Cosa Nostra's longevity is in no small measure due to the shapeshifting nature of the organisation. This agility is not only evident in its modus

operandi and internal structures, but also in the signs and symbols that it appropriates. In the twentieth century, as the world modernised, so did *mafiosi*, rebranding themselves by appropriating modern cultural cues and discarding the archaic ones that no longer served their purpose.

The phenomenon becomes even more evident when one looks at the cross-fertilisation of symbols between movies and *mafiosi*. In 1972 the movie *The Godfather* landed in cinemas worldwide and became a global phenomenon and an inspiration for members of Cosa Nostra, as well as other mafias.

The Godfather was based on a novel written by Mario Puzo, the son of Italian immigrants who lived in New York. He claimed that the novel was based on research and not personal experience, but his book, and subsequently the movies, became a handbook used by *mafiosi* both in the US and Italy.

The story starts in 1945 New York, where the boss of the Corleone crime family, Vito Corleone, holds court during his daughter's wedding, graciously listening to petitioners who were taking advantage of the fact that in Sicily there was a tradition that the father of a bride could not refuse any request on his daughter's wedding day.

One of the people asking for help is his godson, Johnny Fontane, who wants to become a movie star. Don Corleone dispatches his trusted advisor to Los Angeles to convince film producer Jack Woltz to give Fontane a juicy part. Woltz initially brushes off the request, but he quickly comes around when he wakes up one morning and discovers that he is sharing the bed with the decapitated head of his stallion. This scene became iconic, and the Mafia took note.

3.7.1 An instruction manual for murder and mayhem

In a clear case of life imitating art, *mafiosi* started using decapitated horse heads to warn and intimidate victims. In 1991 three employees of a construction company that had refused to pay the *pizzo* found a horse head in one of the company cars.[70] *The Godfather* had become a global blockbuster, and everyone who had watched it understood the symbolism of the find.

When horse heads were not readily available, *mafiosi* improvised by using other animals. In 2012 a severed pig's head was found on the doorstep of a priest who was criticising the 'Ndrangheta during his Sunday sermons. Then in 2016, Fr Antonio Aguanno, the parish priest of Vita, in north-western Sicily, found a donkey's head in a plastic bag at the entrance of the church where he was about to celebrate mass.[71]

More ominously, Cosa Nostra also adopted ideas from the movie when it came to murder, as was the case when mafia killers disguised themselves as doctors to gain access to their targeted victim who was sick in bed.

The movie glamourised the Mafia, impacting not only the perceptions of the general public but also those of *mafiosi* themselves. It deployed the old tropes of honour and love of family that had been central to the mythology of the Mafia from its early days, portraying Don Vito as a respectable man who only did what needed to be done to protect those he loved and the people who depended upon him. The mafia boss was always elegant and composed, ruling his clan with a firm hand, while showing his softer side in scenes where he played with his grandson.

3.7.2 Clothes Make the Man

Later in the book we will speak of Calogero Vizzini, an influential mafia boss in the post-WWII era. Several photos of the man exist, and in all of them he is dressed in a slovenly manner, projecting a peasant-like persona almost to the point of caricature. However, he was not alone in trying to be as inconspicuous as possible. Giuseppe Genco Russo, another powerful *capomafia*, wore dark pants, a simple white shirt and a shabby hat. Paolino Bontade, on the other hand, wore a simple suit made by a local tailor. Their maxim was that "*i colori attirano le mosche*" (colours attract flies) so *mafiosi* made it a point not to attract attention.

However, this all changed after *The Godfather* aired in the 1970s. In the movie, mafia bosses wore elegant clothing and indulged in showy displays of conspicuous consumption. This led to a major shift in the way *mafiosi* behaved and dressed. Instead of trying to blend in with the crowd, they wanted to broadcast their power and virility.

Stefano Bontade, the son of the abovementioned Paolino Bontade, was nicknamed *The Prince* because he dressed like Don Vito and behaved in the same haughty and sombre manner. Tommaso Buscetta, the man who was to become a *pentito* and blow the cover off Cosa Nostra, was always dressed in designer blazers and tailored pants and was a known womaniser. His sartorial style was so admired that Dolce & Gabbana used it as an inspiration for one of their clothing lines.

The practice became even more pronounced toward the end of the twentieth century, when up-and-coming *mafiosi* like Matteo Messina Denaro, who is widely believed to be the current boss of bosses of the Mafia, hit the scene dressed to the nines in Prada and Versace. Messina Denaro drove flashy cars and cultivated his image as a virile playboy, always appearing with a different beautiful woman on his arm.

Incredible though it may sound, *mafiosi* also dressed like fashion models when they were in jail. The Ucciardone prison in Palermo, where many of them were serving their sentences, was known for decades as The Grand Hotel because inmates wore expensive, well-cut silk suits like the ones Michael Corleone wore in *The Godfather*. A good example is Tommaso Buscetta, who was imprisoned in Ucciardone for several years. According to other inmates he was always dressed in the very best designer clothes and used expensive toiletries and perfumes. In addition, all his meals were delivered to the prison from the top restaurants in Palermo.[72]

This went on until 2011, when Rita Barbera became the new governor of the prison. Determined to stamp out the performative displays of wealth and power by mafia bosses in Ucciardone, she banned all high-end fashion labels. Prisoners were no longer allowed to wear Armani, Gucci, Prada or Versace, which were the labels of choice for most of the *mafiosi*.

3.7.3 Talking the Talk

After watching *The Godfather*, *mafiosi* did not only change the way they dressed, but also the way they talked. Several phrases used in the film became a staple part of their lexicon.

"I am going to make you an offer you can't refuse."

"... this isn't personal, it's business."

"... the one who brings you the message will be the betrayer."

"... sleeping with the fishes."

These were all phrases dreamt up by Mario Puzo, but they soon became a hallmark of mafia dialogue in Sicily and gangster speak in the US.

3.7.4 A New Performative Era

Ironically the American crime families had initially been opposed to the movie and had even intervened to make sure that the word mafia never featured in the script. However, when the film became a blockbuster the Mob had a change of heart, with police officers reporting that they invariably found *The Godfather* box sets in all the mafia residences they raided.

Nowadays we hear of mafia weddings and mafia funerals using The Godfather soundtrack, as in the notorious case of the funeral of Vittorio Casamonica in Rome in 2015. The boss of the Casamonica mafia clan was buried with great pomp and splendour, including a live band playing the theme music from the movie as the coffin was carried from the elaborate hearse into the church.

As in the case of the Beati Paoli, it is sometimes difficult to tell where reality begins and fiction ends.

CHAPTER 4

SACRED SYMBOLS AND RITUALS

"You *might smile at it as if it was an archaic ceremony, or you might think of it as a real joke.*

It is instead an extremely serious thing that affects him for the rest of his life.

Entering the mafia is like converting to a religion.

One never stops being a priest.

Nor a mafioso."
Judge Giovanni Falcone

The rituals of a society are imbued with meaning and symbolism, and as such they are of great interest to anthropologists and all those who want to understand people's values and behaviour.

Definitions of what constitutes a ritual vary, however there are some fundamental principles on which there is widespread consensus, namely that ritual behaviour is clearly distinct from day-to-day behaviour, and that it involves elements of the supernatural. Rituals bring people together and are at their core a mechanism that helps build the spirit of a community.

Arnold Van Gennep described ritual as having three stages. During the preliminary stage preparations are made for the special event. Once everything is in place, the participants move on to the liminality stage, where social order is suspended and only the rules of the ritual apply, and finally, in the post-liminality stage, the group emerges from the ritual in a transformed state. Victor Turner developed this concept further, describing the liminality stage as being a time of intense emotion and social bonding occurring within a context of sacredness, a phenomenon that he termed *communitas*. In fact, it is now understood that rituals are one of the most powerful ways to build community spirit. They are so effective that they are considered a differentiator in societal evolution, with groups who regularly participate in community rituals outlasting groups that do not.

To survive and thrive, the Sicilian Mafia needed to ensure strong cohesion within the group, as well as obedience and discipline throughout the ranks. They achieved this by strategically deploying rituals, which partially explains how Cosa Nostra survived and kept its inner workings veiled in a shroud of secrecy for so long.

4.1 The Initiation Ritual – La Punciuta

In chapter 2 we spoke about Dr Galati, the brave doctor who attempted to stand up to the Uditore mafia. As already mentioned, when he finally escaped with his family to Naples in 1875, the doctor sent a memorandum to the Minister of the Interior about the situation in Palermo, which prompted a request to the Chief of Police in Palermo for a report about the situation on the island.

The resulting dossier contained a clear description of an initiation ritual used by the *cosche*, a ceremony where the bandits pricked the aspiring new member's hand and smeared his blood on a picture of a saint or the Madonna. The initiate then swore an oath of allegiance while the picture was burned.

This information was backed up by the 1877 trial of the Stuppagghieri (Fuse Burners). This clan was purportedly brought together by the brother of the Monreale chief of police, who used them as his informants and enforcers. In their testimony they spoke of an initiation ritual that incorporated fire, blood, and a holy picture. They also described the pyramidical hierarchy of their clan, with the overall leader, known as the *capo* (leader), delegating control of different localities to various *sottocapi* (deputies), who in turn had assistants called the *consiglio direttivo*. The *capo* and *sottocapi* ensured that all members of the clan followed the rules of the society, and that any men who broke the rules were severely punished.

The rules were as follows[73]:
1. Clan members were to help each other and avenge each other.
2. Clan members had to answer a call to arms to defend other members of the clan and to free any members who ended up in the hands of the judiciary.
3. The proceeds of any of the activities of the clan, be it robbery or extortion, were to be distributed according to instructions issued by the *capo*.
4. Clan members were to maintain an oath of secrecy on pain of death.

According to a news report about the trial that appeared in the *Giornale di Sicilia* on the 20th of August 1877, *"the person to be initiated enters the room and stands by a table upon which there is the image of a saint. He gives his right hand to the two compari and they prick the tip of his thumb with a needle, drawing a drop of blood to smear the picture of the saint. The initiate takes his oath on this bloody image and then he burns the bloody sacred image in the candle flame. This is how he is baptised and hailed compare."*

A few years later, in 1884, during a trial in Agrigento, the public prosecutor described the initiation ritual of yet another clan – the Fratellanza of Girgenti. The process closely resembled the one described by the Stuppagghieri, with the sole addition that after the holy picture was burned its ashes were ceremonially scattered in the wind. In addition, the testimony also included a mention of a formal oath, in which the initiate swore eternal fealty to the clan.

The abovementioned structure, rules and initiation ritual bear a striking similarity to the ones described by *pentiti* a hundred years later.

4.1.1 Recruiting and initiating mafiosi in the twentieth century

The initiation ceremony is not the beginning of the process of enculturating *mafiosi*, but rather the completion of a stage of careful observation and selection, with older men in the *cosche* keeping an eye out for boys who have the right attributes.

> "*The best of the young ones are carefully watched and studied by the older men. The oldest of the mafiosi, friends of the father, relatives of the mother, keep an eye on the kids, and some of them stand out from the others... These fine male children are studied by the whole group, and when one of them makes an impression because he is smart and sure of himself and bossy he is immediately taken in hand and encouraged by the adult men of honour who teach him and show him the ropes, take him along with them, start giving him things to do.*" Antonino Calderone[74]

> "*It's not as if you get up and join Cosa Nostra. It's a kind of outlook, they keep an eye on you as a child, they bring you up, they teach you how to shoot, to kill, to plant bombs. You're a robot, you're marked out. The way you come into Cosa Nostra is as "avvicinati," hangers-on, for a period that can last twenty years, or five years, or one year, and depending on individuals, then somebody tells you the time has come.*" Leonardo Messina[75]

When the time arrives for recruits to be initiated, they are usually separated from the rest of the group as preparations are made for *la punciuta*. In some cases, they are even locked in a dark room. After a few hours of sitting in darkness the ritual moves to the liminality stage, where the *capomafia* fetches them one by one, taking them to a secluded location. The ritual is performed by the boss in the presence of the whole *cosca*.

> "*I am in a position to describe in detail the initiation into Cosa Nostra, not just because I belong to it myself but also because I took part in several of these ceremonies. ... The person who is deemed to possess the qualities necessary to become a member is monitored to check how able he is to commit serious criminal acts and maintain silence with the police. In certain areas, the candidate is required to commit a serious crime to prove himself and to bind him so that he cannot go back. This does not apply to*

men such as me, who come from families who belong to a long established mafioso tradition.

When the appropriate moment comes, the candidate or candidates are led to a room, in a secluded location, in the presence of the rappresentante and the men of honour of the family. In Catania we used to put all the men of honour on one side of the room and all the candidates on the opposite side. In other towns they shut the candidate or candidates in a room for a few hours and then take them out one by one.

At this point the rappresentante of the family explains the rules of Cosa Nostra, beginning by saying that what is known as "mafia" is, in reality, called Cosa Nostra. These rules are not to touch the women of other men of honour; not to steal from other men of honour or from anyone; not to exploit prostitution; not to kill other men of honour unless strictly necessary; to avoid passing information to the police; not to fight with other men of honour; to behave in a proper manner; to keep silent about Cosa Nostra around outsiders; to avoid in all circumstances introducing oneself to other men of honour but to wait until a third man of honour who knows both parties confirms membership in Cosa Nostra by saying "This is our friend" or "This is the same thing."

Once these "commandments" of Cosa Nostra have been explained and having received confirmation from the initiate that he wants to become a member, the rappresentante invites each candidate to choose a godfather from among the men of honour in attendance, who are designated "amici nostri." Usually, the candidate chooses the man who introduced him to the family.

Then the oath ceremony takes place. Each candidate identifies his shooting hand and the rappresentante pricks the index finger of that hand in such a way as to spill a little blood, which is used to mark a holy picture (generally of the Annunziata, the patron saint of Cosa Nostra and whose feast day is March 25). When the index finger is pricked, the rappresentante informs him that he must take care never to betray the family, because in Cosa Nostra one enters with blood and leaves only with blood.

At this point the holy picture is set on fire, and the novice, preventing the fire from going out and holding the holy picture in his cupped hands, *solemnly vows never to betray the commandments of Cosa Nostra, or else he will burn like the holy picture.*

At the end of the ceremony the rappresentante introduces the new member to the other men of honour as "amici nostri" and informs the new man of honour of the hierarchy and structure of Cosa Nostra in Sicily. He also lets the new mafioso know who his capodecina is, who he must obey no matter what..." Antonino Calderone[76]

4.1.2 The Cosa Nostra Decalogue of Rules

"I had to pronounce the oath whereby I was to say that should I betray the organisation, my flesh would burn like this saint. I was reminded to behave in the appropriate manner. To be silent, not to look at other men's wives or women, not to steal and especially, every time I was called, I had to rush, leaving whatever I was doing." Tommaso Buscetta[77]

On the 6th of November 2007 the Italian Police captured Salvatore Lo Piccolo. Hidden in his hideout they found a formal, typewritten constitution explaining the different roles within the hierarchy of Cosa Nostra, the decalogue of rules to be followed by *mafiosi*, the procedures for selecting the candidates for initiation into the organisation, and the exact wording of the oath of loyalty –

"I swear to be loyal to Cosa Nostra. May my flesh burn like this holy picture if I betray Cosa Nostra."[78]

The decalogue is fashioned in the form of the Ten Commandments of Christianity, with the Mafia rules echoing many of the Commandments themselves in scope. This is a clear attempt to create an aura of mysticism around what is to all intents and purposes a basic list of rules giving clear guidance as to what new *mafiosi* are signing up for.

The Cosa Nostra decalogue of rules:
1. No-one can present himself directly to another of our friends. There must be a third person to do it.
2. Never look at the wives of other *mafiosi*.
3. Never be seen with police officers.

4. Never go to pubs and clubs.
5. Always being available for Cosa Nostra is a duty - even if your wife's about to give birth.
6. Appointments must absolutely be respected.
7. Never cheat on your wives.
8. Never lie to other mafiosi.
9. Money cannot be appropriated if it belongs to other *mafiosi* or other *cosche*.
10. People with a police officer in the family or with loose morals cannot become a member of Cosa Nostra.

Several of the abovementioned rules are closely tied to *omertà,* a code of honour where a *mafioso* vows to never expose any of the secrets of the Mafia to outsiders and to never collaborate with the police. To take some examples, drinking in pubs is forbidden because inebriated people have loose tongues. Similarly, adultery is problematic because spurned wives are angry and keen to extract revenge and could expose mafia secrets. Association with the police is also unacceptable, for obvious reasons. One must also note that *omertà* is a code of behaviour that has extended to the entire Sicilian population, even those not in the Mafia, because of the brutal retribution meted out to those who were accused of talking out of turn.[79]

It is not coincidental that the description of the structure of the organisation, and the rules and punishments of Cosa Nostra, are such an important part of the initiation ceremony. The aim is not only to educate new members as to what joining the Mafia entails, but also to remind all the other participants in the ceremony about the serious consequences should they not toe the line.

The punishment if any of the members betray Cosa Nostra is death.

4.1.3 Mafiosi emerge from the rite of passage totally transformed

Clearly the Cosa Nostra initiation ritual is a rite of passage that is designed to create a strong feeling of community using all the psychological tools

THE BATTLE FOR SICILY'S SOUL

possible, including the appropriation of Catholic saints or the Madonna to fabricate the aura of sacredness that makes such rituals so effective.

"That night everything seemed beautiful, out of ordinary. I was entering into a new world, full of exceptional people ready to risk their lives to help other men of honour, to vindicate them. It was powerful beyond imagination." Antonino Calderone[80]

"Belonging to Cosa Nostra implied being men of honour. This was at the heart of everything. One could then invent hierarchies, positions, commissions, but within each cosca you breathed an air of equality because we all felt that we belonged to a very special elite." Tommaso Buscetta[81]

The initiate emerges from the ritual transformed. He is now a member of the brotherhood of the Mafia, while the other members have their psychological ties strengthened and renewed, reinforcing the power of the *capomafia* and decreasing the risk of them betraying the clan.

"In my imagination, those men characterised by their wisdom and by being the persons to whom people turned when in need of help fascinated me. When I became a member, it was for me a new life, with new rules. For me only Cosa Nostra existed. There were precise rules and what they said was right and just, because it was based on the idea of mutual respect and assistance. I was fascinated by that world." Gaspare Mutolo[82]

4.2 The Introduction Ritual

In the report written by the Chief of Police in 1875 he describes an elaborate introduction ritual used by *mafiosi* who did not know each other. It was a convoluted conversation about toothache, but of course in truth it had nothing to do with teeth, but was a coded introduction, with references such as "your kingdom" and "your god" identifying which clan the *mafioso* belonged to and who he reported to. [83]

This introduction system was inefficient and not sufficiently secure. It was open to misunderstanding, and there was always a risk of someone misrepresenting themselves as a *mafioso*, leading to an actual *mafioso* unknowingly revealing details about his clan, or to a client paying *pizzo* to the wrong person.

In fact, part of the initiation ritual incorporates the introduction ritual, because it is only when the new member becomes a *mafioso* that he can be formally introduced to other *mafiosi*.

After the oath is taken, and only at that point, the man of honour is introduced to the boss of the Family. Before that, he is not supposed to know who the boss is, nor is he supposed to know of the existence of Cosa Nostra as such." Tommaso Buscetta[84]

When Giovanni Brusca was initiated by Totò Riina, the *capomafia* made it clear that Brusca could only reveal his identity as a member of the Sicilian Mafia to *mafiosi* to whom he was formally introduced by another *mafioso* who could vouch for both parties. Driving the point home, Riina formally introduced Brusca to his father, who was a mafia boss. Only then could father and son acknowledge each other as *mafiosi*.[85]

The importance of the introduction ritual is emphasised as the very first rule in the decalogue found at the hideout of Salvatore Lo Piccolo in 2007. The ritualised introduction required the trusted third party to inform the other two *mafiosi* that *"He is a friend of ours"* or *"You are both the same as me."*

4.3 Ritual of Allegiance
In 2015 the Italian police managed to take several photos of a Cosa Nostra ritual of obedience and allegiance in Palermo, while also recording the conversation. Members of the Santa Maria di Gesu clan lined up to kiss the forehead of their boss, Giuseppe Greco, also known as Pino the Uncle, in a ceremony meant to symbolise and reinforce his authority.

Also caught on tape is the *capomafia* ordering a hit on Mirko Sciacchitano, a young *mafioso* who had messed up an assignment he had been given. Clearly the boss wanted to impress on everyone present that any errors, or failure to follow orders to the letter, would result in death.

4.4 Appropriation of Catholic Ceremonies, Sacraments and Language
As discussed, there is no doubt that the use of rituals to create bonds between *mafiosi* and a strong allegiance to the boss is probably one of

the main reasons Cosa Nostra managed to keep its secrets and survive for so long. However, another fundamental requirement for survival was the putting down of roots in the community. One of the ways *mafiosi* achieved this was through the ingenious appropriation and colonisation of several Catholic rituals, using the sacred as part of their arsenal to establish and maintain their position in the community and to create a sense of *communitas* with non-*mafiosi* in their villages and towns.

It is important to note that this enmeshment with the Catholic faith does not only impact the image of the Mafia held by the population at large but is actually a very important part of how *mafiosi* perceive themselves and rationalise their actions. Many *mafiosi* describe themselves as devout Catholics. They never miss mass and are often seen reading the Bible, and on numerous occasions, when mafia bosses were arrested, the police found altars and paintings or images of the Madonna and other saints in their hideouts.

One case in point is Beneditto Santapaola, the mafia boss of the Catania faction, who was accused of having killed hundreds of people and ordering the assassination of General Carlo Alberto Dalla Chiesa in 1982 and journalist Giuseppe Fava in 1984. He was on the run for eleven years, living in a farmhouse outside Catania, where he built a chapel complete with a bell tower, an altar, and a statue of the Virgin Mary. In May 1993, the police raided the farm and arrested him. Before leaving the house Santapaola collected a Bible that lay on his bedside table and kissed it, after which he was led away in handcuffs.[86]

The same happened in June 1997 when the police raided the hideout of Pietro Aglieri, the boss of the Santa Maria di Gesù faction. Aglieri was involved in the assassination of prosecuting magistrate Antonio Scopelliti in 1991, as well as Democrazia Cristiana politician Salvo Lima and antimafia Judge Paolo Borsellino[5] in 1992. In his hiding place the police

---

5 Paolo Borsellino was born in Palermo on the 19th of January 1940. He graduated in law from the University of Palermo in 1962 and became a magistrate a year later. In 1975 he started working with Rocco Chinicci on Mafia investigations. He collaborated with Carabinieri captain Emanuele Basile in an investigation that led to the arrest of Leoluca Bagarella, Totò Riina's brother-in-law, along with another five *mafiosi*. Retribution was swift – Basile was

found a large library with around two hundred religion and philosophy books, as well as a chapel with an altar, a large wooden crucifix, a statue of the Virgin Mary, a holy water font, and a large painting representing the Last Supper. In addition, to their surprise, they found a censer in which incense is burned, along with green and purple vestments, indicating that a priest had visited to celebrate mass in the hideout. It later emerged that three priests regularly visited Aglieri in his hideout to celebrate mass and give him spiritual guidance – they were Father Mario Frittitta, Father Giacomo Ribaudo and Father Lillo Tubolino.[87]

4.4.1 Feasts, Processions and Assertion of Authority
On the 25th of July 1937 the community of Riesi celebrated the feast of St Joseph. As was customary, in the evening the statue of the saint was carried along the streets through town. However, that year something was different. St Joseph was going to become an unwitting protagonist in the transfer of power from a Mafia boss to his son.

Giuseppe Di Cristina, leader of the Riesi mafia clan, had planned the ceremony with care, with the full support of the religious and political leaders of the locality. He walked with the saint through the town, followed by the faithful, until they reached his home where his son Francesco was waiting for him.

The procession stopped in front of the boss' house, and the band stopped playing. The crowd watched as Giuseppe greeted his son and kissed him three times – a ritual that signified the abdication of the old boss and the solemn consecration of his son Francesco as the new *capomafia*. Francesco then bowed to his father and to Saint Joseph (in that order, making it clear who he considered the more important of the two), at which point the band started playing a joyous tune, the crowd cheered and the church bells rang in celebration.[88] This is a clear example of how religious symbols and events are used to feed the mythology of the Mafia, bestowing an aura of respectability upon the men of honour.

---

killed on the 4th of May 1980, after which Paolo Borsellino was put under police protection. He was part of the Antimafia Pool of prosecutors, working closely with Giuseppe Di Lello, Leonardo Guarnotta and of course, Giovanni Falcone, in preparation for the Maxi Trial.

The participation of the Mafia in major religious events in Sicily was by no means restricted to processions or special occasions such as transfers of power. *Mafiosi* were very visible in all public Catholic ceremonies and events, ranging from holy mass, where important *mafiosi* had special pews reserved for them, to Easter Sunday performances. In one case the *capomafia* of Misilmeri, Momo Grasso, was accorded the honour of playing the role of Jesus in the annual performance of The Passion during Easter celebrations.[89]

Performative public appearances in religious events are therefore part and parcel of the strategy of Cosa Nostra. Leonardo Messina, a pentito who was previously one of the top-ranking members of the San Cataldo mafia clan, spoke in 1996 about his role in the procession of Madonna dell'Annunziata (Our Lady of the Annunciation), claiming the Madonna as the patron saint of the Sicilian Mafia.

"I was responsible for the religious procession of Cosa Nostra's patron saint, Our Lady of the Annunciation. I walked in the procession next to the saint. You will understand it if you want to. ... These ritual occasions have a very important role for us. ... The priest? Do you think the priest did not know who organised the processions of the saint?" Leonardo Messina[90]

Even more recent were the events that unfolded in Campobello di Mazara in September 2006. A procession carrying the Holy Crucifix around the town stopped in front of the house of Francesco Luppino, a *mafioso* under house arrest after having been found guilty of murder and mafia association. Several members of the bank and people participating in the procession then entered Luppino's house to greet him and show him respect.

In 2012, during the annual feast and procession of Our Lady of Mount Carmel in Ballarò, Alessandro D'Ambrogio, mafia boss of the Porta Nuova mafia faction of Palermo, was given the honoured and highly coveted role of carrying the statue around the streets of the locality with devout parishioners handing him children to be blessed by the Madonna. Two years later D'Ambrogio was in prison, so he could no longer attend the procession and carry the statue. However, this did not liberate Our

Lady of Mount Carmel from her association with Cosa Nostra. To honour D'Ambrogio the procession stopped for several minutes outside a business owned by his family, embroiling the mother of God in a gesture of deference to the imprisoned mafia boss.[91]

The investment of money, time and effort in these highly visible Catholic events paid very good dividends for Cosa Nostra. It enabled mafia bosses to closely align themselves with the clerical authorities, and through them, with God, setting themselves up as the protectors of morality and social order.

The conspicuous presence of the boss and his fellow *mafiosi* at the front of religious processions, and centre stage at all religious events, enabled Cosa Nostra to monopolise the ceremonies, with the mafia boss usurping the role of the saint and commandeering the deference of the adoring public for himself.

4.4.2 Funerals and Transitions of Power
Processions and other holy celebrations are therefore an excellent opportunity for *mafiosi* to flaunt their position and power publicly and ostentatiously. Also important, however, is the performative opportunity offered by funerals – and the more pomp and circumstance the better.

Catholic funerals are an important rite of passage, symbolising the transition from man's existence on earth to everlasting life in heaven. Mafia funerals, therefore, make an important statement, defiantly propagating the myth of *mafiosi* as men of honour and defenders of the weak, whose place in heaven is assured.

The funeral of a *capomafia* is particularly important because it offers an opportunity to display the transition of power in a form of "The King is dead. Long live the King!" All the mourners at the funeral thus become participants in what is supposed to be a Catholic ritual but is actually a celebration of Mafia power and authority in the community, as well as the coronation of the new boss.

This symbolic handover is even more sensitive and critical when the dead mafia boss was murdered in a feud between mafia factions. The funeral marks an end to that chapter of violence, with the blood of the slain boss washing away enmities and setting the scene for reconciliation between the clans in a not-so-subtle comparison with Jesus Christ, who died on the cross for the forgiveness of humankind's sins.

The collective mourning also creates a sense of *communitas,* which strengthens the bonds of *convivenza* between *mafiosi* and members of the community attending the funeral, both during the ceremony in church and in the subsequent funeral procession. The liturgical part of the funeral celebrated by a priest in a consecrated church, usually with a sermon that extolls the virtues of the dead *mafioso,* also reaffirms the status of the Mafia as an honourable association that submits itself only to the judgement of God and not that of men.

After the funeral mass all the mourners walk slowly behind the coffin as it makes its way to the cemetery, with much weeping and praise for the dead *mafioso.* Once again this is heavy with symbolism, highlighting the fact that *mafiosi* and civil society must co-exist as one community.

A good example of the power of such funerary arrangements is the 1954 funeral for *capomafia* Calogero Vizzini. He was accused of having committed thirty-nine murders, six attempted murders, and several other crimes, but had never been convicted because no witnesses were willing to testify against him.

Vizzini came from a renowned family which included five priests, foremost amongst whom were the Bishop of Noto and the Bishop of Muro. His funeral was a massive affair with a procession of thousands of people dressed in formal black clothing. Amongst the mourners were politicians, policemen and officials of the Church. But in pride of place, walking right in front, next to the coffin, was Giuseppe Genco Russo, mafia boss of Mussumeli, who was establishing his authority and position as Vizzini's successor within the hierarchy of Cosa Nostra. Walking with him in a display of unity was mafia boss Francesco Paolino Bontade, known as Don Paolino Bontà.[92]

Thousands of holy pictures were distributed to commemorate the occasion, carrying the quote - *"Vedi giudizio umano, come spesso erra!"*[93] a subversive statement aimed at the judicial authorities who had dared try to judge the Mafia boss. On the back of the cards:

"He showed with words and deeds that his mafia was not criminality
but stood for respect of the law
defence of all rights
greatness of character.
It was love."[94]

A large funeral notice was affixed to the church door, where under the depiction of the cross the following announcement was made[95] –

"CALOGERO VIZZINI
With the skill of a genius
he raised the fortunes of a distinguished household.
Wise, dynamic, tireless,
he was the benefactor of the workers on the land and
in the sulphur mines.
Constantly doing good,
he won himself a wide reputation
in Italy and abroad.
Great in the face of persecution,
greater still in the face of adversity,
he remained unfailingly cheerful.
And today,
with the peace of Christ
and in the majesty of death,
he receives from friends and foes alike
the most beautiful of tributes:
He was a gentleman."

Seven years later, Francesco Di Cristina also passed away. He was the *capomafia* whose father, Giuseppe Di Cristina, had abdicated and passed him the baton in 1937 during the feast of St Joseph. The main church of Riesi was packed with mourners. After mass, a procession of parishioners, including civil, military, and religious leaders, followed the hearse, drawn by four horses, to give a last farewell to the former mafia boss.

4.4.3 Baptisms, Weddings and Kinship Bonds

The Sicilian Mafia originated in small villages which were often quite isolated, which meant that most marriages occurred between members of the same community (in some cases even between first cousins), a custom referred to as endogamy. This resulted in multiple strong bonds of kinship between villagers, acting as the main sources of societal connections and organisation.

Early Mafia clans were therefore made up of men bound together by family relationships. This had many advantages – fathers, uncles, sons, brothers, and cousins knew each other well and understood each other in ways that outsiders would struggle to do. It was also much easier to define the hierarchy in the *cosca*, because in most cases it reflected the hierarchy within the family, with fathers and uncles having more power than the sons and cousins.[96]

The strong family ties also ensured that the villagers had an interest in aiding and abetting the clan, which was made of men related to them by marriage or blood. The family ties, culture, and activities (both legal and illegal) of the community thus become so intertwined that it became difficult to ascertain where kinship ended and Mafia began, which also explains why *omertà* became so widespread on the island.

As transport and travel around the island became easier, endogamy became more difficult to maintain. Outsiders thus entered the community via marriage, weakening the kinship ties that were so essential for the social order, both within the village or town, and within the *cosca* itself. This meant that *mafiosi* had to find ways of creating bonds that were not solely related to blood and marriage.

The solution was to co-opt the Catholic sacrament of Baptism, using godparenthood, a ritualised kinship bond of extreme importance to Sicilians. The link between godfather and godchild is an indissoluble bond that lasts for an entire lifetime, a form of spiritual kinship that is sometimes claimed to be even stronger than that of kinship by blood.

Furthermore, in the process the godfather and the biological father became *compari* (co-fathers) creating an obligation between the two to always assist and support each other. *Mafiosi* thus used the Catholic Baptism of their children to create strong links within the *cosca*, or even links between *cosche* when peace needed to be brokered or secured.

By appointing a senior *mafioso* as the godfather (hence the name of the famous movie) of their child, a family created a link of kinship with him, increasing the chances of the father progressing up the chain of command in the *cosca*, while also enjoying a measure of protection. The same applied to the baby himself, in the case of boys.

In the 1800s, the Mafia often followed up *la punciuta* of a new *mafioso* with the creation of a spiritual kinship bond by making the *capomafia* the godfather of the *mafioso's* child. Subsequent children would then be given other godfathers from within the *cosca*, creating a resilient interconnected network of spiritual kinship reinforcing the mafia clan structure and hierarchy.

The baptismal bond is, to a certain extent, a temporary measure until the children in question grow up. These children are raised within the mafia culture – the boys are taught to be aggressive, ruthless, and deferent to the boss, while the girls are taught to be submissive and supportive. When they reach marriageable age, inmarriage is encouraged (and in some cases enforced), with a view to forging the most desirable bonds of all – blood ties.

"To this let it be added that Giacomo Giuseppe Gambino was present at the wedding of Giovanni Grizzaffi, nephew of the Corleone man Salvatore Riina, and that one of Gambino's sisters is married to Giovanni Pio, who had been identified as a "man of honour" of Buscetta and Contorno's San Lorenzo family, while another sister is married to Calogero Spina, the son of the well-known mafia capo of the della Noce district mafia." Extract from the first Maxi Trial indictment

4.5 God's Will
Bernardo Provenzano was second-in-command to mafia boss of bosses Totò Riina, succeeding him as overall head of Cosa Nostra when Riina was

arrested in 1993. He was found guilty in absentia for the assassinations of Giovanni Falcone and Paolo Borsellino, as well as for the bombings that occurred in Rome, Milan and Florence in 1993 which left ten people dead. Notwithstanding this, Provenzano styled himself as a devout Catholic, ostentatiously carrying a Bible with him wherever he went.

When Provenzano became the boss of bosses the Mafia was in poor shape, ravaged after a bloody internecine war and reeling from the revelations of the *pentiti* in the run-up to the Maxi Trial. The image of the Mafia as an organisation made up of men of honour was in tatters, and a strong antimafia sentiment had taken hold in Sicily.

Provenzano had to bring warring clans together and rekindle the sense of *communitas* that had all but vanished over the previous fifteen years. To do so he created a new system of communication based on *pizzini*, short type-written notes delivered by hand using trusted couriers. These notes were encrypted using a system like the Caesar cipher, an encryption process used by Julius Caesar to protect important military messages. It also used numeric sequences to conceal the names of people.[97]

The Provenzano code was quite simple, based on assigning a number to each letter by raising by three the value provided to the 21 letters of the Italian alphabet listed in alphabetical order. As a result, A (1+3) becomes 4, B (2+3) becomes 5, C (3+3) becomes 6, etc.

Once decrypted, the *pizzini* were written in a very particular style, using language steeped in spirituality and couched in terminology of the faith. Provenzano presented himself as a wise and religiously devout leader, watching over *mafiosi* and guiding them on the path of righteousness. In his *pizzini* there are repeated mentions of 'Our Lord Jesus Christ' who is often invoked to "*help us to do the right things*," implying that Provenzano had sought divine inspiration and approval before writing the note. "*Con il volere di Dio*" (if God is willing) also appears multiple times, turning God into a willing accomplice of the *mafiosi*, who are doing God's work here on earth. The notes always ended with "*Vi benedica il Signore e vi protegga*" (May God bless you and protect you).[98]

It is also important to note the language used by those who replied to Provenzano with their own *pizzini*. A good example is this extract from a *pizzino* sent by Ignazio Ribisi to Provenzano *"...Before concluding, it is important for me to say this: we live for you, therefore whatever you might need we beg you not to spare us from the pleasure of serving you."* [99] Also interesting is a note from Matteo Messina Denaro, who says *"I have always belonged to you. I follow a way in my life which is your way, I was born this way and I will die this way, I am certain of this. ... you are our master."* [100]

Note the deference and the language used – Provenzano appears to have taken on almost Messiah-like properties, with the *mafiosi* "belonging" to him, and pledging to devoutly serve him for the rest of their lives.

The *pizzini* come across as caricatures of religiosity and loyalty, but one should not underestimate the power conferred upon mafia bosses when they cloak themselves in the Catholic faith, both when it comes to their image in society and to recruiting and controlling their foot soldiers. By invoking God, they sanctify their leadership, creating an aura of invulnerability and authority that burnishes their credentials and solidifies their power.

Timeline of events mentioned in this section

1282	On the 30th of March 1282, during evening Vespers, the Sicilians revolt against the French, ousting Charles of Anjou.
1720	Birth of Francesco Maria Emanuele Gaetani, the Marquis of Villabianca, author of the Opuscoli Palermitani (Palermo Pamphlets), in vol. XVI of which he writes about the legend of the Beati Paoli.
1820s	The first Masonic sects arrive in Sicily, exposing Sicilians to the concept of an initiation ritual.
1836	Vincenzo Linares publishes a serialised account of the Beati Paoli in a Palermitan newspaper called *Il Vapore*.
1840	Vincenzo Linares publishes *Racconti Popolari*, which includes the previously serialised story about the Beati Paoli.
1848	Carmelo Piola writes a poem in Sicilian dialect about the Beati Paoli called *Li Beati Pauli ligenna popolari*.
1863	Launch of *I mafiusi di la Vicaria*, a play by Giuseppe Rizzotto and Gaspare Mosca that refers to the men of honour as *mafiusi* for the first time.
	I Beati Paoli o La Famiglia del Giustiziato, a play written by Benedetto Naselli, is first performed on the 21st of December 1863 in Palermo.
1865	The prefect of Palermo, the Marquis Filippo Antonio Gualterio, pens a report where he refers to the criminals in the city as "*the so-called Maffia or criminal association*".
	Elisée Reclus, a French anarchist in exile, writes an article describing the *maffia* which is published in a French travel magazine. He describes it as a criminal association made up of over five thousand men.

1868	A Catholic-Regionalist bloc wins a decisive victory in local elections. The new mayor, Domenico Peranni, revives the legend of the Beati Paoli to give it a politically convenient slant and names a square in their honour.
1873	Giuseppe Bruno Arcaro publishes an essay entitled *A page of Sicilian History* in which he presents the Beati Paoli as a sect revolting against oppressors, including the Piedmontese.
1875	Giuseppe Pitrè, an Italian folklorist, creates a written record of the oral folkloristic tales about the Beati Paoli, which he described as a secret society made up of brave men from the lower classes who defended the weak and took revenge on those who exploited and tormented them.
	Pasquale Villari publishes *Le Lettere Meridionali*, which focused on the social, cultural and economic gaps between northern and southern Italy.
1877	Trial of the Stuppagghieri, who testify about an initiation ritual that incorporated fire, blood, and a holy picture.
1880	Giovanni Carmelo Verga publishes a collection of stories called *Vita dei Campi*, which includes a story called *Cavalleria Rusticana*.
1890	The opera *Cavalleria Rusticana* by Pietro Mascagni premieres on the 17th of May at the Teatro Costanzi in Rome.
1909	On the 12th of March an Italian American policeman, Joe Petrosino, is assassinated in a square in Palermo.
	In April a witness claims Don Vito Cascio Ferro, the *mafioso* who is suspected of masterminding the killing of Petrosino, sent him to drop off a note at a door leading to the very underground chamber that legend claimed was used by the Beati Paoli for their nocturnal tribunals.
	Luigi Natoli, writing under the pseudonym William Galt, writes a serialised novel about the Beati Paoli for the national newspaper *Giornale di Sicilia*. Two hundred and thirty-nine episodes were released daily between May 1909 and January 1910.

1920   Giovanni Alfredo Cesareo writes a play called *La Mafia*.

1921   Natoli's novel is published in book form, becoming a major bestseller.

The play called *La Mafia* written by Giovanni Alfredo Cesareo is performed for the first time in the Eliseo Theatre in Rome in 1921.

1937   On the 25th of July 1937, the community of Riesi celebrate the feast of St Joseph. The statue of the saint becomes an unwitting protagonist in the transfer of power from a Mafia boss, Giuseppe Di Cristina, to his son, Francesco Di Cristina.

1947   Luigi Natoli's novel about the Beati Paoli is turned into a film called The Black Masked Knights.

1949   Luigi Natoli's novel is reprinted and distributed widely.

1954   Elaborate funeral for mafia boss Calogero Vizzini.

1955   The demand for Natoli's *I Beati Paoli* leads to yet another reprint of the book.

1969   Mario Puzo publishes *The Godfather*, a novel about a crime family in New York, spanning a period of ten years from 1945 to 1955.

1972   *The Godfather*, a movie directed by Francis Ford Coppola, based on the novel by Mario Puzo, premiers at the Loew's State Theatre on the 14th of March.

1973   Leonardo Vitale, a member of the Altarello di Baida Mafia faction, turns himself in to the police after suffering a crisis of faith.

1980   The second mafia war starts – hundreds of people are killed.

1983   Antonino Calderone escapes from Sicily with his wife and three children to avoid being killed by the Corleonesi. He settles in France.

1984   Tommaso Buscetta becomes a *pentito* and uncovers the
        Mafia's secrets, spending 45 days explaining the inner
        workings of Cosa Nostra to Giovanni Falcone.

1986   Antonino Calderone is arrested in Nice.

1987   On the 9th of April Antonino Calderone meets Giovanni
        Falcone in a Marseille prison. Over the course of a year he
        gives over one thousand pages of testimony.

1993   On the 15th of January, Totò Riina is arrested after 23 years
        on the run. He is replaced by Bernardo Provenzano.

        In May the police arrest Beneditto Santapaola, the mafia boss
        of the Catania faction. In the farm where the mafia boss had
        hidden for eleven years, the police find a chapel dedicated to
        the Virgin Mary and a Bible on the bedside table.

1996   Leonardo Messina, a *pentito* who was previously one of the
        top-ranking members of the San Cataldo mafia clan, talks
        about his important role in the procession of the Madonna
        dell'Annunziata (Our Lady of the Annunciation), claiming the
        Madonna as the patron saint of the Sicilian Mafia.

1997   In June the police raid the hideout of Pietro Aglieri, the boss
        of the Santa Maria di Gesù *cosca*, where they find a chapel
        with an altar, a large wooden crucifix, a statue of the Virgin
        Mary, a holy water font, and a large painting representing the
        Last Supper.

2006   In September 2006 a procession carrying the Holy Crucifix
        around the village of Campobello di Mazara stops in front
        of the house of Francesco Luppino, a *mafioso* under house
        arrest, in a mark of respect.

2007   The Italian police capture Salvatore Lo Piccolo. In his hideout they find a formal, typewritten constitution explaining the different roles within the hierarchy of Cosa Nostra, the decalogue of rules to be followed by *mafiosi*, the procedures for selecting the candidates for initiation into the organisation, and the exact wording of the oath of loyalty.

2012   Alessandro D'Ambrogio, mafia boss of the Porta Nuova mafia faction of Palermo, is given the honoured and highly coveted role of carrying the statue of Our Lady of Mount Carmel in Ballarò.

2014   The procession of Our Lady of Mount Carmel stops for several minutes outside a business owned by Alessandro D'Ambrogio's family, embroiling the mother of God in a gesture of deference to the imprisoned mafia boss.

2015   The Italian police manage to take several photos of a Cosa Nostra ritual of obedience and allegiance in Palermo.

            In August the funeral of Vittorio Casamonica, the boss of the Casamonica mafia clan, becomes a case of life imitating art when a live band plays the theme music from the movie as the coffin is carried from the elaborate hearse into the church.

SECTION III
THE TURN OF THE TWENTIETH CENTURY

"To all free and strong men who in this grave hour feel the duty to cooperate for the good of the country without prejudice and preconceptions, we call for ideals of justice and freedom." Manifesto of the Italian People's Party, 1919

CHAPTER 5
THE SOCIAL PRIESTS VS COSA NOSTRA

" The Mafia will become even more cruel and inhumane. From Sicily it will make its way up the entire peninsula, perhaps even managing to reach beyond the Alps." Fr Luigi Sturzo

The Sicilian Mafia's tentacles are entwined around Sicilian culture and religious faith. Much as brands embellish their popular appeal through endorsements from celebrities and influencers, *mafiosi* have used the sacred symbols and rituals of the Catholic Church to bolster their image as protectors of the weak, fighting a righteous war against the evil and the powerful.

Since the inception of Cosa Nostra, priests have been initiated in the Mafia, priests have covered for the Mafia and priests have denied the Mafia existed. This, however, does not tell the whole story, for there have also been priests who were very aware of the evil of the Mafia and sought to educate and protect their parishioners, in some cases paying for their bravery and social conscience with their lives.

5.1 Fr Sturzo and the Partito Popolare Italiano
In chapter 2 we spoke about the Fasci movement, made up of activists pushing for better conditions for workers in Sicily. The leaders of the

Catholic Church were wary of this type of activism, viewing it as a clarion call to disrupt the socio-political order and lead Italy into the quicksand of Socialism or Marxism.

However, while there were priests who threatened Fasci with excommunication, there were many others who sympathised with the mission of the Fasci. They could see that many of their parishioners were being oppressed by the landowners and *gabellotti*, and agreed that working conditions, taxes and rents needed to be improved in the interest of social justice. In some cases, there were even priests who hosted Fasci meetings in their churches, equating the activists' socialist ideals with those of Christian social justice.

In October 1893, as the battle between the Fasci and the landowners escalated and workers went on strike and took to the streets, Bishop Guttadauro of Caltanissetta penned a pastoral letter about the situation developing in Sicily. He took a stand in favour of the poor - *"The reasons for the discontent exist and they cannot be disguised. The rich mostly abuse the needs of the poor, who are forced to live a life of fatigue, hardship and disillusionment."*

Guttadauro urged parish priests to help parishioners negotiate with owners and *gabellotti* to improve the terms and conditions of land rental contracts and to ensure that workers were paid fairly and freed from the tyranny of usury.

However, when Prime Minister Crispi sent in the army in February 1894 and the Fasci movement was decimated by the violence unleashed by the soldiers and the *mafiosi*, the leadership of the Church sided with the powers-that-be, which implicitly included the Mafia. The bishops justified the brutal campaign waged by General Roberto Morra di Lavriano as necessary to control the anarchists and insurrectionists who had tried to destabilise the island. Bishop Guttadauro also fell into line, joining the chorus of praise for the General and speaking out in favour of the status quo.

That said, notwithstanding the final position taken by the Holy See and senior clergy, the seeds had been sown for a generation of priests committed to alleviating the lot of the poor, heeding Bishop Guttadauro's initial call to get actively involved in issues such as land contract negotiations and other practical ways of improving the peasants' quality of life.

Leading the charge was Don Luigi Sturzo. Born in Caltagirone in 1871, he was ordained into the priesthood in 1894. Influenced by the exploitation of workers and the brutal suppression of the peasants he had just witnessed, he became very active in the social and political scene. Not one to limit himself to sermons and theories, Don Sturzo rolled up his sleeves and got to work. He founded credit unions to enable peasants to borrow money without having to resort to usurious *gabellotti* and *mafiosi*. He set up worker unions and cooperatives to give peasants and labourers collective bargaining power. Over and above all that, he also got actively involved in politics, founding the newspaper *La Croce di Constantino* (The Cross of Constantine) in 1897 to spread his message. He even served as deputy mayor of Caltagirone from 1905 to 1920.

Don Sturzo was outspoken about the scourge of the Mafia, regularly writing articles about the topic in La Croce di Costantino.

"...the Mafia, which grips justice, police, administration and politics in its tentacles; that Mafia that today serves to be served tomorrow, protects to be protected, has its feet in Sicily but also seizes Rome, penetrates the ministerial cabinets, the corridors of Montecitorio, violates secrets, steals documents, ensnares men believed to be paragons of integrity, into committing dishonourable and violent acts. By now doubt, mistrust, sadness, abandonment invades the soul of the good, and one ends up in despair. (…) It is the frightening revelation of the moral pollution of Italy, it is the gangrenous wounds of our homeland, the triumphant immorality in the government." Fr Sturzo, in an article entitled Mafia, published on the 21st of January 1900.

In 1919, Don Sturzo was one of the founders of the Partito Popolare Italiano PPI (Italian Popular Party), a political platform for Catholic Social Reform, which was to a great extent a Catholic interpretation of Socialism. Sturzo's vision of Christian Democracy was well-received in the country, which at that point was torn between anticlerical liberals, clerical conservatives, and insurrectionary Marxists, so the Partito Popolare rapidly became the second largest party in Italy, acting as a kingmaker in the formation of government coalitions between 1919 and 1922.

In a book Fr Sturzo published in 1939, called *Church and State*, he explains his ideology, which he called Popularism, explaining that this differed from a liberal democracy in that it favoured an organic, decentralised state as opposed to the individualist, centralised one that liberal democracies promoted. It took a stance on civil and political liberty, which it maintained as equal for all, without party monopolies and without persecution of religion, race, or classes. He stressed that it differed from socialism in that it accepted the concept of private property, while focusing on the social function of such property, thus being social because it represented a shift from the predominant capitalist system.

Fr Sturzo emphasised that above all, his Populism was Christian, because according to him that was the only foundation on which a healthy and fair society could grow.

5.2 The Social Priests

Don Sturzo was not alone. He was one of a cadre of priests determined to bring about change in Sicily. Collectively referred to as *social priests*, they were Catholic activists pushing for reform and social justice. But as they did so, they inevitably came up against the Mafia, which was just as determined to stop the change from happening. In some of these cases, the result was a tragedy foretold.

Fr Giorgio Gennaro was the parish priest of Ciaculli, a small hamlet in Palermo. This was the stronghold of the Greco mafia *cosca*, which also controlled Croceverde Giardini on the south-eastern outskirts of Palermo. The Grecos were a very powerful mafia family whose influence extended throughout Sicily. Giuseppe Greco, also known as *Piddu u tinenti* (Piddu the lieutenant) was *capomafia* and also the *gabellotto* who controlled *I Giardini* (The Gardens), 300 hectares of citrus orchards heaving with tangerines that were the source of great wealth.

In 1916, the Grecos were infuriated when Fr Gennaro denounced them during a Sunday sermon for misappropriating church finances. The priest made it clear that the *mafiosi* had stolen funds that had been destined for charity, exposing the supposedly devout men of honour for what they truly were – leeches stealing money from the poor. This was dangerous for the *mafiosi*, who were determined not to allow the priest to dent their religious credentials and standing in the community, so Salvatore and Giuseppe Greco issued an order for his assassination.

Fr Giorgio Gennaro was killed on the 16th of February 1916, becoming the first priest on record to lose his life to Cosa Nostra. [101]

Three years later, on the 28th of June 1919 another priest was attacked and left for dead. He was Fr Costantino Stella, a beloved social priest committed to improving the lot of the poor and disenfranchised in his parish. Fr Stella was ordained in 1897 and, like Fr Sturzo, he was greatly influenced by the lack of social justice in Sicily and the harsh repression suffered by the Fasci. In his very first year as parish priest, he set up a *Monte Frumentario* (Wheat Mountain), a cooperative that distributed seeds, fertiliser, and other items essential to the agricultural process to support poor tenant farmers and prevent them from falling victim to usury. Once the *Monte Frumentario* was up and running and benefiting his parishioners, Fr Stella also established a fund to organise collective renting and empower his parishioners to negotiate as a bloc, as well as a consumer cooperative to create purchasing power and drive down the price of essential foodstuffs. These initiatives were an inconvenience for the landowners, *gabellotti* and *mafiosi* who profited from the misery of the oppressed workers. Any gains made by the peasants and the workers impacted their bottom line and in their eyes this was unacceptable.

Fr Stella was also politically active, regularly publishing articles in several Sicilian newspapers and running for City Council elections in 1902 and 1904. The good priest was making headway and had become an irritating thorn in Cosa Nostra's side, so on the 28th of June 1919 they sent assassins who stabbed him in front of his house. His injuries were so serious that doctors were not able to save him, and he died eight days later in hospital, at the young age of 46.[102]

Fr Stefano Caronia was another hands-on activist and social priest who was just as committed as Fr Sturzo and Fr Stella to helping his parishioners. He too became involved in setting up cooperatives to empower his parishioners to have more of an influence in local affairs. He also collaborated with Fr Sturzo in the Italian Popular Party. Fr Caronia was very outspoken, pushing the authorities to expropriate the feudal lands in the environs of Gibellina in favour of the local Agriculture Cooperative, thus benefitting workers in his parish.

Fr Caronia's activism was starting to bear fruit, and hundreds of people in Gibellina had joined the Italian Popular Party to support his aims. This made him a serious threat to the local *mafiosi* and the powerful men they protected, so on the 17th of November 1920, Fr Stefano Caronia was executed. They shot him three times in broad daylight in the centre of town near the Consumer Cooperative he had set up for his parishioners. The message was clear – anyone who came in between the Mafia and their money would be killed.

The following message was engraved on Fr Caronia's tombstone.

"He distinguished himself for study and discipline in the Seminary of Mazara. He was ordained a priest on May 23, 1900, and devoutedly cared for the Church of San Nicolò. A fervent champion of Catholic Action, he supported democracy and was one of the leaders of the movement. Elected Archpriest of Gibellina on 6 July, 1914, he was welcomed by all as a messenger of God. A cultured and hardworking priest, he held high the faith in the people and the dignity in the clergy. Tireless apostle organised an active section of the Italian Popular Party, he was instrumental in gaining... the first victory in the province while the most difficult problems for the religious and economic settlement of the classes were maturing. Struck by a murderous hand, he fell on the evening of November 17, 1920, and was martyred for peace."

Notwithstanding the tyranny of the Mafia and the lack of support by the ecclesiastical authorities, Fr Sturzo and the social priests were making a positive impact on the lives of the poor in their parishes. The Partito Popolare Italiano was also a ray of hope for southern Italy because it brought with it the possibility of meaningful social reform. Unfortunately, however, the social priests and the PPI were soon to be overtaken by events, as a massive political storm was about to hit Italy.

CHAPTER 6
THE FASCISTS VS COSA NOSTRA

"Our program is simple: we want to rule Italy."
Benito Mussolini

On the 28th of October 1922 thousands of fascist demonstrators entered Rome. The next day King Vittorio Emanuele III appointed Mussolini as Prime Minister, thereby capitulating without a fight and transferring political power to the fascists. This was the beginning of a dictatorship that would last until Mussolini was deposed in 1943.

6.1 The Roman Question
In February 1922 Pope Pius XI took over the reins of the Holy See. He was an authoritarian with a visceral hatred of communism, formed after witnessing the Bolshevik attack on Warsaw while he was based there as the emissary of Pope Benedict XV.

It was a turbulent year for the Kingdom of Italy. A new government was elected, and Luigi Facta was appointed Prime Minister on the 22nd of July. However, three months later, Benito Mussolini, the leader of the National Fascist Party, set the wheels in motion for a coup d'état.

Thirty thousand fascists (known as Blackshirts because of their uniform) marched on Rome to demand a change in government. Luigi Facta wanted to declare a state of emergency, but King Vittorio Emanuele III refused to sign the order, fearing that it might spark off a civil war. Facta

119

resigned, and on the 29th of October 1922 the King invited Mussolini to form a new Italian government.

Mussolini knew that to achieve his goals he needed to neutralise Don Sturzo's PPI, so he started making overtures to the Holy See. Gradually, Pius XI came to see Mussolini as a bulwark against socialism and communism, as well as the man who could finally bring an end to the Roman Question in a manner that would be acceptable to the Pope.

Fr Sturzo was a fervent anti-fascist, and this put him on a collision course with the Holy See. He coined the phrase "clerical fascism" or "filo-fascists" to refer to the faction of the Roman Catholic Partito Popolare Italiano which supported a collaboration with Benito Mussolini and his regime. In 1923 he resisted pressure from Pope Pius XI to vote in favour of the Acerbo Law, which had been proposed by Baron Giacomo Acerbo to give Mussolini's fascist party a majority of deputies in parliament. Clearly the priest had become a problem, so Mussolini conspired with his supporters in the Vatican to push him out of the Partito Popolare Italiano, and Fr Sturzo was forced to resign as General Secretary in July 1923. The Acerbo law was passed in November 1923 and the following year the National Fascist Party won the election, securing two-thirds of the seats in parliament thanks to the new legislation.

Now that he was securely installed in the seat of power, Mussolini pressured the Holy See to get rid of Fr Sturzo. Cardinal Pietro Gasparri acceded to his wishes and the priest was forced to leave Rome on the 25th of October 1924, living in exile for the next 22 years.

In 1926 Pope Pius XI started negotiations with the Italian Government, culminating in the signing of the Lateran Pacts on the 11th of February 1929. The Holy See acknowledged Italian sovereignty over the former papal states, while Italy recognised papal sovereignty over Vatican City. The Roman Question was finally laid to rest.

6.2 Cesare Mori

Cosa Nostra *mafiosi* were initially very pleased with this turn of events. Fr Sturzo and all the people he inspired had slowly managed to create a wave of opposition against them on the island, challenging the status quo and their power. However, they soon discovered that they had jumped from the frying pan into the fire, because Mussolini had no intention of sharing power with anyone, let alone a criminal organisation which had strong links to his political rivals. Instead of working with *mafiosi* to establish and maintain control of Sicily as his predecessors had done, the *Duce* (a title used by Mussolini) decided to eliminate them, asserting the fascists' monopoly over the use of violence in the process.

Mussolini entrusted Cesare Mori with the mission of eradicating the Mafia from Sicily in June 1924. The instructions were to do stop at nothing to achieve this aim.

"Your Excellency has carte blanche, the authority of the state must absolutely, I repeat absolutely, be re-established in Sicily. If the laws still in force hinder you, this will be no problem, as we will draw up new laws." Telegram sent by Mussolini to Mori

The Mafia had flourished in the years since the unification of Italy by acting as the intermediary between the landowners / proprietors and the peasants / labourers. The fledgling state had been unable to guarantee security and the protection of assets and investments on the island, thus creating an opportunity for Cosa Nostra to take over. However, the fascists required no intermediaries to impose their will on the people, and they had no qualms about using violence to achieve their aims. Mori was adamant that his goal was to establish a direct line of communication between the people and the government, thus abolishing the system of intermediaries that meant that the population obtained as a favour that which was actually theirs by right.

Mori took up the challenge and set up a police militia that unleashed a reign of terror on Sicily. Torture, extrajudicial arrests and executions, mass deportations of suspects and, in some cases, entire villages – there was nothing that Mori, now known as the Iron Prefect, was not willing to do. At one point his militia forcefully occupied the entire village of Gangi, conducting house-to-house searches and terrorising peasants to force them to expose *mafiosi*.

"These operations were carried out in considerable numbers and on a massive scale: and the speed with which they followed one another and the exactness of evidence on which they were based completely strangled the criminal associations which for so many years had flourished with impunity. And the whole island chanted a hymn of liberation." Cesare Mori

Mori arrested thousands of low-level *mafiosi*, although several escaped to countries such as America or Tunisia. Of these, it is estimated that five hundred moved to the US, including *mafiosi* such as Carlo Gambino, Joe Bonanno, Joe Masseria, Joe Profaci and Stefano Magaddino – essentially creating the nucleus for the genesis of the American Mafia.

In total, eleven thousand arrests were made, although in some cases the accusation of mafia association was just a convenient excuse to arrest people who were seen as a threat to the hegemony of the Fascist Party.

Mussolini did not want to pick a fight with the landowners, so in the great majority of cases their close collaboration with the *Mafia* was overlooked. However, Mori's dedication to the cause of eradicating Cosa Nostra meant that he followed evidence wherever it led, even when it took him right up to influential state officials and members of the Fascist party. This made him a lot of enemies and ultimately led to his downfall. In 1929 Cesare Mori was relieved of his post and the government announced that he was no longer needed because the Mafia had been exterminated.

The truth, however, was that Mori had only eliminated the lower levels of the mafia hierarchy. Cosa Nostra was just like a lizard that self-amputates its tail when caught by predators – it allowed the foot soldiers to be sacrificed and lived to fight another day. Once Mori was out of the picture, the landowners returned to their previous modus operandi and in the 1930s the management of the great estates returned into the hands of *gabellotti* and their coteries of strongmen.

What Mori had done was prune old wood from Cosa Nostra, clearing the way for a new generation of even more ruthless *mafiosi* to seize power. One of these was young Michele Navarra of the Corleonesi, who had just graduated as a physician in 1929. With the removal of the Iron Prefect, everything cranked back into motion, with police records showing that mafia and related criminal activity picked up considerably in the 1930s, with a proliferation of crimes such as arson, theft, and execution-style murders.

The stage was set for Cosa Nostra to blossom in the post-war boom.

Timeline of events mentioned in this section

1916   Assassination of Fr Giorgio Gennaro by the Ciaculli mafia.

1919   Founding of the Partito Popolare Italiano.

Fr Costantino Stella is stabbed to death on the 29th of June and dies eight days later in hospital.

1920   Assassination of Fr Stefano Caronia – a social priest advocating for social justice and active in the Italian Popular Party with Fr Sturzo.

1922   Fascist demonstrators and Blackshirt paramilitaries enter Rome on the 28th of October. The next day, King Vittorio Emanuele III appoints Mussolini as Prime Minister, transferring political power to the fascists.

1923   Fr Sturzo refuses to be pressured to vote in favour of the Acerbo law. He is forced to resign as the General Secretary of the PPI on 10th of July 1923.

The Acerbo law is passed in November, setting the scene for Mussolini to seize total control of parliament.

1924   Italy goes to the polls on the 6th of April. Thanks to the Acerbo law, the Fascist National Party gets two-thirds of the seats in parliament.

Cesare Mori is tasked with eradicating the Mafia from Sicily in June 1924.

Mussolini pressures the Holy See to get rid of Fr Sturzo, who is sent into exile.

1929   On the 11th of February the Holy See and the fascist government sign the Lateran Pacts.

Cesare Mori is relieved from his post because his investigations had come too close to influential state officials and members of the Fascist party. It is claimed he is no longer needed because the Mafia had finally been destroyed.

SECTION IV
PICKING UP THE PIECES AFTER WORLD WAR II

"Those who receive gift packages from uncles and cousins in the United States have been warned that they will not get another dollar if Italy turns communist." Don Luigi Sturzo

CHAPTER 7

THE WINDS OF CHANGE

In May 1943 the Allied Forces, led by the British and the Americans, defeated the Axis army in the Battle of Tunisia, taking over 250,000 German and Italian soldiers as prisoners of war. The logical next step was to cross the Mediterranean Sea to Sicily in a direct attack on one of the three main Axis partners in the war – fascist Italy.

The Germans were aware of the likelihood of a move by the Allies into Italy, and they identified Sicily, Corsica, and Sardinia as the likely entry points for the attack. They were, however, misdirected by a corpse dressed as a Royal Marine carrying false documents planted by British intelligence off the coast of Spain. As a result, they shifted their main strength from Sicily to Sardinia and Corsica, leaving only two German divisions on the island.

7.1 Operation Husky

On the 10th of July 1943 the Allies launched Operation Husky, a massive amphibious attack on the southern shores of Sicily. Over a period of three days 150,000 soldiers disembarked onto Sicily off 3000 ships which had made the crossing protected by more than 4000 aircraft.

In the early hours of the 25th of July, the Grand Council of the fascist government voted to transfer some of Mussolini's power to King Vittorio Emanuele in a clear vote of no confidence in their leader. Immediately after the vote, Mussolini met the King, who informed him that Italy had lost the war and that General Pietro Badoglio was taking over as prime minister. The police then arrested the former dictator, holding him under house arrest.

Prime Minister Badoglio immediately started negotiating with General Eisenhower, and the Armistice of Cassibile was signed on the 3rd of September 1943 and made public on the 8th of September. Operation Avalanche, the Allied invasion of Italy, immediately kicked off and within hours Allied troops landed in Salerno. This was the beginning of a series of bloody battles waged against the Nazis who were attempting to occupy Italy and keep out the Allies.

In September 1943 Nazi paratroopers rescued Mussolini from the Apennine Mountains ski resort where he was being detained, setting him up as the figurehead of the newly formed Social Republic of Italy, a puppet state in German-occupied northern Italy.

The Italian Resistance and the pro-Allied divisions of the Italian Royal Army, the Italian Royal Navy, and the Italy Royal Airforce (which came to be known as the Esercito Cobelligerante Italiano) fought alongside the Allies, while the pro-Axis and fascist divisions of the Italian forces came together as the National Republican Army and fought with the Germans. The result was a civil war that ran alongside the world war until the 2nd of May 1945, when the German forces finally surrendered.

7.2 The Allies and the Sicilian Mafia

A popular theory attributes the resurrection of the Sicilian Mafia towards the end of WWII to a secret agreement made with the Allied Forces. This narrative originated from a Sicilian journalist called Michele Pantaleone who wrote an article in the Palermo newspaper *L'Ora* in 1958, claiming that the Mafia provided protection and support for the Allies to invade the island in 1943.

In 1962 Pantaleone published a book called *Mafia e Politica, 1943-1962*, in which he stated that on the 10th of July 1943 a US Army plane flew over Villalba and scattered yellow silk scarves embroidered with a big letter L, which Pantaleone believed was a reference to Lucky Luciano, a prominent *mafioso* in the US. Pantaleone further stated that a few days later, American tanks arrived in Villalba and mafia boss Calogero Vizzini climbed aboard and started coordinating mafia support for the American troops, protecting them from snipers and providing guides to help them make their way through the mountains.

In truth, however, there has never been any evidence that this happened. When questioned regarding his sources, Pantaleone stated that he had witnessed the events in person.

Historians such as Salvatore Lupo and Tim Newark have thrown cold water on these claims. They cite the fact that although the Mafia still existed at the end of the war, it was a shadow of its former self, and the Allies did not consider the *mafiosi* to be strong enough to offer them any support, even had they desired it. Furthermore, the ruse to draw the Germans to Sardinia and Corsica was successful, and the massive contingent of 150,000 soldiers that disembarked in Sicily was able to overthrow the two remaining German divisions and take over the island with relative ease. They did not need any help from the Mafia.

It is also important to note that although Calogero Vizzini was the boss of the Villalba *cosca*, the Sicilian Mafia network had broken down during the years of fascist repression, so he was hardly known beyond the region of Caltanisetta, let alone in the US. It is therefore highly unlikely that he would have had the connections required to coordinate the type of mafia support Pantaleone described.

In the book *Mafia Allies: The True Story of America's Secret Alliance with the Mob in World War II*, Tim Newark cites a different interpretation of the events that happened in Villalba that fateful day. According to historian Luigi Lumia, when the American tanks rolled in, a crowd of people led by Calogero Vizzini greeted the Americans, chanting 'Long Live America', 'Long Live the Mafia', 'Long Live Don Calo'.

One of the US army officials approached Vizzini, who was clearly the leader of the pack, and took him to the Allied command post for an interrogation. Acting through an interpreter the Americans questioned

Vizzini about a recent firefight, but he was then released because they decided he had no useful information to contribute about the matter. In a bid to save face, Vizzini threatened the interpreter to ensure that the embarrassing episode would never be made public. He then returned to Villalba in triumph, claiming that the Allies were grateful and indebted to him for his contribution to the invasion.

Those who favour Pantaleone's version of events point to the considerable knowledge that the Allies had of local culture, and the fact that they would have needed help to make it through the difficult mountainous terrain in Sicily. The claim is that it would have been impossible for the Americans and the British to take over the island as rapidly as they did without having insiders showing them the ropes.

This is indeed true, and in fact the Americans did have the benefit of a group of insiders guiding them – but that does not necessarily mean that the insiders were *mafiosi*. Over four million Sicilians had emigrated to America by 1924, including several outspoken anti-fascist Italians who escaped the country when Mussolini came to power. One such Sicilian American was Biagio Massimo Corvo, who was born in Sicily in 1920. His father, Cesare Corvo, was an anti-fascist journalist who escaped to the US in 1923, leaving his wife Giuseppina and three-year-old son behind. In 1929 Cesare was granted American citizenship, which made it possible for his family to join him in the US.

In 1932 Cesare Corvo founded *Il Bolletino*, a weekly newspaper in Italian, focusing on the political situation in Italy. As his son got older, he too became involved in the paper and the network of anti-fascist Italian exiles, thus retaining strong roots within his Sicilian heritage. When the US joined the war, young Corvo joined the army. Working on his own initiative he started to draft a topographical map of Sicily that showed ports, docks, rivers, cities, railroad networks, valleys, mountains, bridges, tunnels, and everything else that an invading force would need to know to succeed in taking over the island.[103]

News about Corvo's work reached Colonel Earl Brennan of the American Office of Strategic Services (OSS), which had just been created by US President Franklin D. Roosevelt to coordinate the collection and analysis of strategic intelligence required for special operations, with a particular focus on espionage and sabotage. Upon making enquiries with the Pentagon, the Navy, the State Department, and the college at Fort McNair, Colonel Brennan discovered that the US did not currently have in its possession a topographical relief map of Sicily, thus greatly increasing the value of Corvo's contribution and earning him a promotion.

Max Corvo was appointed the chief of Sicilian and Italian OSS operations. He tapped into his father's network of Italian exiles for in-depth knowledge about Sicily and built a team of trusted Italian Americans to assist him with his work. The collaborators included Fr Sturzo, who at the time lived in Brooklyn.

The Italian OSS team trawled through reams of documents, books, and maps to glean as much information as possible for the topographical maps they were developing. They also set up a course for OSS operatives, teaching them the history and geography of Sicily, including an overview of the fascist administrative setup on the island.

When the Allies defeated the Axis forces in Tunisia, Corvo and his team spoke to refugees and Sicilian prisoners of war, using the information acquired to build a credible disinformation programme to psychologically influence Sicilians. Two weeks before Operation Husky the Allied Forces started radio broadcasts from Tunis in Italian. They also scattered leaflets from planes over Sicily, with a mix of real and fake news designed to encourage Sicilians to support the Allies and revolt against the Nazis.

In his book *The Office of Strategic Services and Italian Americans - The Untold History*, Dr Salvatore La Gumina, the director of the Centre for Italian American Studies at Nassau Community College, throws cold water on the theory that the Allies had a quid pro quo deal with Lucky Luciano. He described his communications about the issue with Corvo, who had acknowledged that he had been approached regarding the possibility of enlisting Luciano's help. However, the OSS had concluded that there was little to gain from the association given that Mussolini's crackdown on the criminal organisation in the 1920s had all but wiped it out. In addition, he was clear that he would have considered any such collaboration disgraceful, believing it would have reflected very poorly on his team.

Carlo d'Este, a renowned military historian and author who has been awarded the Pritzker Literature Award for Lifetime Achievement in Military Writing, also assessed the claims of a collaboration between the OSS and the Mafia. In the book *Bitter Victory, The Battle for Sicily*, D'Este concludes that there was simply no evidence to corroborate the claims made by Pantaleone. Furthermore, it was his opinion that the head of the OSS, General William Donovan, who he described as a *"crusading prosecutor"* would never have agreed to work with *mafiosi*.

The stories put forward by Pantaleone and Lumia have the same core points. The Americans arrived and Vizzini got into a vehicle and was driven off somewhere. The truth of what happened once they left Villalba probably went to the grave with Vizzini and the interpreter, however the fact remains that the OSS and American Army had their own intelligence sources and did not require support from the Mafia when it came to the invasion. The stories that circulated after the war probably originated from *mafiosi* who wanted to puff up their own importance and were then amplified by their landowner patrons who wanted to wash their hands of responsibility for the resurgence of the Mafia.

That said, it cannot be disputed that once the Allies were in Sicily, there were clear signs of collaboration with the Mafia, which by now had aligned with the Separatist movement that was supported by the Americans.

"I have the honour to report that on November 18, 1944 General Giuseppe Castellano, together with Maffia leaders including Calogero Vizzini conferred with Virgilio Nasi, head of the Nasi clan in Trapani and asked him to take over the leadership of a Maffia-backed movement for Sicilian autonomy ... General Castellano ... has developed close contacts with the Maffia leaders and has met them on frequent occasions ... prominent members of the Maffia met in Palermo and one of the results of this meeting was the decision to ask Virgilio Nasi to head the movement with the ultimate intention of him becoming High Commissioner. The Nasi family have been

well known in the Province of Trapani for at least two generations and are highly respected by all classes." Letter from the American Consul General to the US Secretary of State in 1944[104]

Returning to the article that Michele Pantaleone wrote in 1958 and the subsequent book published in 1962, it is worth noting that almost twenty years had passed since the invasion, and a lot of water had flowed under the bridge in the interim. During that time, Pantaleone, who was the leader of a peasant cooperative in Villalba, had been embroiled in many confrontations with Vizzini. On one occasion the Mafia even tried to kill the journalist and peasant leader, in which attempt they were fortunately unsuccessful.

As a socialist and later a communist, Pantaleone experienced first-hand the terror unleashed by the Mafia after the war to stamp out communism in Sicily, with the tacit support of the Americans, the Democrazia Cristiana Party, and the Church. The years of bloodshed and the active role taken by the Americans in the propaganda against communists would undoubtedly have coloured his interpretation of events twenty years earlier, making it all too easy for him to conclude that the collusion had started before, and not after, the Allies landed in Sicily.

7.3 The Surrender

On the 27th of April 1945, Benito Mussolini was captured by communist partisans as he attempted to escape to Switzerland with his mistress Clara Petacci. When news about their capture reached the American OSS, they demanded that the prisoners be handed over, as per the terms of the armistice.

"Benito Mussolini, his main fascist associates and all persons suspected of having committed war crimes or similar crimes, whose names are on the lists that will be delivered by the United Nations and which now or in the future are in territory controlled by the allied military command or by the Italian government, will be immediately arrested and handed over to the United Nations forces." Clause 29 of the armistice.

The partisans ignored the agreement and the requests from the OSS, summarily executing Mussolini, Petacci and the rest of their entourage on the 28th of April. Their dead bodies were loaded on a truck and dumped in Piazzale Loreto in Milan in the middle of the night.

As soon as the Milanese heard the news they rushed to the square, which had been the scene of the Massacre of Piazzale Loreto, referring to the public execution of fifteen innocent Milanese civilians on the 10th of August 1944 as revenge by the Gestapo for an attack by partisans on a German military convoy. In a chilling message to the Italians from the Nazis, the corpses of the Martyrs of Piazzale Loreto had been hung upside down for several days from the roof of an Esso service station overlooking the square. The crowd of infuriated Milanese set upon the corpses of Mussolini and his minions, kicking and spitting on them. They strung them up in the same way the fifteen martyrs had been displayed and left them dangling for several days as proof that finally the fascist dictatorship was over.

Four days later the Social Republic of Italy surrendered.

7.4 The Cold War
On the 17th of July 1945, the three leaders of the Allied powers – Joseph Stalin for the Soviet Union, Winston Churchill (who was then replaced by Clement Attlee due to a change in government in Britain) and Harry Truman for the US met in Potsdam to discuss how to deal with Germany and establish a new post-war order.

One of their decisions led to the formation of a Council of Foreign Ministers, made up of representatives from the United Kingdom, the Soviet Union, China, France, and the United States. Its mission was to finalise peace treaties with the countries that had formed part of the Axis Alliance, including Italy, and to resolve any outstanding issues regarding territorial borders.

Trouble was brewing between the former Allies, with the West and the Soviet Union increasingly at loggerheads with each other. The meetings of the Council of Foreign Ministers became more and more confrontational, and by December 1947 the parties could not agree on the terms for the peace treaty with Germany and Austria.

The situation was exacerbated by a coup d'état in February 1948 by the Communist Party in Czechoslovakia, in a move supported by the Soviet Union. The country descended into chaos as the communists set up action committees and armed militias which were sent out to forcibly control the population. A purge of anti-communists was soon underway, with people getting arrested or losing their jobs, and thousands of Czechs desperately tried to flee the country.

On the other side of the divide, on the 17th of March the United Kingdom, France and Benelux countries signed the Treaty of Brussels, establishing the Western Union (WU), a defence alliance that also aimed to promote economic, cultural and social collaboration between its members.

In March 1948 the US government passed the European Recovery Program, which came to be known as the Marshall Plan. This was an extensive economic recovery programme financed by the US to rebuild Europe and prevent the spread of communism.

The face-off between the West and the Soviet Union came to be known as the Cold War, in that it was not a military confrontation, but rather a battle based on propaganda and backroom deals in a bid to shape the geopolitical future of Europe. The tensions between the US, with its Western allies, and the Soviet Union and the Eastern Bloc, were to last for over forty years, until the dissolution of the Soviet Union in 1991.

CHAPTER 8

THE FIGHT AGAINST THE COMMUNISTS

'o con Cristo o contro Cristo'

The seeds for the Catholic Church's behaviour and the position they took in the post-war years in relation to the peasant uprisings in Sicily were sown in February 1917, when thousands of workers went on strike and marched through the streets of Petrograd in the former Russian Empire.

The fall of the Romanov dynasty sparked a wave of extreme violence towards religious groups, particularly those pertaining to the Russian Orthodox Church, which had supported the Tsar. Bolsheviks attacked Orthodox churches and monasteries, butchering any clerics, monks, and nuns they found in their way.

8.1 Ominous Rumblings of Land Expropriation

Within eight months of Tsar Nicholas II's abdication, the Bolsheviks, led by Vladimir Ilich Lenin, seized power. The Communist Party of the Soviet Union (CPSU) was the founding and ruling political party of the Union of Soviet Socialist Republics, commonly known as the USSR or the Soviet Union, which came into being in 1922.

Lenin knew that to retain the support of the peasant class he had to initiate serious land reform. Russian peasants wanted agricultural land to be expropriated, split into small holdings and distributed amongst the people, but this never materialised. Instead, large collective farms were set up and the peasants were employed to cultivate food for the nation. While this was not exactly what the peasants had demanded, they nonetheless acknowledged that their circumstances had improved dramatically and that they now had at least some say in how the farms were run.

Landowners in Sicily observed these events with alarm. It was clear that they had to do anything in their power to prevent communism from taking root in Sicily.

8.2 The Eradication of Religion
One of the stated goals of the communists was the eradication of religion as the first step towards becoming a fully atheist state, and to achieve this aim they kicked off an extended period of terrible religious persecution.

Within a year the Communist Party had seized all the property owned by the various religious organisations in the country. In a show of power and disdain, they converted some of these properties into communist offices. Other places of worship became shops, warehouses, or even public toilets.[105] In one particularly notable case, they converted the Petersburg Cathedral of Our Lady of Kazan into a Museum of the History of Religion and of Atheism, which focused on the folly of religion, the opiate of the masses.

The Communist Party did not only destroy churches, synagogues, and mosques in its quest to destroy religion. It also launched an extensive anti-religious propaganda campaign designed to re-educate the masses and foster what they called *scientific atheism*. Rumours were spread around the country that people were contracting syphilis after kissing the religious icons that were so central to Russian Orthodox tradition. School curricula were also adapted to prioritise anti-religion education, with the propaganda permeating lessons in unrelated subjects, including grammar and mathematics.

By the 1930s the communists believed that the job was done, and in a spirit of self-congratulation they included a religion question in the

1937 census. They came to regret this move when the results showed that over 56 percent of the population still identified as believers. The results shocked the government and led to a dramatic shift in Soviet policy.

Unable to explain how religious belief had endured, they declared religion to be the cause and not merely the symptom of societal problems, which according to them explained the failure of the comprehensive re-education of the masses. In essence, the argument was that the people had not become atheists because religious leaders were thwarting communism by preventing the achievement of perfect social justice. To end this subversion, it was decided that all religious organisations needed to be exterminated.[106]

This change in policy coincided with the Great Purge unleashed by Soviet dictator Joseph Stalin between 1936 and 1938. Historians estimate that over seven hundred and fifty thousand people were killed, and more than one million people were sent to forced labour camps known as Gulags. Records kept by the Russian Orthodox church show that 168,300 clergy were arrested, of whom 106,300 were executed. The Roman Catholic Church also suffered heavy losses - 422 Catholic priests, 962 Catholic monks and countless Catholic nuns and laypeople were killed.[107]

In 1914 Russia had 55,173 Russian Orthodox churches and 29,593 chapels, 112,629 priests, 550 monasteries and 475 convents with a total of 95,259 monks and nuns. By 1939 only one hundred Russian Orthodox churches were still operational, and only four bishops survived. The Roman Catholic church initially had 1240 places of worship, but by 1939 only two Roman Catholic churches were still open.[108]

During World War II and in its immediate aftermath, the religious persecution died down and religious communities slowly started re-emerging. This brief respite ended in 1959 when Khrushchev launched a renewed campaign of persecution of all religious denominations.

Once again there was a concerted drive to close churches and monasteries, along with seminaries and any other institution teaching theology. Citizens requesting baptisms, weddings or religious funerals had to be reported to the state, and any parents found teaching their children religious doctrine were to lose their parental rights. Furthermore, it became illegal for children to attend any church service or receive the sacraments.

Given these events it is understandable that the Catholic Church believed that communism was an existential threat. The ecclesiastical authorities were thus at one with landowners in their determination to keep the communists out of Sicily. This meant that, possibly unwittingly, the Church was now aligned not only with the landowners, but also with their enforcers, the Mafia.

8.3 Ecclesiastical Blinkers

There is no better example of the Church's obsession with communism that Cardinal Ernesto Ruffini, who became the Archbishop of Palermo on the 11th of October 1945, at a time when the United States and the Soviet Union were starting to square off in a widespread political, economic and propaganda struggle.

Ruffini was only too aware of the fact that Lenin had used the peasants to prop up his weak Bolshevik government. This led him to view any mention of the suffering of Sicilian peasants as an attempt to mobilise the masses against landowners and the Church. In his eyes any mention of land reform was tantamount to a declaration of war.

In the meantime, the landowners returned to the same playbook they had successfully used to suppress the Fasci Siciliani. Once again, they deployed the Mafia to target peasant leaders on the forefront of the movement demanding land reform and better conditions for farm workers and labourers. This led to the execution of communist and trade unionist Andrea Raia in 1944. That same year the Mafia also tried to kill Girolamo Li Causi, the regional secretary of the *Partito Communista*, during a rally in Villalba.

In Ruffini's eyes, the end justified the means. He conflated any claims made about the violence unleashed by the Mafia with leftist propaganda, so he publicly declared that the *"mafia existed only in the minds of those who wished Sicily ill"* and that any claims to the opposite was disinformation *"spread around by communists."* [109]

In the runup to the local election of 1947 the situation became even more dangerous for activists and politicians committed to improving the lot of the poor and the disenfranchised in Sicily. On the 4th of January the Mafia assassinated Accursio Miraglia, secretary of the local Chamber of Labour and communist leader. A few days later, on the 17th of January, *mafioso* Francesco Paolo Niosi executed Pietro Macchiarella, a communist activist advocating for better conditions for peasants in the Palermo area. On the very same day the Mafia staged a shooting in the Palermo shipyard, with Mafia boss Salvatore Celeste shouting, *"You know who I am! Whoever votes for the People's Block will have neither father nor mother!"*[110]

The following month, on the 13th of February, the Mafia killed Vincenzo "Nunzio" Sansone, a communist advocating for agrarian land reform and secretary of the local Chamber of Labour, as well as another communist activist, Leonardo Salvia.

In the book *Stories from Villabatesi,* Edoardo Salmeri shares the story of the assassination of Nunzio Sansone, who he had first met on a day when Mussolini had happened to pass through Villabate. That day, Vincenzo ran towards the car of the Duce to give him a letter when it stopped briefly on the road to accept a gift of a branch carrying oranges from the town authorities. At that point the police caught him, severely beating him for having the temerity to approach the fascist leader. From that day Salmeri and Sansone became good friends. According to the author, Vincenzo was a dedicated literature teacher who wanted to rescue the working and peasant masses from the material and moral squalor in which they were trapped. However his activism was an irritation for Cosa Nostra and the men they served, so they shot him as he walked home one evening – *"he had been crushed by the Mafia, by that so-called "honoured society" which had the audacity to claim it represented the ideals of justice of the ancient sect of the Beati Paoli, but who instead safeguarded the interests of the barons and the agrarians, of the exploiters, of human slave drivers. That's why the Mafia had killed him."*[111]

The killings did not stop there. On the 2nd of March 1947, Federterra Epifanio Li Puma, sharecropper and socialist, was also killed, while

Calogero Cangelosi, the socialist secretary of the Chamber of Labour, was assassinated a few weeks later.

Notwithstanding the executions and terror unleashed by the Mafia, the activists and peasants persevered and on the 20th of April 1947 the People's Block, a coalition of the Italian Communist Party and the Italian Socialist Party, won 29.15 percent of the vote in the elections for the Constituent Assembly of the autonomous region of Sicily, soundly beating Democrazia Cristiana, which only got 20.52 percent of the vote.

On the 1st of May 1947, hundreds of families congregated at Portella della Ginestra in a rally organised by the Communist Party to mark International Workers' Day and celebrate their recent electoral victory. A gang of bandits led by Salvatore Giuliano sprayed the crowd with machine gun fire, killing a total of 11 people and wounding many more. The victims of the Portella della Ginestra massacre included several women and children – Vincenzina La Fata (8 years old), Giovanni Grifò (12 years old), Giuseppe Di Maggio (13 years old), Serafino Lascari (15 years old), Giovanni Megna (18 years old), Castrense Intravaia (18 years old), Vito Allotta (19 years old), Francesco Vicari (22 years old), Margherita Clesceri (37 years old), Giorgio Cusenza (42 years old) and Filippo Di Salvo (48 years old).

The very next day the Democrazia Cristiana Minister of the Interior Mario Scelba announced in Parliament that the Portella della Ginestra shooting was not a political or terrorist act, but rather an attack by bandits who had no political affiliation. The claim was immediately rebutted by Girolamo Li Causi, the leader of the Sicilian arm of the Communist Party, who had survived the assassination attempt by the Mafia two years earlier. The discussion became so heated that it ended up in a fist fight, with two hundred members of parliament punching and kicking each other.

The truth about the Massacre at Portella della Ginestra has never been determined, although it must be said that it would never have happened without the consent of the local *capomafia*. It is also important to note that when Li Causi publicly called on Giuliano to name the masterminds of the massacre, the bandit replied in a signed letter that he knew that

Scelba wanted him dead, because he knew his secrets and could destroy his political career. [112]

Salvatore Giuliano's letter was prophetic - he was indeed killed on the 5th of July 1950, just as the trial of the perpetrators of the massacre was starting. His lieutenant Gaspare Pisciotta testified that Giuliano had received a letter offering an amnesty for the whole gang in return for attacking the May Day celebrations. He pointed the finger at several illustrious political figures as the ones who had ordered the attack, singling out Bernardo Mattarella, Prince Alliata, Giuseppe Marchesano and Mario Scelba. However, the men he implicated were later cleared after trial.

At Portella della Ginestra, a plaque was put up in memory of the victims of the massacre.

"On May 1, 1947, here, on the rock of Barbato, celebrating the working class festival and the victory of April 20, the people of Piana degli Albanesi, San Giuseppe Jato, and San Ciprirello, men, women and children, fell under the ferocious barbarity of the bullets of the Mafia and the landed barons, who mowed down innocent victims in order to put an end to the struggle of the peasants for liberation from the servitude of feudalism. The slaughter horrified the world. The blood of new martyrs consecrated in the conscience of the people the resolve to continue the struggle for the redemption of the land in a world of liberty and peace."

In the aftermath of the massacre, Archbishop Ernesto Ruffini sent a letter to the Pope where he expressed no regret about the loss of life, or empathy for the suffering of the families who had lost loved ones, but instead justified what had happened.

"It is a fact that the reaction to left-wing extremism is taking on impressive proportions. Indeed, we could have predicted as inevitable this resistance and rebellion against the arrogant pretences, the calumnies, the disloyal thinking and the anti-Italian and anti-Christian theories of the communists. We are still overly afraid of these deluded masses manipulated by godless men"[113]

Clearly, in the eyes of Ruffini and the ecclesiastical authorities of the time, there were no holds barred in the war against communism, and the deaths of innocent people attending a peaceful rally were simply to be written off as collateral damage.

The attacks and murders continued unabated until the general election in 1948. In total, between 1944 and 1948, more than forty trade unionists, socialists and communists were killed by the Mafia in Sicily. The Church and the State remained silent in the face of the carnage.

8.4 The Propaganda War

The tensions of the Cold War, the disaster unfolding in Czechoslovakia, and the determination of the Holy See to keep communism at bay formed the background to the events that unfolded in Italy in 1948 as the Italians prepared to go to the polls on the 18th of April to elect the first Parliament of the Italian Republic. The election was a contest between the governing Democrazia Cristiana Party (Christian Democratic Party) led by Alcide de Gasperi and the Popular Democratic Front, an alliance between the communists, led by Palmiro Togliatti, and the socialists, led by Pietro Nenni.

Concerned by the possibility that the Soviet Union would use the Italian Communist Party to influence and control Italy, the US, the UK and the Catholic Church mobilised to support Democrazia Cristiana (DC),[6] a centrist party with an ideology based on Catholic doctrine.

The leaders of DC understood that the funding and support they were receiving were contingent on them acting as a bulwark against the Communist Party. So far, they had collaborated with the communists as equal partners in government, but now they made a swift volte-face. They kicked the communists out of the government coalition and signalled their determination to never again collaborate with them or the socialists.

---

6 On the 9th of November 1926 the fascist regime forced the dissolution of the Partito Popolare Italiano. However, the network of relationships between the members of the party remained alive, thanks in no small measure to the efforts of Don Luigi Sturzo. In 1942 several exponents of the defunct PPI started meeting in secret with members of other organisations such as Azione Cattolica (Catholic Action) and Federazione Universitaria Cattolica Italiana (Federation of Italian Catholic Universities). On the 19th of March 1943, the group approved the founding document of the Democrazia Cristiana party, written by Alcide De Gaspari.

According to historian Francesco Renda, the DC made a conscious decision to accept the Mafia's assistance, taking a formal vote about the matter. Senior party officials used the Cold War as an excuse for their decision to join forces with the criminal group, because they needed to control the masses in Sicily. In the process Cosa Nostra became the military arm of a powerful political entity, a position it had never held before. This elevated the Mafia, aligning it with the government and expanding its influence to include not only political and social issues but also economic ones.[114]

Thus began the unholy alliance between Democrazia Cristiana and Cosa Nostra.

8.4.1 American Intervention

The Americans launched a strong propaganda campaign, leveraging all the tools at their disposal. They used both the carrot and the stick. On one hand they showered the Italians with their kindness and largesse – promising to help them improve the terms of the peace treaty, returning gold stolen by the Nazis, and gifting them with merchant ships. On the other hand, they threatened that if the communists won the election, Italy would be excluded from the Marshall Plan and would not receive any funds to rebuild the country.

Democrazia Cristiana and the Italian government received considerable financial support from the Americans, who also equipped the police with modern equipment to empower them to break up any demonstrations by peasants and workers calling for change and better work conditions.

A *Friendship Train* was organised to travel all over Italy, distributing gifts as a sign of the strong relationship and respect between Italy and the US. Prominent Italian Americans such as Frank Sinatra recorded radio appeals that were transmitted all over Italy.[115]

In parallel with the official channels, the Italian American community also sprang into action. Generoso Pope, the owner of the most widely read Italian newspaper in the US, *Il Progresso* (Progress), came up with the idea of encouraging Americans of Italian descent to write to their friends and family in Italy, urging them not to vote for the communists. Pope used his newspaper to encourage readers to send letters, and soon other newspapers picked up the idea and ran with it.

Victor L. Anfuso, a New York lawyer and Commander of the Knights of the Holy Sepulchre, was a great supporter of the initiative. He distributed a quarter of a million template letters to Americans of Italian descent, in collaboration with the Bishop Lithographing Corporation and Divagando Magazine.[116]

The following is a translation of Congressman Anfuso's 1948 letter regarding the Italian election.[117]

"Dear _____,

It is Easter Sunday and the bells are pealing joyously. In this country where people of every race and creed live together in harmony, we would like to be able to celebrate this Holy Day singing hymns thanking God for the peace and prosperity of all peoples.

We are thinking especially of our beautiful and dear Italy, which after so much suffering, we finally want to see rebuilt and free from all tyranny and injustice. This is why we are anxiously thinking of all those of you who will be going to vote on April 18th, deciding not only your destiny but perhaps that of the whole world.

Therefore, it shouldn't surprise you, if we ask, if we implore you not to throw our beautiful Italy into the despotic arms of communism. America hasn't anything against communism in Russia, but why impose it on other people, other lands, in the process dimming the light of liberty? Above all, Italy should be able to surmount the repulsive oppression and violence which are enemies of God and of the family.

The United States has shown its friendship for Italy in an indisputable manner, sending ships laden with food, coal and medicine for the sick, as well as ships and materials for reconstruction. In return for this the country has not asked for anything, instead cancelling Italy's debt, while further plans to help the country are being formulated in Washington.

That isn't all; the Americans want Italy to have Trieste and to become a member of the United Nations. If this hasn't already happened, it is because Russia has opposed it.

Have faith in America's proven friendship; don't reject the aid that this nation wishes to continue sending; don't destroy in one day the stupendous work which you have already done in directing Italy towards its reconstruction!

For your good and for those who want to live in peace, throw off the threat of communism!

This is the prayer which all of us Americans of Italian origin direct to you on this Easter day, in the hope that the Resurrection of Our Lord may always be celebrated in the land that is the centre of Catholicism."

Catholic priests also joined the charge, using their Sunday sermons to encourage the faithful to urge their relatives back in Italy to vote against the communists, and distributing tens of thousands of templates for their parishioners to copy. Fr Monteleone in Jersey City drafted a form letter of his own, full of fire and brimstone and exhortations, and with clear instructions regarding who to vote for.

He was so determined to make sure the letters were sent to Italy that he even took over the logistics of the campaign. He distributed 3000 letters to be signed by parishioners, and then collected them and took care of postage, ensuring that they were sent on time to be delivered before the 18th of April. He also signed over five thousand letters himself, sending them to priests in Italy to give out to parishioners in localities that leaned towards the communists. [118]

A Committee to Aid Democracy in Italy was also set up by Italian Americans in New York. They designed and printed half a million illustrated postcards for Italians to be sent to Italy. One of the postcards showed two pictures side by side. In the first one a woman is hugging her husband as her children play at her feet, with the caption "Democracy: Peace and Happiness," while the second showed the same woman and children crying as the man marched to war, with the caption "Dictatorship: War and Tears." Another, more ghoulish postcard showed a procession of skeletons walking out of a cemetery after rising from their graves, shouting that *"We are the martyrs who died for Italy's independence. We are going to remind those who have forgotten us that we did not die in vain!"* A third appealed to those who depended on support from their relatives in America, showing a high iron wall between themselves and their relatives, who are shouting *"Brother, if God forbid the communists win, how I will be able to help you with this iron wall between us!"* as they stand helplessly by a pile of supplies addressed to Italy. [119]

Ten million letters, cards and telegrams were sent by Italians in the US to their families back home. The letters were delivered by air on special Freedom Flights organised by the US Post Office and TWA airlines.[120]

8.4.2 Lobbying by the Holy See
"essere con Cristo, o contro Cristo; e tutta la questione"
Pope Pius XII

One year before the election the entire strength of the Vatican was put behind Democrazia Cristiana, with Pope Pius XII declaring from the balcony of St Peter's Basilica that a vote for the Christian Democrats was a vote for Christ, while a vote for the Popular Front was a vote against Christ. This was a very strong message in a country that at the time was devoutly Catholic.

The Holy See was so concerned that it even called upon the mother of God to campaign for Democrazia Cristiana, with processions carrying a statue of the Madonna organised in towns and villages all over Italy. Fervent Catholics thronged around the statues, singing hymns and reciting the rosary, begging the Madonna to protect them from the scourge of communism.

A wave of Marian devotion washed over the country and several apparitions and miracles were reported in quick succession in towns and villages all over Italy. In December 1947 a woman called Annunziata Gentile, who lived in Montopoli Sabina, claimed to have had several dreams in which a sad Virgin Mary, sometimes dressed in black as if in mourning, urged her to find her. Gentili asked the villagers for help and indicated a spot where they should dig. One month later the diggers finally found something – a small, weathered statue that appeared to be a woman holding something in her arms. That evening Gentile dreamed that the Madonna told her that she had been found. Pilgrims flocked to the site, and two brothers called Silvio and Oreste Antonini, blind since birth, claimed they could now see, after asking the Virgin Mary to intercede with God on their behalf.[121]

On the 10th of February 1948, a woman from Assisi announced that the statue of the Madonna on the roof of the church of Santa Maria degli Angeli (Holy Mary of the Angels) moved her head and sighed. The woman told her family and friends about her vision and soon the news reached a radio station that reported the apparition as fact, attributing the Virgin's sighs to sadness at the popularity enjoyed by the Popular Front and fear that communism was going to eradicate Catholicism. [122]

Pilgrimages started being organised to Assisi as Italians thronged to visit the sighing Madonna, kicking off mass hysteria with dozens claiming to have seen the statue move. This evolved into stories about miracles, with devotees claiming the sighing Madonna had healed them. In one case, the doctor of a 48-year-old woman called Filide Gori claimed that after three years of unsuccessful medical treatments, she was fully cured after praying to the sighing Virgin on top of the church. [123]

In Ancona a woman called Maria Gobbi reported that she had seen a 20 cm long cross, crowned with the Holy Eucharist, at the bottom of a large bowl which she used to ferment olives. Once again people flocked to see her house and the event was reported as fact by the national newspaper Il Messagero.[124]

It must be said that the ecclesiastical authorities did not encourage the faithful to believe in these apparitions. Bishops and priests spoke out, saying that the reported episodes were likely optical illusions or the result of troubled minds. That said, it is an interesting sign of the times that so many people believed the Madonna was regularly making trips to Italy, and notable that so many reputable newspapers and radio stations reported these claims as facts.

The Vatican also mobilised *Azione Cattolica* (Catholic Action), a militant lay organisation that plastered every wall all over Italy with posters targeting the faithful with messages such as *"In the secret of the ballot-box God sees you, Stalin doesn't."* The posters used strong imagery to reach the entire population, including the illiterate. Azione Cattolica also organised mass meetings all over Italy, exhorting the faithful to save the country from the scourge of communism.[125]

All the above, however, pales into insignificance when compared the impact of cinema on the campaign. The Italians absolutely loved going to the cinema, and there were over 6500 theatres open in 1948. That year a total of 588 million tickets were sold, equivalent to 1.6 million tickets daily. At that time the minister responsible for cinema was Giulio Andreotti, who invested heavily in the distribution of films that promoted a pro-American message. He also arranged for *Ninotska*, a 1939 anti-communist film by Ernst Lubitsch starring Greta Garbo, to be shown multiple times a day in Italian movie theatres all over the country.

The medium was so popular that every parish had a projector in its church hall, making available 'parish cinemas' that were perfect for political messaging. Catholic activist Luigi Gedda set up several committees to create Catholic propaganda films. Several were produced, but there was one that was particularly effective - *La Strategia della Menzogna* (The strategy of the lie). The movie shows clips of various leftist leaders addressing crowds, as a voiceover warns the viewer that these men are liars, promising jobs and a fairer society while bringing hunger and destruction (illustrated with clips of war ruins). The movie then shows scenes of armed insurrections in European countries as the voiceover explains that communists want people to be unemployed and hungry, organising strikes that paralyse industry and lead to even more unemployment. Comparing Palmiro Togliatti (the leader of the Italian Communist Party) to Benito Mussolini, the voiceover warns – *"They talk of life but demand death in their slogans; talk of peace but prepare instruments of war."* The final scene of the movie then switches to footage of riots in Spain with people pillaging and burning churches, with the voiceover intoning the importance of keeping the communists out of power. [126]

8.5 The Election Results

The Christian Democrats clearly had some seriously important players fighting on their behalf. The communists, on the other hand, did not get much support from the Soviet Union. Events in Europe also did not help – the communist takeover of Czechoslovakia, the escalating violence in Greece as the military branch of the Communist Party of Greece (KKE) forced the country into civil war, and the violent communist opposition in France. All these became factors that inevitably influenced voters in Italy, who were observing what was happening around them in Europe with increasing concern.

As a result, Democrazia Cristiana won a decisive victory with 48.51 percent of the vote. The Popular Democratic Front, on the other hand, emerged bruised and humiliated, with only 31 percent. The Italians had spoken, and their choice was a resounding repudiation of the machinations of the Soviet Union.

8.6 The Aftermath of the Election

The communist and socialist parties had lost the election, but the situation in Sicily was still dire for many of its inhabitants, so the social unrest continued. The Catholic Church was aware of the very real injustices that were being perpetuated against the weak and the poor on the island. In December 1951, during a meeting of bishops of the Sicilian plenary council, Pope Pius XII appealed to them to assist their communities and help workers and trade unions by any means possible. [127]

However, when the Bishop of Agrigento, Giovanni Battista Peruzzo, proposed to include a chapter in the plenary's documents about the social doctrine of the Church on matters that impacted their poor parishioners, such as agrarian land reform and decent wages, the proposal was shot down, because the spectre of a peasant uprising still haunted several senior clergymen.[128]

Cardinal Ruffini was still as obsessed with communism as ever. In a pastoral letter called *Il Vero Volto della Sicilia* (The True Face of Sicily), read out from pulpits on Palm Sunday 1964, Ruffini condemned the media. *"Recently, we have witnessed a great conspiracy organised to dishonour Sicily; the three main contributing factors are the Mafia, Il Gattopardo and Danilo Dolci."*[129] The Mafia, the letter insisted, was *"nothing more than an insignificant minority of criminals"* whose impact and power was inflated by the media.

Il Gattopardo, the novel that had incurred Ruffini's displeasure, was written by Giuseppe Tomasi di Lampedusa and published in 1958. It chronicled the changes in Sicilian life and society through the eyes of Don Fabrizio Corbera, a 19th-century Sicilian nobleman, as he lived through a civil war and revolution. Don Fabrizio had to choose between upholding the continuity of upper-class values, and breaking tradition to secure the continuity of his family's influence. It is nowadays considered one of the most important novels in modern Italian literature and has won several international awards.

Danilo Dolci, on the other hand, was an Italian activist, sociologist, educator and poet. He was one of the leaders of the non-violence movement in Sicily, protesting against poverty, social exclusion and the Mafia. Ruffini was angry because Dolci had published a report entitled *Inchiesta a Palermo* (1956) where he described the terrible conditions suffered by peasants and fishermen in Sicily, and the power of Cosa Nostra.

According to the Cardinal, stories of social strife, violence and mafia activity were all part of a conspiracy. Ruffini was convinced that acknowledging the truth about the misery and poverty suffered by a large swathe of Sicilians was grist for the communist mill, so he stuck his head in the sand and ignored the reality that surrounded him. When a journalist once asked him *"What is the Mafia?"* he responded, *"As far as I know, it could be a brand of detergent."*

However, while the Holy See and the senior clergymen of Sicily had their eyes trained on the communists, priests in Sicilian parishes were facing the horror of the Mafia every day. A new generation of priests were coming face to face with Cosa Nostra and battling to save their parishioners from the yoke of criminality.

Foremost amongst them was a priest call Fr. Pino Puglisi, but there were also others who, often singlehandedly, fought to safeguard their parishioners and keep their children out of the clutches of Cosa Nostra. Unfortunately, their path was not easy, as explained by Father Ennio Pintacuda, who in later years said that those priests who, like him and Fr Puglisi, were working against the Mafia, were viewed very negatively by the ecclesiastical authorities, who saw them as agents of communism and not proponents of Christianity.[130]

CHAPTER 9

THE RESURGENCE OF COSA NOSTRA

"*The most conspicuous causal factor behind the persistence and expansion of mafia power in Sicily is undoubtedly the relationships which the Mafia was able to establish with the public sector, above all with administrative and bureaucratic structures and then with political power.*"

Antimafia Commission 1972 [131]

In 1950 the government of the newly created Republic of Italy set up the *Cassa del Mezzogiorno* (Fund for the South), with a budget to be used to stimulate economic development in southern Italy through public works, infrastructure projects and credit subsidies to incentivise investment in the region. The Cassa funded several projects between the 1950s and the 1990s, spending over 140 trillion lire on the construction of aqueducts, hospitals, and schools, as well as the reclamation of millions of hectares of land, the improvement of the road network, and upgrading and expansion of the electrical grid.

The large amounts of money made available for projects in the south attracted the Mafia like blood in the water attracts sharks. The *mafiosi* systematically bribed and corrupted city planners and other decision makers to come up with pork barrel projects which were contracted to mafia-connected companies that were often paid in full for work that was never completed.

9.1 The Sack of Palermo

Salvatore Achille Ettore Lima aka Salvo Lima, the son of a Palermo *mafioso*, became the mayor of Palermo in 1958. During the five years he was mayor (1958 to 1963) he conspired with Vito Alfio Ciancimino, a corrupt assessor for public works with close Corleone mafia ties, to sign off 4,000 building permits, kicking off a period that came to be known as *The Sack of Palermo*. Lima and Ciancimino also ensured that most of the construction licences on the island were given to *mafiosi*, even when the recipients had no construction experience whatsoever. This meant that most of the *Cassa del Mezzogiorno* money that poured into Sicily for infrastructure projects ended up in the pockets of the Mafia.

The construction frenzy that ensued led to the destruction of swathes of agricultural land, including the beautiful mature orchards surrounding Palermo, and the demolishing of several lovely Art Nouveau villas, including Villa Deliella, a masterpiece of the great Sicilian architect Ernesto Basile, which was demolished in the middle of the night a few hours before it was to be formally declared a protected building. In their place rose ugly, low-quality apartment blocks built by *mafiosi* masquerading as builders, who cut corners at every turn.

In return, the Mafia ensured that their political patrons faced no competition at the ballot, using every trick in the book to rig elections in their favour. The Mafia controlled blocks of votes and manipulated electoral lists to ensure a victory for the politicians they were supporting. Voters were routinely stopped, threatened, and sometimes even physically assaulted as they approached the voting booths, where several *mafiosi* lingered, intimidating people as they entered the polling stations.[132] There was no such thing as a free and fair election in Sicily.

9.2 Pork Barrels and Narcotics

Gaetano Badalamenti was the boss of the Cinisi *cosca* and a well-known *mafioso* who had been deported from the US. In one of the most infamous cases of pork barrel projects created solely to direct funds to Cosa Nostra, he bribed government planners to have an airport built 33km away from western Palermo. Punta Raisi was not conveniently located for passengers and the location was very windy so not ideal for take-offs and landings, but it was perfect for the Cinisi mafia for two reasons. The first was that they were granted the contract for the provision of the stone to be used in the construction of the airport, as well as the contract for the construction itself. The second was that it was perfectly located for the coordination of shipments of heroin to be flown between Cinisi and Detroit, where Badalamenti's brother lived.

The building of the Punta Raisi airport was a crucial element in the formation of the *Pizza Connection*, a Mafia drug trafficking and money laundering operation that operated in Sicily and the US, created and led by Badalamenti.[133]

The drug ring imported morphine from Turkey and southwest Asia, processed it into heroin in Sicily, and then exported it to the United States, where it was distributed using a network of pizzerias in several US cities, creating unprecedented drug revenues which then flowed back to Sicily. In setting up this massive operation Cosa Nostra managed to cut out major drug rings which manufactured heroin in France, thus taking over a larger share of the international narcotics market. In total, it is estimated that the *Pizza Connection* drug business exported circa US$1.65 billion of heroin to the United States between 1975 and 1984.

9.2.1 The Drug Mules

Badalamenti came up with an ingenious scheme for the transportation of drugs from Palermo to the US. Every week the Palermo-Rome-New York flight carried housewives travelling to New York for a short holiday in a luxury hotel in the city. Each woman wore a body belt stuffed with drugs on the way to New York and then returned to Palermo laden with wads of dollars. Most of the drug mules were middle-aged and poverty-stricken, living in a *catoi*, a windowless basement apartment in the filthy centre of old Palermo, or in one of the ugly tower blocks on the outskirts of the city.

The women were given a $150 allowance for each day they spent in New York, and an overall payment of 25 million lire once the deliveries were complete. This was a pittance compared to the value of the drugs and the money they smuggled in and out of the country, and it also came at a great personal price that they most likely were not aware of until it was too late. The following is an extract from testimony given to Judge Giovanni Falcone by Salvatore Allegra.

"Totuccio explained why it was better using them. First of all there were fewer risks with them carrying the goods ... Then for him, Totuccio, there was an ulterior motive. Before "dressing" them, he would "have" them all. The ritual would be carried out in a villa at Costa Corsara, not far from Punta Raisi. The woman would have to be there the evening before departure to get her instructions, and she would spend the night there... that night or perhaps on the morning of departure, the courier would have to pay the obligatory "lovemaking" tax: a coupling imposed by the mafioso."[134]

9.2.2 Giuseppe "Peppino" Impastato

On the night between the 8th and 9th of May 1978, a young man was stretched out over a railway line with a bomb under his body. The man was Giuseppe "Peppino" Impastato, a communist activist who was the son of a *mafioso* in the Cinisi *cosca*. He refused to follow in his father's footsteps and instead founded a radio station called *Radio Aut*, which he used to denounce injustice and the Mafia.

The local authorities and the media claimed that Impastato was killed in an explosion that occurred while he was organising a terrorist attack on the railroad. The truth, however, was that the killing was ordered by the Cinisi mafia boss Gaetano Badalamenti. Public Prosecutor Gaetano Costa was the first to flag the death as a mafia crime, as opposed to terrorism or suicide.

The inscription of Peppino's gravestone describes him as a *"revolutionary and communist militant killed by the Christian democratic mafia."*

9.3 The First Mafia War

According to *pentito* Tommaso Buscetta, several meetings were held between top Sicilian and American *mafiosi* between the 12th and the 16th of October 1957 in Palermo. During these meetings the US gangsters

Joseph Bonanno and Lucky Luciano explained how the American Mafia Commission functioned and recommended that the Sicilians set up a similar structure. The Sicilians immediately saw the merits of such a setup, and the resulting organisation structure was a key innovation that facilitated the rapid growth of the Sicilian Mafia after the war.

A confidential report of the carabinieri dated the 28th of May 1963 includes mention of the existence of a Mafia commission composed of fifteen mafia bosses – six from Palermo city and the rest from surrounding towns. Initially the *commissione* functioned well, maintaining a strong hold on all the operations of the Mafia. However, its success was short lived. On the 26th of December 1962, Calcedonio Di Pisa, the boss of the Noce Mafia *cosca* and a member of the Sicilian Mafia Commission, was assassinated because of a dispute relating to the loss of a shipment of heroin being transported by a waiter on a transatlantic ship voyage. This kicked off a period of intense fighting between rival clans in what came to be known as the first mafia war.

On the 30th of June 1963, an automobile loaded with explosives was left outside the home of Salvatore Greco aka Ciaschiteddu Greco, head of the Sicilian Mafia Commission and the boss of the Ciaculli Mafia family. Seven police and military officers were killed as they tried to defuse the bomb after receiving an anonymous tipoff. Their names were Mario Malausa, Silvio Corrao, Calogero Vaccaro, Eugenio Altomare and Mario Farbelli from the Carabinieri, and Pasquale Nuccio and Giorgio Ciacci from the Italian Army.

This came to be known as the Massacre of Ciaculli and was a major turning point for the Italian State, prompting it to finally take serious action against the Mafia. Over a period of three months, 1200 *mafiosi* were arrested, many of them ending up in prison for several years. The heat was turned up to such a degree that the Sicilian Mafia Commission disbanded, with many senior *mafiosi* escaping to countries such as the United States, Venezuela or Canada.

On the 31st of May 1965, Judge Cesare Terranova[7] signed the order to send 114 *mafiosi* to trial in relation to crimes associated with the first mafia war. The charges included murder, kidnapping, theft and smuggling, public massacre (the Ciaculli bombing) and organised delinquency, in what came to be known as the *Trial of the 114*. The judge ruled that the crimes and those accused of carrying them out were all linked, and that the accused should be tried as members of an organised criminal association. In December 1967 the Trial of the 114 commenced. It lasted an entire year, but the results were very disappointing. Of the 114 accused, only 10 were found guilty by the Court of Catanzaro, and many of those only for organised delinquency.

Also in 1965, Cesare Terranova ordered the prosecution of sixty-four Corleone *mafiosi*, including Luciano Leggio, the boss of the Corleone *cosca*, for a series of murders in Corleone from 1958 to 1963, including the assassination of the previous boss of the Corleonesi, Michele Navarra. The Bari court acquitted the 64 Corleonesi. It later emerged that the judges and prosecutors had all received death threats from the Mafia.

9.4 The First Antimafia Commission
The Ciaculli massacre galvanised the *Commissione Parlamentare d'Inchiesta sul Fenomeno della Mafia in Sicilia* (Parliamentary Commission of Inquiry on the Mafia phenomenon in Sicily).

The first Antimafia Commission, as it came to be known, was originally constituted by the Italian Parliament in February 1963. However, it remained dormant due to an impending general election, which was held in April of that year. It was then reconstituted on the 5th June 1963 under the leadership of a Democrazia Cristiana politician called Donato Pafundi, finally meeting for the first time on the July 1963.

---

7 Judge Cesare Terranova was born in 1921 in a small town close to Palermo. In 1946 he joined the judiciary and by 1958 he became the Chief Investigative Prosecutor in Palermo. He was one of the first prosecuting magistrates to seriously investigate the Mafia and links between *mafiosi* and prominent politicians. In 1972 he was elected as a member of the Italian Parliament for the Independent Left on the Italian Communist Party ticket and he became heavily involved in the Antimafia Commission. On the 25th September 1979 he was assassinated along with his driver and bodyguard, policeman Lenin Mancuso.

THE BATTLE FOR SICILY'S SOUL

Pafundi was very cautious, deciding that some of the findings of the Commission were explosive. After five years of work the first report was finally submitted in March 1968 – but it consisted of only three pages full of inconsequential findings.

In 1968 the leadership of the Commission passed from Pafundi to Francesco Cattanei, a Christian Democrat from the north of Italy. Unlike his predecessor, Cattanei was determined to achieve tangible results, but he soon ended up under attack from his own party. The official party newspaper, *Il Popolo* (The People), attempted to destroy his reputation and branded him as a tool of the communists. Notwithstanding the pressure, Cattanei and the Antimafia Commission continued their investigations and in July 1971 they published an interim report which named prominent *mafiosi* and outlined the characteristics of the Sicilian Mafia - *"... magistrates, trade unionists, prefects, journalists and police officials agreed about the existence of intimate links between the Mafia and the public authorities ... some trade unionists actually said that 'the mafioso is a man of politics.'"*[135]

The Antimafia Commission was then dissolved in anticipation of a general election on the 7th of May 1972. When it was reconstituted, Cattanei was not reappointed. The new leader of the Commission was Luigi Carraro, a Democrazia Cristiana politician whose main concern was protecting the party at all costs, even if that meant turning a blind eye to corruption and association with Cosa Nostra.

Another newcomer in the Commission was Cesare Terranova, who had just been elected for the Independent Left as a member of the Italian Parliament and had been appointed the secretary of the Antimafia Commission. Pio La Torre, the leader of the Communist Party of Italy, was also involved and in 1976 the two men published a minority report highlighting the links between the Mafia and several politicians, particularly ones from Democrazia Cristiana -

".. it would be a grave error on the part of the Commission to accept the theory that the Mafia-political link has been eliminated. Even today the behaviour of the ruling DC group in the running of the city and the

provincial councils offers the most favourable terrain for the perpetuation of the system of Mafia power."

The final report of the first Antimafia Commission was published in 1976, a full thirteen years after the commission was first constituted, and it pointed directly at Salvo Lima, a Democrazia Cristiana politician, as a major enabler of the Mafia. The report was totally disregarded by the government, leading to Terranova referring to the Commission as *"thirteen wasted years."*

CHAPTER 10

THE END OF THE ENTENTE CORDIALE

Dr Jane Schneider and Dr Peter Schneider were anthropologists who conducted extensive fieldwork in Sicily in the sixties. During that time Peter Schneider attended a series of exclusively male banquets that give us an insight into how *mafiosi* built their *intreccio* (tightly woven strands) of networks of friendship and obligation with politicians and other men they might one day require.

10.1 Weaving a Web of Intrecci

One day Peter Schneider struck up a friendship with a butcher, who also happened to be a powerful *mafioso*. At the time there was an escalating conflict between the Mafia butchers in the town and a meat wholesaler in another town who claimed that the *mafiosi* were not honouring the terms of a deal regarding the quantity of meat they would order annually.

The leader of a *cosca* from a third town took on the role of mediator in the dispute, bringing together the parties to broker a truce. The re-negotiation was successful and when the parties finally came to a new agreement, the mediating *mafioso* announced that he would organise a *tavoliddu* (banquet) to seal the deal. Since Dr Schneider fortuitously happened to be in the shop when the announcement was made, an invitation was extended to him too, so he got to experience the celebration first-hand.

The *tavoliddu* was organised at a remote country estate where the guests gorged on meat, fish, and copious amounts of wine. The main host was Don Totò, whose nickname was *il Vescovo* (Bishop) because of his close connections to the diocese in his town as well as with Democrazia Cristiana politicians. Assisting him in his hosting duties were his lieutenants, Mimo and Pippo. During the feast Don Totò sat at the centre of a massive U-shaped table with the meat wholesaler and his mafia connections on one side, and the butchers and their *mafiosi* on the other. *Il Vescovo* toasted the guests, first honouring the senior *mafiosi* at the table, and then their friends who had joined them, announcing that friendship was more important than money.

When supper was over, Don Totò and his two lieutenants dressed up in white tablecloths, impersonating priests. Mimo sang a mass, assisted by *il Vescovo*, while Pippo held a beach umbrella over their heads. The liturgy sounded like a traditional Latin service but was in fact a ribald story sung in dialect about the shenanigans that wives and daughters probably got up to when the men were away. The audience, acting as the congregation, was instructed to chant *mincchia* (dick) at the conclusion of each verse in place of amen. Once the mass was over, several of the *mafiosi* enacted sexy parodies of female strippers, as their audience dissolved in gales of laughter. [136]

The banquet was declared a great success, and the butchers announced that they would organise one themselves to reciprocate the excellent hospitality of the mediator. Several additional guests were invited the second time round, and the feast was held at a mountainside restaurant where the *mafiosi* served octopus, roast lamb and goat stew. The entertainment once again featured the ribald mass, to the delight of all the guests.

A few weeks later a third feast took place, this time hosted by the *mafiosi* associated with the meat wholesaler. By now the guest list had expanded to over fifty people, including three Palermo football players and a jazz drummer. Also in attendance were the local veterinarian (a crucial contact in the meat trade), two priests, and the communist mayor and vice-mayor of Villamaura. Guests were treated to free-flowing wine delivered through hoses with spigots, and much merriment ensued. This time the ribald mass was accompanied by fireworks, just like the ones set off during important religious village feasts.[137]

According to the Schneiders these feasts were a very common occurrence at the time, since *mafiosi* were quick to take any opportunity available to organise such networking events. In some cases there were also women in attendance, such as at a *schitticchia* (feast) to celebrate a baptism, a good harvest, or the annual sheep shearing.

Depositions from *pentiti* after the second mafia war in the 1980s also described poker games, feasting, and other entertainment held every weekend from the 1950s to the 1970s at a hotel called the Zagarella, hosted by Nino Salvo, a *mafioso* who used these events to bring together a powerful network of friends, including many politicians and state officials. In 1995 the Zagarella became the focus of the spectacular trial of Italy's former prime minister Andreotti, who was charged with working with the Mafia and was pictured in a 1979 photo at the hotel alongside Nino Salvo and Salvo Lima.

What was most notable about these feasts was the conviviality and connections fostered between the guests, as well as the spirit of complicity that arose from the oftentimes sacrilegious entertainment. Veterinarians who were supposed to certify meat cavorted with butchers who required the certification. Priests who had the power to reserve privileged (and highly visible) seating arrangements in church and dispense prestigious roles in religious processions feasted with *mafiosi* who needed these status symbols to reinforce their position and authority in the town. Politicians who needed votes laughed uproariously or played poker with *mafiosi* who controlled thousands of votes but wanted lucrative government contracts in return. And carabinieri who were supposed to ensure that all citizens upheld the law got drunk with *mafiosi* who broke the law daily.

These connections, made by the *mafiosi* in a spirit of "scratch my back and I will scratch yours," were designed to foster a spirit of cooperation. The unspoken agreement was that the State and the Church would turn a blind eye to the illicit activities of the Mafia, while the *mafiosi* would not attack the State or the Church. It was a friendly understanding of sorts, sealed with mountains of meat and lakes of wine.

10.2 The Season of Excellent Cadavers

In the late 1970s, Luciano Leggio, the boss of the Corleone clan, started manoeuvring to take over control of Cosa Nostra and the highly lucrative narcotics trade. These were the years when men like Totò Riina and Bernardo Provenzano were straining at the leash to make their presence felt in the Mafia. The entente cordiale between Cosa Nostra, the Church and the State was shattered as Leggio mowed down anyone, friend or foe alike, who stood in his way.

On the 26th of January 1979, Leoluca Bagarella (the brother-in-law of Totò Riina) of the Corleonesi *cosca*, killed Mario Francese, shooting him five times outside his home in Palermo. Francese was an investigative reporter with the *Giornale di Sicilia* who had covered the Ciaculli massacre, the murder of Carbinieri Colonel Giuseppe Russo and the 1969 trial of the Corleonesi. He had also interviewed Ninetta Bagarella, the wife of Totò Riina, and traced the evolution of the Corleonesi clan and the corruption and collusion in construction projects such as the Garcia dam.

Twenty-two years later the courts found Totò Riina, Francesco Madonia, Antonino Geraci, Giuseppe Farinella, Michele Greco, Leoluca Bagarella, Bernardo Provenzano and Giuseppe Calò guilty of Francese's murder.

In their final judgement the judges described Mario Francese as having a remarkable ability to draw connections between the most important news stories, to bravely interpret them, and to do so in a way that allowed for the reconstruction of the structure and methods of Cosa Nostra with exceptional clarity, during a period in which Cosa Nostra's strategy on government contracts was slowly emerging. They described the killing as an attempt by the Mafia to prevent the journalist from shining a light on their criminal activities and evolving business model. Francese was a serious threat to the Mafia because there was a good chance that he would have managed to expose its illegal character, organisation and rules with his knowledge and investigations years before such information became available to the public and law officials.

The verdicts were confirmed on appeal. In the final ruling the judges stated that - *"his death opened the season of excellent cadavers."* [138] The assassination of Mario Francese marked the beginning of a two-year killing spree of anyone who tried to save Sicily from the Mafia. A few weeks after Francese was killed, Cosa Nostra targeted Michele Reina, the secretary of the Sicilian section of Democrazia Cristiana. Tommaso Buscetta would later testify that this assassination was ordered by Totò Riina to intimidate any DC politicians who were trying to enact reforms to stop corruption and break the ties that bound their party to the Mafia. Riina's message was clear - their political affiliation would no longer protect them from Cosa Nostra.

The next high-profile assassinations took place in July 1979. Giorgio Ambrosoli was an Italian lawyer who had been appointed by the courts to liquidate the *Banca Privata Italiana* (Italian Private Bank), which had been set up by a Sicilian banker called Michele Sindona as a vehicle to launder the proceeds of the Mafia narcotics trade. Ambrosoli had uncovered evidence that incriminated Sindona, and he was collaborating with Giorgio Boris Giuliano, the head of the Palermo squadra mobile (investigative squad). The two men were getting very close to uncovering the Mafia's money laundering network, so they were both killed within days of each other.

Cosa Nostra was on the warpath. In September 1979 Judge Cesare Terranova, the Head of the Investigations Division within the Public Prosecutor's Office of Palermo, who had bravely led several investigations into the Mafia and indicted several *mafiosi*, was shot in his car along with his driver and bodyguard Lenin Mancuso.

Judge Rocco Chinnici bravely stepped into Terranova's shoes and took over leadership of the Investigations Division. He was fully committed to investigating the Mafia, but he also knew that to truly win the battle against Cosa Nostra, it was essential to reach the hearts and minds of common Sicilians to break the culture of *omertà*. Chinnici often spoke at public events, urging the audience to resist the Mafia, and he visited schools where he talked about his vision of a society that was not tyrannised by Cosa Nostra.

Chinnici assigned the investigation into the heroin trafficking network set up by the Spatola-Inzerillo-Gambino mafia clans to Giovanni Falcone. This was the same case that had led to the murder of Giorgio Ambrosoli and Giorgio Boris Giuliano a few months earlier.

The murderous spree unleashed by the Mafia showed no signs of abating. On the 6th of January 1980 the Mafia assassinated a high-profile politician. Piersanti Mattarella was the Democrazia Cristiana President of the Regional Government of Sicily. He was enacting reforms that would end the mafia public contracts racket, and he also passed laws that enforced building standards, throwing a spanner into the Mafia's lucrative construction business.

Thirteen years later, Francesco Marina Mannoia, a *pentito* who had started a new life in the US witness protection programme, claimed that after Mattarella's assassination, Senator Giulio Andreotti and Salvatore Lima met mafia bosses Salvatore Inzerillo and Stefano Bontate. When Andreotti berated the *mafiosi* for the killing, Stefano Bontate made it clear that it was Cosa Nostra, and not the politicians, who ruled Sicily. He warned Andreotti that if any DC politicians stood in the way of the Mafia, they would lose all the mafia-controlled votes in southern Italy. Clearly the shift of power between the politicians and Cosa Nostra was finally complete. [139]

After a brief lull of four months, Cosa Nostra struck again. Emanuele Basile was a young carabiniere who was investigating the murder of Giorgio Boris Giuliano, collaborating with Judge Paolo Borsellino. On the 4th of May 1980, Basile was shot multiple times in the back as he walked through the streets of Monreale carrying his four-year-old daughter, who fortunately was not injured in the attack.

On the 6th of August 1980, Judge Gaetano Costa, the Chief Prosecutor of Palermo, was killed by Cosa Nostra in a drive by shooting as he chose a book from a bookstall. Costa had bravely signed the indictments of 55 *mafiosi* when other prosecutors had refused to do so, which led to Cosa Nostra singling him out for retribution.

It is impossible not to be in awe of these brave men who knew that they were standing in line to be assassinated by the Mafia but kept stepping forward and continuing the work of their fallen colleagues. They knew they had a target on their back, but they were determined to do whatever they could to liberate Sicily from the scourge of the Mafia. They paid for their integrity and patriotism with their lives.

10.3 The Second Mafia War

In 1980 the machinations of the Corleonesi broke out into full on war with opposing clans. The resulting carnage is commonly referred to as the second mafia war. In 1981 there were 251 murders in Palermo alone. One hundred of those bodies were never found, indicating *lupara bianca* assassinations.

One of the aces up Totò Riina's sleeve was the fact that nobody knew the identity of the Corleone foot soldiers, so it was much easier to catch his adversaries unawares. Furthermore, while the bosses of the *cosche* targeted by the Corleonesi lived openly in their territories, and participated actively in everyday life, the whereabouts of fugitive Corleone leaders such as Totò Riina and Bernardo Provenzano were unknown.

The three towns of Bagheria, Casteldaccia, and Altavilla became known as the *triangle of death*, because of the rampant bloodshed in 1981. According to Father Stabile, a Catholic priest from Bagheria, in August 1981 a total of fifteen people were killed over a period of fifteen days. There was a new corpse every day. That was when the parish priests of the three towns decided that the time had come for them to break their silence.[140]

Fr Stabile and his peers from Casteldaccia and Altavilla publicly denounced the mafia killings. They also joined forces with politicians from both the communist and Democrazia Cristiana parties to create an antimafia committee in Casteldaccia.

On the 31st of October 1981 the Archbishop of Palermo, Salvatore Pappalardo, gave a sermon during a mass held in memory of all the victims of Cosa Nostra, where he described the Mafia as *"a complex and entangled combination of common delinquency which operates in the open and occult manipulators of sordid affairs who act under careful cover and protection."*

A month later Pope John Paul II publicly urged Sicilian bishops to get involved in the battle against Cosa Nostra. Pressure was also mounting on the government to take decisive and concrete action.

It so happened that at the time the government of Italy was not led by a Christian Democrat. The Prime Minister was Giovanni Spadolini, the leader of the Republican Party. Spadolini was concerned about the escalating violence in Sicily, so in March 1982 he asked General Carlo Alberto Dalla Chiesa to become the Prefect of Palermo. The general consensus was that Dalla Chiesa's experience in rooting out terrorism made him eminently suitable to finally exterminate the Mafia. The general also had strong links with Sicily and had been involved in several antimafia investigations prior to his appointment as Head of the Special Anti-Terrorism Unit of the Republic of Italy. Appointing such a high-profile general as the chief law enforcement officer in Palermo was seen as a clear sign that the government was finally going to clamp down on Cosa Nostra.

Dalla Chiesa accepted the post with some misgivings. He believed that to truly stop the Mafia, he would need the authority to coordinate antimafia activities throughout Sicily, and not in Palermo alone. This was discussed at great length in Rome, and vague promises were made that Dalla Chiesa would be given additional powers in the indeterminate future.

In the meantime, however, Cosa Nostra was gearing up for another high-profile assassination.

Pio La Torre, the leader of the Communist Party and a member of Parliament, was an outspoken antimafia campaigner and proponent of agricultural land reform in Sicily. Two years earlier he had proposed a law to criminalise any form of association with the Mafia and to make it possible for the courts to confiscate the assets of convicted *mafiosi*. On the 30th of April 1982, a mafia kill squad trapped and killed Pio La Torre and his driver Rosario Di Salvi in their car in a one-way street close to the Communist Party's Headquarters in Palermo.

Dalla Chiesa's first official duty as Prefect of Palermo consisted of attending La Torre's funeral. It soon emerged that his thinking about the

Mafia was aligned with that of the assassinated leader of the Communist Party. In an interview with Giorgio Bocca of the newspaper La Repubblica, he was clear that one of the ways of getting Cosa Nostra was to follow their money trail.[141]

However, the Mafia had no intention of letting anyone stand in their way. Four months after General Dalla Chiesa's appointment, on the 3rd of September 1982, the general, his wife of two months Emanuela Setti Carraro, and their protection agent Domenico Russo, were killed in a hail of bullets in what came to be known as the Via Carini massacre.

The next day a handwritten sign was attached on a wall at the scene of the assassination.

"Here the hopes of honest Palermitans have died".

At the funeral of General Dalla Chiesa and his wife, the Archbishop of Palermo, Salvatore Pappalardo, condemned the violence but did not mention the Mafia by name, instead criticising the Italian political establishment for not imposing law and order in Sicily. The sermon was important because it marked a break from the position taken by Pappalardo's predecessor, Cardinal Ernesto Ruffini.

"A well-known phrase is appropriate here, it comes from Sallustio, I believe: "Dum Romae consulitur ... Saguntum espugnatur" – while Rome decides on a course of action, Saguntu is conquered. And this time it is not Saguntu but Palermo! This poor Palermo of ours!"[142]

Reactions to the sermon were mixed, with many, including the editor of the *Giornale di Sicilia,* opining that Archbishop Pappalardo should not have made such a political statement.[143] A few months later the archbishop went to the Ucciardone prison, as he did every year, to celebrate Easter mass, but this time he was greeted by an empty room. The Mafia had made it clear that all prisoners, *mafiosi* and non-*mafiosi* alike, were to boycott Pappalardo's visit. The fact that nobody turned up for the mass was proof of the iron grip the Mafia had over all the prison inmates and their power in the criminal community.

The criticism and backlash cowed the ecclesiastical authorities and when Pope John Paul II visited Sicily in November 1982, he skipped the paragraph in his speech (which had already been given to journalists) referring to the Mafia. It was almost ten years before the bishops made their voices heard again, when the Bishop of Agrigento called the Mafia "*a symbol of Satan's power*" in 1989 and the Bishop of Catania announced the excommunication of *mafiosi* in 1990.[144]

The assassinations of Pio La Torre and General Dalla Chiesa increased the pressure on the Italian Parliament to finally do something tangible to fight the Mafia. This led to new legislation being passed in September 1982. The Rognoni-La Torre law (named because it included proposals made by both Pio La Torre and Democrazia Cristiana Minister Virginio Rognoni) criminalised membership in mafia-type associations and empowered the State to confiscate the property of convicted *mafiosi* as the proceeds of crime. It gave law enforcement wider powers to access financial information about suspected *mafiosi* and their associates, and made it possible for state officials to conduct stringent and invasive due diligence on any company awarded a government contract.

The Italian Parliament also created the role that General Dalla Chiesa had requested but not received. The person holding the post of high commissioner for mafia investigations would be able to coordinate and oversee all mafia investigations in Sicily. Unfortunately, the man who was best suited for this position was now dead, killed by Cosa Nostra.

The Rognoni-La Torre law gave investigators increased power to follow Mafia money trails, but as soon as the police and judges started using these new tools, Cosa Nostra sprang into action to make its displeasure felt. On the 14th of November 1982, Cosa Nostra assassinated Calogero Zucchetto, a member of the Palermo Mobile Squad who was investigating the Corleonesi, shooting him five times in the head. Two months later, on the 25th of January 1983, three men armed with submachine guns executed Judge Giangiacomo Ciaccio Montalto, who had been investigating the Minore mafia clan in Trapani using the Rognoni-La Torre Law. The assassination occurred just one week after Montalto helped lead investigators to 87 kilos of heroin in a shoe factory in Florence, thus disrupting a node in the Mafia's narcotics distribution network. It was as clear as crystal that Cosa Nostra wanted to intimidate police officers and magistrates who were thinking of using the new investigative tools at their disposal. [145]

At the beginning of July 1983, Judges Rocco Chinnici and Giovanni Falcone issued arrest warrants for the murder of General Dalla Chiesa. Then good news came in from Thailand. The Italian Police had managed to trace Cosa Nostra's heroin supplier in Bangkok and one of the traffickers had agreed to testify in Italy. Giovanni Falcone and Francesca Morvillo flew to Thailand together, hoping to relax and enjoy each other's company for a few days before the judge met the trafficker and started interrogating him. However, it was not meant to be. On the 28th of July, Judge Rocco Chinnici was killed by a car bomb as he left home to go to work. Also killed were his two bodyguards, Mario Trapassi and Salvatore Bartolotta, as well as the caretaker of the apartment block, Filippo Li Sacchi.

When the dust settled after Chinicci's death, the investigative magistrates waited to see who would be appointed to replace him. Falcone was eminently qualified for the job, but he did not even apply, knowing that in Italy it was not competence that mattered in appointments such as these. The man who finally got the job was Judge Antonino Caponetto, a 63-year-old Sicilian who had spent most of his career in Florence and had no experience in mafia investigations. At face value this was not good news, but the facts proved otherwise. Caponetto left his family in Florence and moved to Palermo, where for his own safety his lodgings consisted of a small cell-like room in the Treasury Police Barracks, where he lived under constant guard. The man was driven by his love of Sicily and he was totally committed to continue what Cesare Terranova and Rocco Chinicci had started.[146]

One of Caponetto's first decisions was to set up a pool of magistrates focused on mafia investigations. This concept had been used successfully in the prosecution of terrorism cases. The idea was to facilitate the sharing and responsibility for mafia investigations, avoiding a situation where one man became the sole repository of institutional knowledge regarding any one case. The move was also designed to reduce the risk of Cosa Nostra singling out any one of the judges for assassination.

The Antimafia Pool included Giovanni Falcone, Paolo Borsellino, Giuseppe Di Lello and Leonardo Guarnotta. Caponetto relieved the four men of all non-mafia investigations, taking on the bulk of the resulting workload himself. The four magistrates were now free to focus solely on their mafia cases and they divided the work in a way that enabled each one of them to play to their strengths. Giovanni Falcone focused on building relationships with investigators all over the world, constantly travelling to countries such as France, Thailand, the US and Turkey in his quest to unravel the international drug trafficking routes set up by Cosa Nostra. Paolo Borsellino oversaw all the investigations relating to the assassinations of judges, police officers and state officials. Leonardo Guarnotta took over financial investigations, using the powers granted by the Rognoni – La Torre law, while Di Lello followed up on all the other mafia murders and crimes that needed to be investigated.

There were also other changes afoot. In August 1983 Bettino Craxi became Prime Minister of Italy. He was a socialist and was in no way beholden to Cosa Nostra. He appointed Mino Martinazzoli as the Minister of Justice. Martinazzoli was a Christian Democrat, but he was not from the south, so he did not need the Mafia's support to get elected. Finally, the Antimafia Pool could count on the support of the people in power.

The judges had up to then been working in offices with no security measures in place. They also did not have any computers. Within months the team had new furniture and computer equipment to aid their financial investigations. Falcone and Borsellino were moved to secure offices with bulletproof doors and closed-circuit cameras. They were also provided with armoured cars and were under constant police protection. The Antimafia Pool became an investigative powerhouse, uncovering the secrets of Cosa Nostra and preparing the scene for the Maxi Trial in 1986.[147]

10.4 Pentiti and the Buscetta Theorem

"I trust you, Judge Falcone, and I trust deputy police chief Gianni De Gennaro. But I don't trust anyone else. I don't believe the Italian State has the real intention of fighting the Mafia. … I want to warn you, Judge. After

this interrogation you will become a celebrity. But they will try to destroy you physically and professionally. And they will do the same to me. Never forget that you are opening an account with Cosa Nostra that will only be settled when you die. Are you sure that you want to go ahead with this?" Tommaso Buscetta warning Judge Giovanni Falcone in 1984

The second mafia war and the relentless campaign of assassinations shattered the carefully constructed façade of Cosa Nostra, while also breaking the bonds between *mafiosi* that had held for over a hundred years. In 1983 Giovanni Falcone started to cultivate *mafiosi* from the losing factions of Cosa Nostra, encouraging them to turn state's witness in return for protection. He also built a strong collaboration with the Justice Department in the US, in a move to capture Sicilian *mafiosi* who had moved to the United States. This marked the beginning of the *pentiti* programme, set up in collaboration with the US Witness Protection Programme.

Several key *mafiosi* from the losing factions defected, collaborating with the State in return for a reduction in jail term for the crimes they had committed and a new life for themselves and their family in witness protection in the US. In villages like San Giovanni, located in the valley of Spicco Vallata, there were so many *pentiti* that the locality almost became a ghost town as entire families were spirited away and relocated elsewhere with a new identity.[148]

These *pentiti* broke the code of silence known as *omertà* and lifted the lid on Cosa Nostra, a secret society of men with a formal statute, bound together by an oath of allegiance and organised in a strictly hierarchical organisation with a decalogue of rules that were violently enforced.

In 1984 Tommaso Buscetta spent forty-five days explaining the inner workings of Cosa Nostra to Judge Falcone, including the hierarchical structure of the organisation and the existence of a governing council known as the Commission or Cupola. This enabled the prosecutor to construct a sociology of Cosa Nostra which he called the *Buscetta Theorem*. Like the Rognoni-La Torre Law, the theorem emphasised the organised and structured nature of the Sicilian Mafia.

At the bottom of the hierarchy of each *cosca* were the *soldati* (soldiers), commonly referred to as *uomini d'onore* (men of honour). Soldati were organised in groups of ten, known as *decine*, led by a *capodecina*. At the top of each *cosca* was the *capo* (boss), and directly reporting to him was the *vice capo* (deputy) and *consigliere* (advisor). The *capo* also appointed a *reggente* (regent) to take over the reins should the boss be indisposed.

The structure of a *cosca* is as follows, starting from the top:
1. *Capo*
2. *Vice Capo, Consigliere, Reggente*
3. *Capodecina*
4. *Soldati*

Each *cosca* had its own territory, but it also cooperated closely with other *cosche* in the vicinity. This cooperation was facilitated by a council called a *mandamento*, where each *cosca* was represented by its *capo*, who in this role was known as the *rappresentante* (representative).

The *rappresentanti* of the *cosche* in the *mandamento* elected a leader as *capo mandamento*, who then got to represent the region in the *Commissione Provinciale*. One of the *mafiosi* on the *Commissione Provinciale* was then elected to represent all the *cosche* in the province in the *Commissione Interprovinciale*, where one man was elected as the *Capo dei Capi* (boss of bosses), at the very pinnacle of the organisation of Cosa Nostra.

The full management structure of Cosa Nostra as described by Buscetta starting from the very top, is as follows:
1. *Capo dei Capi*
2. *Commissione Interprovinciale*
3. *Commissione Provinciale*
4. *Mandamento*
5. *Cosca*
6. *Decina*

Buscetta also described the initiation ritual used when recruiting new *mafiosi*, along with the knowledge and instructions passed on to them during the ceremony. Based on this information, Giovanni Falcone was able to show that upon joining Cosa Nostra all *mafiosi* become aware of the criminal nature of the organisation. Therefore, this meant they were complicit in all the crimes committed by the Mafia, even if they were not directly involved themselves. This became the central premise of the Buscetta Theorem.

"Before him [Buscetta], I had – we had – only a superficial understanding of the mafia phenomenon. With him we began to understand its structure and how it operated on the inside. He confirmed for us numerous ideas about the structure, recruitment techniques, and the functions of Cosa Nostra. But above all he gave us a broad, wide-ranging, global vision of the organisation. He gave us an interpretative key, a language and a code. He was for us like a language professor who allowed us to go among the Turks without having to try to communicate with our hands." Giovanni Falcone

The information provided by Buscetta, along with Falcone's interpretation and conclusions, supported the theory that the Mafia was *mala in se* (wrong in and of itself) - an unlawful association based on the anticipatory expectation of committing crimes. This meant that by becoming a member one was joining a conspiracy of criminality, implying collective responsibility for every crime committed by members of the organisation.[149] In addition, Buscetta's revelation that assassinations of high-profile people such as police officers, judges and politicians, commonly referred to as excellent cadavers, had to be approved in advance by the Commission, meant that mafia bosses could be held collectively responsible for these murders. This became the foundation of the legal argument used by the antimafia prosecutors in the Maxi Trial in 1986.

On the 29th of September 1984, the Antimafia Pool issued 366 arrest warrants. These were given to Ninni Cassarà, the deputy chief of the judicial police, who led a massive operation in the dead of night to capture the *mafiosi*. The operation was successful, with the great majority of the targets ending up in custody.

The next day, the Italian magazine Panorama revealed that Tommaso Buscetta had turned state's witness. The news created a tectonic shift in the world of *mafiosi*. Breaking *omertà* and collaborating with the forces of justice had previously been unimaginable, but here was a high profile *mafioso* doing exactly that. The very next day, Salvatore Contorno (aka Totuccio), a *mafioso* who knew he was marked for death by the Corleonesi, asked to speak to Falcone, who flew to Rome on the 1st of October to interrogate him.

According to unconfirmed reports, Contorno also met Buscetta when he asked to talk to Falcone. Upon seeing Buscetta, Contorno supposedly fell to his knees and kissed his hand, and Buscetta told him, "*Totuccio, you can talk now.*"

"*I intend to collaborate with the justice system telling everything that I know about Cosa Nostra ... because I realise that it is nothing but a band of cowards and murderers.*" Salvatore Contorno[150]

Salvatore Contorno was able to shed light on several murders committed during the second mafia war, as well as the machinations of Totò Riina and the Corleonesi in their quest for power. He had also witnessed several meetings between Sicilian and New York *mafiosi*, providing crucial evidence for the *Pizza Connection* case in the US. Falcone had finally closed the circle of his investigations into the international drug trafficking network of Cosa Nostra. Based on Contorno's testimony, the Antimafia Pool was able to issue a further 120 arrest warrants.

10.5 The Bloody Summer of 1985

"*Let's face it, we are walking cadavers.*"
Ninni Cassarà

In 1985 the police force of Palermo was investing heavily in its antimafia operations. Giuseppe "Beppe" Montana was the chief of the newly created *Sezione Catturandi* (Fugitive Capture Team), that focused on hunting down mafia fugitives. One of his missions was the arrest of the *mafiosi* who had evaded capture in the raids led by Ninni Cassarà in September 1984, as well as the execution of the new warrants issued based on Contorno's revelations.

The *Catturandi* team worked closely with the investigative magistrates of the Antimafia Pool, tracking down *mafiosi* who were trying to evade justice and executing arrest warrants. Beppe Montana focused on the Greco clan and in July 1985, two years after the murder of Chinicci, his team captured 8 Greco *mafiosi* who were on the run.

Three days later Montana went on a boat trip with his girlfriend and some friends. When they returned to the marina at the end of the day, they were greeted by a mafia kill squad. Montana was shot four times and he died on the spot. He was only 34 years old.

Montana's colleagues were infuriated. They soon identified a suspect, Salvatore Marino, and they raided his house, where they found a bloodied shirt and 34 million lire (circa USD30,000) wrapped in a newspaper. They arrested Marino and took him in for interrogation. Fifteen hours later the suspect was dead – he was covered in bruises and had several broken bones.[151]

It later transpired that during the interrogation Marino refused to divulge the names of the other members of the kill squad. The police beat him up and forced him to drink salt water, until Marino lost consciousness. He was rushed to hospital, only to be pronounced dead on arrival. The head of the police investigative division and ten of his officers were later charged with murder.

The death of the young *mafioso* was grist to the mill of Cosa Nostra. On the 4th of August they organised a massive funeral, carrying the coffin through the streets of Palermo, in a show of contempt for the police.

Two days later, Ninni Cassarà, the deputy chief of the judicial police, who worked hand in hand with Giovanni Falcone and the Antimafia Pool, was killed alongside his bodyguard, Roberto Antiochia, in a hail of bullets shot by a squad of eight mafia hitmen using AK-47 rifles. Cassarà's wife Laura and one of his three children witnessed the ferocious attack from the balcony of their seventh-floor apartment. He was the fourteenth senior police officer to be assassinated by the Mafia in Palermo in a period of six years. According to the testimony of *pentiti*, this was such an important assassination that the kill team included four members of the Mafia Commission – Bernardo Brusca, Francesco Madonia, Giuseppe Gambino and Pino Greco.

Betrayed and fearing for their lives, several police officers raged that the government had abandoned them. At Cassarà's funeral, plainclothes policemen screamed at the politicians who were in attendance and spat on Interior Minister Scalfaro.

A few days after the assassination of Ninni Cassarà, Giovanni Falcone and Paolo Borsellino received a visit from the police in the dead of night. They were told that credible intelligence had been received about an assassination plot targeting them, but that the State could not guarantee their safety and that of their families. So it had been decided to evacuate them to an unknown destination. Shocked, the judges woke their families and they packed their bags, before being taken straight to a military plane awaiting them at the airport.

The flight was not a long one, and Paolo Borsellino, his wife Angela and their three children, Lucia, Manfredi and Fiammetta, along with Giovanni Falcone, his fiancée Francesca Morvillo and her mother, soon found themselves on the island of Asinara, just off the coast of Sardinia. They were to stay in a wing of a maximum-security prison until they were given the all-clear to return to Palermo. This episode highlights something that is often forgotten when discussing the events in Sicily so many years ago. Giovanni Falcone and Paolo Borsellino were incredibly brave and committed, but they were not alone. They both had people they loved and who loved them, who suffered with them through those terrifying years. Paolo and Agnese were very worried about their daughter, Lucia, who was so traumatised by the constant tension and fear that she developed anorexia. Giovanni, on the other hand, was concerned about the safety of Francesca, who was soon to become his wife. These family members and loved ones, who stood by the two judges until the bitter end, deserve due credit and appreciation for the crucial and excruciating supporting roles they performed in the battle against Cosa Nostra.

In total, the two families spent thirty-three days on the prison island, returning to their homes in late September.[152] In a surreal turn of events, the prison billed the two men for their board and lodging. The judges were shocked, but the bills were duly paid.[153]

By now Falcone and Borsellino had almost finished working on the indictment documents for the Maxi Trial. On the 8th of November 1985, after years of painstaking investigative work, the Antimafia Pool presented its indictment against 475 defendants in court. The document was bound in 40 volumes, with a total of 12,607 pages of analysis, supporting documentation and photographs.[154]

10.6 The Maxi Trial

"This is the trial of the mafia organisation called 'Cosa Nostra,'... which, with violence and intimidation, has sowed, and continues to sow, death and terror." The introduction to the indictments for the Maxi Trial[155]

On the 10th of February 1986, the Mafia Maxi Trial kicked off in Palermo in the high-security bunker that had been built specifically for this purpose next to Ucciardone prison. On that fateful day a long procession of men in handcuffs and chains filed through a 50-metre tunnel connecting the prison to the new courtroom, where they were locked up in thirty steel cages at the back of the courtroom.

The large octagonal courtroom was nearly the size of a football stadium. The facility was known as the *aula-bunker* (bunker courtroom) and was built to withstand bombs or even missile attacks. In the middle of the courtroom there was seating for over one thousand lawyers and witnesses and on the balcony there were yet another thousand seats to accommodate the press and members of the public. Adjoining the courtroom was a room for the storage of court documents, equipped with advanced computerised document filing systems which were essential considering the mountain of paperwork generated both before and during the trial.

In total, the Italian government spent over $18 million to build the *aula-bunker* and a further $72 million on security, including the deployment of an army tank outside the courtroom and 3500 policemen and soldiers to secure Palermo during the proceedings. Special measures were also put in place to protect Falcone, Borsellino and their fellow judges. Streets were cleared before they drove by, and helicopters were deployed to monitor their homes and travel routes.

The trial was a massive undertaking, predicated on the premise that the accused did not commit crimes as individuals, but rather as part of one unified criminal organisation. Critical to the prosecution was the testimony of two *pentiti* (Tommaso Buscetta and Salvatore Contorno) and the findings of the Antimafia Pool, who had made extensive use of the powers granted to them by the Rognoni-La Torre Law.

The Presiding Judge Alfonso Giordano sat under a large Crucifix with two alternate judges sitting beside him, ready to step in if anything happened to Giordano. In total, 475 *mafiosi* were facing charges, but of those, 119 were fugitives so they were tried in absentia.

The Maxi Trial took almost two years, ending on the 16th of December 1987. Of the 475 accused, 338 were convicted and 114 were absolved. Michele Greco, the head of the Mafia Commission, was found guilty of ordering 78 homicides, including the assassinations of several government officials. He was sentenced to life in prison. In total, the *mafiosi* found guilty were sentenced to 2,665 years of prison, which did not include the life sentences meted out to the 19 leading Mafia bosses and killers.

The Antimafia Pool, however, knew that although this was a landmark victory, Cosa Nostra was far from being defeated. Work had already started on Maxi Trials 2, 3 and 4. Just a few months earlier, on the 9th of April 1987, Giovanni Falcone had first met Antonino Calderone in a prison in Marseille. For a whole year the antimafia prosecutor flew to Marseille weekly. He collected over one thousand pages of testimony from Calderone. The *pentito*'s claims were painstakingly cross-referenced and checked, leading to the issuing of one hundred and sixty arrest warrants.

However, destiny was once again to intervene. On the 14th and 15th of June 1987 the Italians went to the polls, once again putting Democrazia Cristiana in the driving seat of government. Amintore Fanfani, who was known to have strong connections with Vito Ciancimino and Salvatore Lima, became the minister of interior, while Giuliano Vassalli became minister of justice. The latter appointment was particularly ominous for the Antimafia Pool in Palermo, because Vassalli was known to be totally against the practice of negotiating with *mafiosi* to turn state's witness. In a later interview, Antonino Caponetto, head of the judicial investigative office, said that at that point the department lost all state support – they no longer had access to new computers or helicopters to protect Giovanni Falcone and Paolo Borsellino. It all stopped.

Timeline of events mentioned in this section

1917   In February the people take to the streets of Petrograd and spark a revolution that leads to the fall of the Romanov dynasty and a wave of extreme violence towards religious groups.

1919   Founding of the *Partito Popolare Italiano*.

1923   Cesare Corvo, a stridently anti-fascist Sicilian journalist, escapes to the US.

1926   On the 9th of November the fascist regime forces the dissolution of the Partito Popolare Italiano.

1929   Cesare Corvo is granted American citizenship. His wife Giuseppina and son Biagio Massimo Corvo aka Max are finally able to join him in the US.

1932   Cesare Corvo founds *Il Bolletino*, a weekly newspaper in Italian, focusing on the political situation in Italy. His son, Max, is also involved in the paper and becomes well connected in the network of anti-fascist Italian exiles.

1937   A census in the Soviet Union finds that just over 56 percent of the population still describe themselves as religious. This leads to a decision to exterminate all members of religious groups in the country.

1942   Max Corvo starts working on a topographical relief map of Sicily.

1943   In May the Allied Forces defeat the Axis armies in Tunisia, taking over 250,000 Italian and German prisoners of war.

On the 10th of July the Allies launch Operation Husky, an amphibious attack on southern Sicily.

On the 25th of July Mussolini loses a vote of confidence of the Grand Council of Fascism and the dictator loses power.

On the 3rd of September an armistice between the Kingdom of Italy and the Allies is signed in Cassibile (Sicily). The agreement is made public on the 8th of September 1943.

1944   On the 5th of August the Mafia assassinates Andrea Raia, a
        communist and trade unionist who opposed the Mafia in the
        fight for peasants' rights.

        On the 10th of August fifteen innocent Milanese civilians are
        publicly executed in Piazzale Loreto in Milan, in what came to
        be known as the Massacre of Piazzale Loreto.

        On the 16th of September the Mafia attacks Girolamo Li Causi,
        the regional secretary of the *Partito Communista*, during a rally
        in Villalba. Fortunately, he survives.

        On the 18th of November General Giuseppe Castellano, of the
        US army, meets Mafia bosses Calogero Vizzini and Virgilio Nasi
        to discuss the creation of a movement for Sicilian autonomy.

1945   On the 27th of April Benito Mussolini is captured as he
        attempts to escape Italy with his mistress Clara Petacci. The two
        are summarily executed and their bodies are hung in Piazzale
        Loreto in Milan.

        On the 2nd of May the German forces and the Social Republic
        of Italy surrender.

        On the 11th of October 1945, Ernesto Ruffino is made
        Archbishop of Palermo by Pope Pius XII.

1947   On the 4th of January the Mafia kills Accursio Miraglia,
        secretary of the local Chamber of Labour and a communist
        leader.

        On the 17th of January, *mafioso* Francesco Paolo Niosi executes
        Pietro Macchiarella, a communist activist calling for better
        conditions for peasants in the Palermo area.

        On the 17th of January the Mafia stage a shooting in the
        Palermo shipyard. Mafia boss Salvatore Celeste shouts: *"You
        know me! Whoever votes for the People's Block will have neither
        father nor mother!"*

On the 13th of February the Mafia assassinates Leonardo Salvia and Nunzio Sansone, two communists advocating for agrarian land reform.

On the 20th of April, the People's Block, a coalition of the Italian Communist Party and the Italian Socialist Party win 29.15 percent of the vote in the elections for the Constituent Assembly of the autonomous region of Sicily. Democrazia Cristiana only gets 20.52 percent of the vote.

Massacre at Portella della Ginestra on May Day. Salvatore Giuliano and his gang of bandits attack a rally organised by the Communist Party to mark International Workers' Day. They kill eleven people and injure close to a hundred.

Relations between the former Allies sour, kicking off the Cold War.

1948   A wave of Marian devotion sweeps over Italy. Several people claim to have seen or heard the Madonna.
Coup d'état in February by the Communist Party in Czechoslovakia, in a move supported by the Soviet Union.
On the 2nd of March the Mafia kills Federterra Epifanio Li Puma, a sharecropper and socialist.

On the 10th of March Luciano Leggio kidnaps, and subsequently murders, Placido Rizzotto, a socialist peasant and trade union leader.

A steady stream of pro-US and anti-communist films are shown in the 6500 movie theatres in Italy. Village priests use projectors in church halls to screen propaganda movies created by Catholic Action activists.

In March the US government passes the European Recovery Program, which came to be known as the Marshall Plan, an extensive economic recovery programme financed by the US.

The Italians go to the polls on the 18th of April to elect the first Parliament of the Italian Republic. Democrazia Cristiana wins a decisive victory with 48.51 percent of the vote.

1950   The Italian Government sets up the *Cassa del Mezzogiorno* to stimulate economic development in southern Italy through public works, infrastructure projects and credit subsidies to incentivise investments in the region.

1957   Top-ranking Sicilian and American *mafiosi* meet in Palermo on the 12th of October. Joseph Bonanno and Lucky Luciano explain how the American Mafia Commission functions and recommend that the Sicilians set up a similar structure.

1958   Michele Pantaleone publishes an article in the Palermo newspaper *L'Ora* in 1958, claiming that the Mafia provided critical support for the Allies to invade Sicily.

In early 1958, the Sicilian Mafia forms its first Mafia Commission, initially including the 46 Mafia *cosche* in Palermo. Salvatore Greco is appointed as its first *rappresentante regionale*.

Salvo Lima, the son of a Palermo *mafioso*, becomes the mayor of Palermo, kicking off a period that came to be known as The Sack of Palermo.

1962   Pantaleone publishes a book called *Mafia e Politica, 1943-1962,* in which he claims that the Allies colluded with the Mafia during the invasion of Sicily.

The first mafia war erupts after the assassination of Calcedonio Di Pisa on the 26th of December.

1963   The first Commissione Parlamentare d'Inchiesta sul Fenomeno della Mafia in Sicilia (aka the Antimafia Commission) is formed in February but remains dormant because of an impending general election.

On the 5th of June the Antimafia Commission is reconstituted under the leadership of Christian Democrat Donato Pafundi.

On the 30th of June an automobile loaded with explosives is parked outside the home of Salvatore Greco. Seven police and military officers are killed as they try to defuse the bomb, in what came to be known as the Massacre of Ciaculli. This event galvanises the Antimafia Commission, which meets for the first time on the 6th of July.

1965   On the 31st May Judge Cesare Terranova signs the order to send 114 *mafiosi* to trial in relation to crimes associated with the first mafia war.

Judge Cesare Terranova orders the prosecution of 64 Corleonesi, including the boss, Luciano Leggio, for a series of murders in Corleone.

Dr Peter Schneider attends a series of mafia tavoliddi (banquets) where he witnesses politicians, carabinieri, priests and state officials cavorting with senior *mafiosi*.

1967   The Trial of the 114 starts in December. It lasts an entire year, but the results are very disappointing. Of the 114 accused only 10 are found guilty by the Court of Catanzaro, of which many were only for Organised Delinquency.

1968   The Bari court acquits the 64 Corleonesi. It later emerges that the judges and prosecutors had all received death threats from the Mafia.

Five years after it came into being, the Antimafia Commission finally submits its first report to Parliament. The document is three pages long.
A new leader is appointed for the Commission – Francesco Cattanei, a Democrazia Cristiana politician from northern Italy.

1970   Inauguration of the Punta Raisi airport, built after Gaetano Badalamenti bribed city planners to locate an airport 33km away from Palermo.

The Corleone clan, led by Luciano Leggio, starts manoeuvring to take over control of Cosa Nostra and the highly lucrative narcotics trade.

1971   In July the Antimafia Commission publishes an interim report that names prominent *mafiosi* and highlights the Mafia's links with politicians and public authorities.

1972   Cesare Terranova is elected as a member of the Italian Parliament.

1976   Cesare Terranova and Pio La Torre publish a minority report of the Antimafia Commission, highlighting the links between the Mafia and several politicians, particularly ones from Democrazia Cristiana.

1978   On the 9th of May Cosa Nostra assassinates Giuseppe "Peppino" Impastato, a young communist activist who had founded a radio station called *Radio Aut* that he used to denounce injustice and the Mafia.

1979   On the 26th of January Leoluca Bagarella kills Mario Francese, an investigative reporter, shooting him five times outside his home in Palermo.

On the 9th of March, Michele Reina, a Democrazia Cristiana politician, is assassinated by Cosa Nostra.

Giorgio Ambrosoli, who was appointed to liquidate Italian banks involved in money laundering, is assassinated on the 11th of July.

On the 21st of July, Leoluca Bagarella kills Giorgio Boris Giuliano, the head of the Palermo Mobile Squad.

Judge Cesare Terranova is assassinated on the 25th of September. Also killed is his driver and bodyguard Lenin Mancuso.

Judge Rocco Chinnici takes over leadership of the Investigations Office at the Palermo Court.

1980   On the 6th of January the Mafia assassinates Piersanti Mattarella, the President of the Regional Government of Sicily.

The beginning of the second mafia war.

On the 4th of May Cosa Nostra assassinates Emanuele Basile, a Carabinieri Captain, shooting him multiple times in the back as he walked in the streets of Monreale carrying his four-year-old daughter (who escaped uninjured).

On the 6th of August Judge Gaetano Costa, the Chief Prosecutor of Palermo, is killed by Cosa Nostra in a drive by shooting.

The new Chief of the Investigative Office in Palermo, Judge Rocco Chinnici, assigns Judge Giovanni Falcone the investigation of the heroin trafficking case of the Spatola-Inzerillo-Gambino *Mafioso* clan.

1981   The violence of the second mafia war results in 251 murders in 1981 in Palermo alone. Of these, 100 people simply disappeared, indicating *lupara bianca* assassinations.

On the 31st of October Archbishop Pappalardo celebrates a mass in memory of all the victims of Cosa Nostra.
In December Pope John Paul II publicly urges Sicilian bishops to get involved in the battle against the Mafia.

1982   Assassination of Pio La Torre, a communist member of Parliament, and his driver Rosario Di Salvo, on the 30th of April.

On the 1st of May Carabinieri General Carlo Alberto Dalla Chiesa is appointed Prefect of Palermo, tasked with stopping the violence and bloodshed of the second mafia war.
On the 3rd of September, General Dalla Chiesa, his wife Emanuela Setti Carraro and their protection agent Domenico Russo are assassinated. At their funeral the Archbishop of Palermo, Salvatore Pappalardo, condemns the violence and criticises the government for not imposing law and order in Sicily.

In September the Italian Parliament passes the Rognoni-La Torre Law, which criminalises membership in mafia-type associations, and empowers the State to confiscate the property of convicted *mafiosi*.

On the 14th of November Cosa Nostra assassinates Calogero Zucchetto, a member of the Palermo Mobile Squad, shooting him five times in the head.

Pope John Paul II visits Sicily but avoids mention of the Mafia.

1983   On the 25th of January the Mafia kills Judge Giangiacomo Ciaccio Montalto, who had been investigating the Minore mafia clan in Trapani.

At the beginning of July, Rocco Chinnici and Giovanni Falcone issue arrest warrants for the murder of General Dalla Chiesa.

On the 29th of July, Judge Rocco Chinnici is killed by a car bomb as he leaves home to go to work. Also killed are his two bodyguards, Mario Trapassi and Salvatore Bartolotta, along with the caretaker of the apartment block, Filippo Li Sacchi.

Antonino Calderone escapes from Sicily with his wife and three children, to avoid being killed by the Corleonesi. He settles in France.

1984   Tommaso Buscetta turns state's witness, spending 45 days explaining the inner workings of Cosa Nostra to Judge Giovanni Falcone.

1985   On the 28th of July Cosa Nostra assassinates Giuseppe "Beppe" Montana, the Police Chief of the newly created Sezione Catturandi.

On the 6th of August Cosa Nostra kills Ninni Cassarà and his bodyguard Roberto Antiochia, deploying a team of eight hitmen with AK-47 rifles.

1986   On the 10th of February the Maxi Trial commences.

1987   On the 16th of December the Maxi Trial ends. Of the 475 accused, 338 are convicted and 114 are absolved.

SECTION V
THE PALERMO RENAISSANCE

"Men come and go, ideas remain. They continue to walk on the legs of others."
Giovanni Falcone

CHAPTER 11
THE TIPPING POINT

"My life is mapped out.
It is my destiny to take a bullet by the Mafia someday.
The only thing I don't know is when…"
Giovanni Falcone

On the 16th of December 1987, the Maxi Trial ended with 338 convictions. However, the prosecutors and *mafiosi* were both aware that it was not yet game over, but rather the beginning of a long process of appeals. The next step was the Palermo Appeals Court, presided over by Judge Antonio Saetta, a man of principle who refused to be corrupted by the Mafia. On the 25th of September 1988 the judge and his son were killed as they drove back to Palermo after attending a baptism in Canicatti. Two years later, in December 1990, the new president of the Palermo Appeals Court overturned 86 of the convictions of the Maxi Trial and reduced the sentences of several *mafiosi*.

After the Maxi Trial the pressure on Giovanni Falcone did not ease up. Several magistrates and politicians felt threatened by his success and his investigations, particularly because he did not hesitate to unearth links between the Mafia and the State. It was these internal forces that conspired to deny Falcone the role of Chief Prosecutor in Palermo. The situation was exacerbated in June 1989 when a sports bag containing 58 sticks of dynamite and a remote-controlled detonator was discovered by a bodyguard below a beach house Falcone had rented for a vacation.

The constant stress and the lack of support by some of his colleagues led the magistrate to decide that he needed a change. Falcone's relationship with the new Chief Prosecutor, Pietro Giammanco, had broken down completely. He was often kept in the dark regarding developments in mafia investigations and had come to believe that Giammanco had an interest in obstructing certain Cosa Nostra leads, possibly because of his close links to Salvo Lima and Giulio Andreotti of Democrazia Cristiana.

In February 1991, under pressure because of the rising wave of criminality in southern Italy, Prime Minister Andreotti appointed Claudio Martelli as the minister of justice, tasking him with burnishing the government's antimafia credentials. One of the first people Martelli called was Giovanni Falcone. The following month Falcone accepted the post of Director-General of Criminal Affairs and he moved to Rome. Initially his colleagues and friends in Palermo thought that he had thrown in the towel, but they were soon proven wrong because it did not take long for Falcone to start making his mark. Within months he had initiated reforms in the system of judicial appointments, in a process designed to weed out judges who were suspiciously soft on mafia crimes. He also totally reorganised mafia investigations all over the country, creating twenty-six organised crime district offices, similar in concept to the Palermo Antimafia Pool. These district offices were to focus solely on investigating mafia crimes, creating a collaborative network of investigative magistrates spanning the country. Falcone also proposed the setting up of an Italian FBI to support the judiciary on local and international investigations, liaising with authorities in other countries to unravel the complex web being woven by Cosa Nostra and other Italian mafias worldwide.

While Falcone was busy in Rome, the Maxi Trial appeal was making its way to the Supreme Court. Antonio Scopelliti, a prosecuting magistrate of impeccable integrity who had rebuffed all attempts to corrupt him, was to preside over the final appeal. Once again Cosa Nostra moved to liquidate the threat, and on the 9th of August 1991 Judge Antonio Scopelliti was ambushed and killed.

The Mafia exerted pressure on Salvatore Lima to ensure that Scopelliti would be replaced by Corrado Carnevale, who over the years had earned the nickname of *l'ammazza-sentenze* (the sentence-killer). Time and time again, Carnevale had overturned mafia convictions and freed *mafiosi* from prison, only for them to go on the run and disappear into thin air. According to the testimony of Giuseppe Marchese, a *pentito* who had had previously been loyal to Riina, Lima had been warned that if he did not ensure that the sentence-killer was assigned to the case, his days would be numbered.[156]

However, Giovanni Falcone intervened, using his new powers as Director-General of Criminal Affairs. The Ministry of Justice started an investigation into Carnevale's rulings and issued a report highlighting several breaches of ethics by the judge, which led to Carnevale stepping down from the Maxi Trial appeal.

While all this was happening, Minister Martelli was trying to get Falcone's proposals approved in Parliament, which was a mammoth undertaking. However, on the 29th of August 1991, the Mafia killed Libero Grassi, a Sicilian businessman who had spoken out publicly about the extortion racket in Sicily, to the point of even issuing an open letter in a local newspaper informing the Mafia that he had no intention of paying them. The Confederation of Italian Industrialists issued a public statement reminding the government of its responsibility to protect law-abiding citizens and get criminals behind bars. Within ten days of Grassi's assassination the Council of Ministers approved Falcone's proposals. Two thousand of the best police officers in Italy were handpicked and given the resources needed to conduct state-of-the-art investigations. And finally, Falcone and Martelli started the ball rolling on the creation of a national office coordinating organised crime investigations in Italy, to be led by a super-prosecutor.

Four months later, the man who ultimately came to preside over the final stage of the Maxi Trial appeal process, Judge Arnaldo Valente, issued his final verdict. On the 30th of January 1992, he overturned the decision of the Palermo Appeals Court and reinstated all the convictions of the Maxi Trial. Totò Riina was found guilty in absentia and given two unappealable life sentences.

Infuriated, the boss of bosses ordered the assassination of Salvatore Lima and Judge Giovanni Falcone. He also made it clear that Falcone's assassination was to be of spectacular ferocity, showcasing the might of Cosa Nostra.

Salvatore Lima was gunned down on the 12th of March by a mafia kill squad as he was busy organising a political rally for Giulio Andreotti. His assassination marked the end of the corrupt alliance between Democrazia Cristiana and the Mafia, forged forty-four years earlier, just before the national election of 1948.

11.1 The Capaci Massacre

Although Giovanni Falcone was now working in Rome, his wife Francesca was still working in Palermo, so every Friday he flew back to Sicily for the weekend. On the 23rd of May 1992, Francesca happened to be in Rome so they flew back home together. When they arrived, they got into an armoured car and set off for Palermo, with another two police cars as an escort. Giovanni Falcone insisted on driving himself, while Francesca sat next to him in the front passenger seat. At two minutes to six o'clock the three cars drove past Capaci and were swallowed up in a massive explosion.

The police escorts in the first car - Vito Schifani, Rocco Dicillo and Antonio Montinaro – died instantaneously. Giovanni Falcone and Francesca Morvillo, who were in the second car, were mortally injured. They were rushed to the hospital, but Falcone died upon arrival. The doctors desperately tried to save Francesca, but she too died later that evening.

The whole world held its breath in horror when the news of Giovanni Falcone's assassination hit the airwaves. Cosa Nostra had obtained around 500kg of TNT and plastic explosive taken from unexploded WWII bombs and packed them in 13 barrels, hiding them in a drainage tunnel under Highway A29, close to the junction to Capaci. This was the route taken by Falcone as he drove from the airport to Palermo and back every weekend.

Giovanni Brusca, one of the trusted lieutenants of Totò Riina, waited on a nearby hill for Falcone and his entourage to drive past and then he detonated the bombs. The explosion ripped up the highway, leaving a 15-metre crater. In total, five people were killed - Giovanni Falcone, his wife Francesca Morvillo, and three police escort agents, Vito Schifani, Rocco Dicillo and Antonio Montinaro.

Paolo Borsellino was devastated. He rushed to the hospital as soon as news of the bomb broke and witnessed the passing of his friend. Distraught, he wept, as he hugged his daughter Lucia outside the emergency room. After the assassination, Paolo Borsellino fell into a deep depression and refused to leave the house for several days. However, he then returned to work, where he threw himself into interrogating mafia witnesses at a manic pace, almost as if he knew that he was running out of time.

11.2 The Mobilisation of Civil Society
On the 25th of May 1992 it was raining heavily. However, this did not stop thousands of Sicilians from braving the weather in order to honour Giovanni Falcone, his wife Francesca Morvillo, and the three police agents, Vito Schifani, Rocco Dicillo and Antonio Montinaro, as they made their last journey in a funeral cortege from the courthouse to the Basilica of San Domenico. A crowd congregated outside the church while the funeral mass was being held, breaking into loud applause when the five coffins were carried out after the ceremony.

However, it was not only despair that the people were feeling. They were also furious and determined to make their voices heard. As ministers and other government officials left the Basilica the crowd howled "Assassins!" and "Justice!"

The funeral mass was transmitted live on television and millions of people were watching when Rosaria Costa, the young widow of Vito Schifani and mother of a one-month-old child, wept and made an impassioned appeal during the mass - *"In the name of all those who have given their lives for the State, I ask that justice be done. Then I turn to the men of the Mafia, because they're here, yes here, inside this church! You should know that even now there is the possibility of forgiveness. I will forgive you, but you must go down on your knees if you have the courage to change! ... too much blood, no love here, there's no love here, there's no love here, there's no love at all."*

Rosaria's words reverberated throughout Sicily and their impact was felt even in the higher echelons of Cosa Nostra. Leonardo Messina, a mafia *vice capo* from Caltanisetta, credits her plea with his change of heart and decision to collaborate with Paolo Borsellino - *"when I heard the speech of the widow of Vito Schifani ... her words struck me with the weight of rocks, and I decided to leave the organisation in the only way possible, by collaborating with the justice system."* Leonardo Messina[157]

Borsellino threw himself into interrogating Messina, whose *cosca* had been aligned with the Corleonesi, thus giving him considerable access to what had been happening at the very centre of Cosa Nostra. He explained that every single government contract awarded in central Sicily had to be approved by the Mafia, who took a cut from the winning bidder. He also described some of the tactics used by government officials to ensure that contracts were awarded to Cosa Nostra. In one particularly egregious case, Gianfranco Occhipinti, a Sicilian Member of Parliament, had removed the antimafia certificate from the bid of the strongest contender for the tender and inserted it into the bid of a company with mafia connections. This led to the disqualification of the former company and the award of the contract to the latter. Messina was even able to produce the misplaced certificate as evidence. The *pentito* also pointed at several high-profile businessmen who acted as go-betweens between the Mafia and politicians, distributing kickbacks after bids went Cosa Nostra's way. Messina's testimony led to the issuing of around two hundred arrest warrants.[158]

Messina also spoke about a house full of money. Cosa Nostra was generating so much revenue through the narcotics trade that it had to rent an apartment in which to store its cash. The rooms of the apartment were packed with bank notes from the floor to the ceiling – so much cash that the *mafiosi* did not know what to do with it.[159]

While Paolo Borsellino was working frenetically, civil society in Sicily was reacting to the Capaci tragedy. Grassroots initiatives started to take shape. The Ficus tree outside Falcone's apartment block in via Notarbartolo became a shrine, commonly referred to as the Falcone tree, with a steady stream of visitors leaving messages and flowers.

One month later, on the 23rd of June, at two minutes to six o'clock, the same time the bomb had exploded at the Capaci intersection, a human chain made up of one thousand people holding hands wound around the streets of Palermo from the Palace of Justice (which the press referred to as the Palace of Poison, due to corruption and mafia infiltration of the institution) to via Notarbartolo where Giovanni Falcone and Francesca Morvillo had lived.

Palermo was in deep mourning, with shop shutters lowered and journalists interviewing heartbroken Palermitans in the squares of the city. Joining them in their grief were other cities such as Capo d'Orlando, where at two minutes to six o'clock all the anti-racket stores lowered their shutters while their owners and workers stood outside in silence.

The Human Chain kicked off an entire week of activities to commemorate Falcone, Morvillo, Schifani, Dicillo and Montinaro. Five thousand scouts marched in torchlight through the streets of the city. In Piazza Politeama there was a public screening of a video called *C 'era un magistrato che ...* (There was a magistrate who ...) featuring Falcone's life using images and footage from the archives. The children of Borgo Vecchio sat with their parish priest in protest in front of the Ucciardone prison, carrying placards – *"Sicily and the mafia are enemies!"*

Police officers laid wreaths on the tomb of General Dalla Chiesa, telling journalists that they had just received six second-hand armoured cars that were already on the brink of breaking down. [160]

One hundred Palermo lawyers published an antimafia appeal, publicly declaring their opposition to the Mafia.[161] They also committed to organising a series of events aimed at drafting a code of ethics that took into consideration the particular realities of a city infiltrated by organised crime.

ARCI, the Associazione Ricreativa Culturale Italiana, a national leisure and cultural organisation founded by the Italian Communist Party, printed forty thousand posters with photos of fugitive *mafiosi* wanted by the police and plastered them on walls all over Sicily. Privately financed antimafia commercials aired on various television stations, showing a long list of mafia victims with a voiceover at the end declaring – *"That's enough: the Mafia cannot rule our lives anymore."*

The youth section of the Democratic Left launched a petition asking that assets confiscated from *mafiosi* be used for social purposes, submitting it to the government with over twenty thousand signatures.

The week of events culminated in a national demonstration on the 27th of June. A large coalition of trade unions and political parties joined forces with youth, cultural and community associations to organise a massive public demonstration in Palermo, with over one hundred thousand people flocking to the city from all over Italy to call for justice and stand up to the Mafia.

The first sight that greeted the protesters when they arrived in Palermo was a display of sheets bearing antimafia messages hanging from windows and balconies all over the city. The residents of the mafia capital were expressing their rage through handmade signs painted on bedsheets, in what was to become a symbol of the stand that civic society was taking against Cosa Nostra. Every person who was hanging the sheet outside their home was making a clear declaration of intent, telling both the authorities and the Mafia – you know who we are and you know where we live, but we are no longer willing to be silent. This carnage must stop.

The grassroots campaign took on a life of its own and soon entire communities were coming together to create sheets to hang on their buildings, involving their children and spreading their antimafia message.[162] The sheets became such a central part of the protests that a group of 26 people formed The Sheets Committee, which organised antimafia activities and called for institutional reform, government accountability, and respect for the law.

What started off with bedsheets grew to include T-shirts, television adverts and pamphlets advertising *"Nine uncomfortable guidelines for the citizen who wants to fight the Mafia."*[163]

1. Learn to do your duty, respect your environment, and preserve it from vandalism and destruction.
2. Educate your children to respect legality and teach them solidarity and tolerance.
3. If you suspect bribery or corruption at your place of work, do not hesitate to do the right thing. Go to a judge if necessary.

If you are a teacher, take every opportunity to talk to your students about the Mafia and the harm it does to society.

If you are a student, insist on punctuality from your teachers, report them if they are absent and protest about favouritism.

If you are a business and you receive malicious offers of protection, turn to one of the anti-racketeering associations. If you are already paying, go to these associations anyway.

4. When dealing with public administration, insist on transparency. Do not ask for favours, but for your rights.
5. Always ask for a receipt from your doctor, mechanic, or in a restaurant.
6. If you witness an attack, help the authorities with their enquiries.
7. Boycott Mafia businesses.

Explain to drug-takers that their behaviour is only doing the Mafia a favour.

Don't buy contraband cigarettes.

8. Refuse to exchange votes for any kind of favour.
9. Intervene to prevent young people from acquiring a mafia mentality.

11.3 The Via d'Amelio Massacre

'E' finito tutto'[8]

Judge Antonino Caponetto

On the 19th of July 1992, Paolo Borsellino woke up at five o'clock to talk to his daughter Fiammetta, who was calling from Thailand. She had initially planned to go to Africa, but her father had asked her to go to a country where it would be easier for the family to communicate with her. He phrased it as a joke – "*How am I going to let you know if I've been*

---

8 "It's all over."

killed?"[164] – but his request, and his daughter's acquiescence, give a heart-breaking insight into both his and his family's frame of mind.

After speaking to his daughter, he wrote a letter to a schoolteacher who had asked him to visit her pupils. She had asked many questions, and seeing as he could not visit in person, he tried to answer them all in writing, explaining that he had chosen to take a stand against the Mafia because of his love for Sicily. He also expressed how hopeful he felt when he saw that the up-and-coming generation was not showing the same indifference to the corruption and criminality that his generation had.

It was a Sunday, so Paolo and his wife drove to their little house by the seaside, where the judge went on a boat trip with a friend. The family then had lunch with a neighbour, returning home for an afternoon siesta. However, the judge was worried about his mother, Maria Pia Lepanto Borsellino, who had spent the day alone in Palermo because his sister was away, so he drove back to the city with his police escort to visit her.

When they arrived outside his mother's house in Via D'Amelio, Paolo Borsellino exited the car with five members of his police escort - Agostino Catalano, Emanuela Loi, Vincenzo Li Muli, Walter Eddie Cosina and Claudio Traina. As he approached the door to ring the doorbell, a powerful car bomb detonated, killing the judge and his escort agents instantaneously. The blast was so strong that the first four floors of his mother's apartment block were severely damaged, and the explosion was heard for miles around.

It was now amply clear that Cosa Nostra would stop at nothing to continue operating with impunity. It was no longer tenable for politicians or the Catholic Church to sit on the fence about the Mafia.

11.4 Hunger Strike
"We are fasting because we are hungry for justice."

Immediately, thousands of Sicilians, horrified by the violence and death unleashed by the Mafia and furious that the State had allowed yet another massacre to happen, took to the streets in towns all over the island, marching with banners calling on the authorities to do something to curb the Mafia.

A plaque was put up in front of the Borsellino home in Via Cilia, inscribed with a famous quote by Paolo Borsellino – *"I never liked this city, and so I learned to love it. Because real love consists in loving what you don't like in order to change it."* Every day a constant stream of people visited the plaque, laying flowers and candles to honour the brave judge.

On the 21st of July soldiers from northern Italy, armed with rifles, created a barrier to hold back the public during the state funeral of the five escort agents who died with Borsellino. Infuriated, the crowd pushed right through them, screaming *"Get the Mafia out of the State!"*

A few days later Paolo Borsellino, whose wife, Agnese, had refused a state funeral, was laid to rest in a private ceremony held in the church of Santa Luisa De Marillac. Antonino Caponetto, who had uttered words of despair - *"It's all over"*- after visiting the scene of the Via d'Amelio massacre, was now determined to honour his fallen colleagues by continuing what they had started – *"Dear Paolo, the struggle you have supported must and will become the struggle of each of us."*[165]

The day after the funeral all the antimafia prosecutors in the Palermo office submitted their resignations, making it clear that they had no intention of working under Pietro Giammanco, who they said had obstructed the important work done by Falcone and Borsellino.

On the 23rd of July the Association of Sicilian Women against the Mafia announced a three-day vigil and fast. They published a *Manifesto for Rebel Citizens* and signed it as *le donne del digiuno* (The Fasting Women), announcing that they were calling for Prefect Jovine, Chief of Police Parisi, Chief Prosecutor Giammanco, High Commissioner to the Fight Against the Mafia Finocchiaro and Interior Minister Mancino to take responsibility for the assassinations and resign.

The Fasting Women set up camp in Piazza Castelnuovo, living and sleeping in an assortment of tents and caravans. Thousands of people signed their petition, giving their full name and address, in a massive collective act of repudiation of *omertà*. The vigil and hunger strikes continued to be organised every month for a whole year, with more and more people joining the demonstrations to make their voice heard.

On the 1st of August the employers' association, Confindustria, published an open letter to President Scalfaro and Prime Minister Giuliano Amato in all the main Italian newspapers. It was a hard-hitting missive calling on the government to take real and demonstrable action against the Mafia, and to clean up and strengthen the institutions that had failed so miserably at curbing the corruption and impunity of *mafiosi* and those who colluded with them and protected them.

A month later, on the 8th of September, five Sicilian bands gave a concert in the Palermo football stadium, with all proceeds going towards the building of a new school named for the two slain judges. In Catania, on the other hand, a musical festival to honour Bellini donated all its takings to the children whose fathers lost their lives trying to protect Borsellino.

The three trade union confederations in Italy collaborated with the police and magistrate unions to draw up a document with concrete proposals for meaningful antimafia reforms. This was presented to the government on the 29th of September.

11.5 Piera and Rita, Witnesses of Justice

Piera Aiello was born in Partanna in western Sicily in a non-mafia family – her father was a bricklayer while her mother was a seamstress. She was still a child when she met a young man called Nicolò and started to date him, not knowing he was the son of Vito Atria, the local mafia boss. A few years later the couple had an argument and decided to break off their relationship, but Don Vito decreed otherwise. He visited the young girl at her home and threatened to kill her parents if she did not marry his son.

Fearing for her family, Piera reunited with Nicolò and in 1985 the couple got married. A few days after the wedding, Don Vito was murdered.

Nicolò had a younger sister called Rita. She was only ten when her father was killed, but having grown in a mafia family she was very aware of the danger that her family was in. She was very close to her brother, who told her that one day he would avenge their father. The tension in the town was palpable and people feared for their lives.

Six years passed. Nicolò and Piera had a child, but their marriage was very unhappy. The young *mafioso* was involved in drug trafficking and he often beat his wife. In the meantime, Rita had become a young woman and started dating a *mafioso*. However, the men who had killed Vito Atria were aware of the risk that one day his son would come after them, so they killed him before he could make good on his threats. They executed him with a sawn-off shotgun, spraying his head, arms, and abdomen with bullets as he cleaned up after a party celebrating the opening of his pizzeria in Montevago. During the autopsy the coroner found more than 1.4kg of bullets in his gut alone.

The very next day his wife turned to the authorities to denounce his murderers. When she spoke to the carabinieri they sent her to Marsala, which was 60km away from Partanna, telling her that the district attorney in that town was a man who could be trusted.

The man was Paolo Borsellino.

Rita was distraught. Her beloved brother, Nicolò, had been murdered in cold blood, but her mother and the entire village were pretending that they did not know who was guilty of the murder. It took her a few months to make the decision, but she finally followed in her sister-in-law's footsteps, giving a deposition to Borsellino and naming the *mafiosi* who had killed her father, Vito Atria, in 1985, as well as those who were responsible for the death of her brother and dozens of other people, victims of a bloody internecine war between mafia clans in Partanna. She also implicated a former mayor and Christian Democrat member of parliament, Vincenzino Culichhia, in the assassination of his deputy in 1983.

Borsellino took Piera and Rita, who was just sixteen at the time, under his wing, and they formed a strong bond with the magistrate, who they called Uncle Paolo.

Piera and Rita's testimony was damning, and it was corroborated in full by the testimony of Nicolò's murderer's mistress, Rosalba Triolo. Their depositions led to the arrest of thirty *mafiosi*. Upon finding out what her daughter had done, Giovanna Cannova threw Rita out on the street for having broken *omertà*. She branded her daughter and her son's wife as *infami* (*ignoble*) and claimed that Borsellino had kidnapped them and forced them to give false witness against the Mafia.

Fearing for their safety, Borsellino arranged for Piera and Rita to be moved to a safe house on the outskirts of Rome, where they could be suitably protected. He also made it a point to visit them every time he was in the capital city and often spoke to them on the phone to make sure that they were doing well. When Paolo Borsellino was assassinated, the two young women were heartbroken and terrified. The man who had helped them and protected them had himself fallen victim to the Mafia.

"I am devastated by the killing of Judge Borsellino. Now there's no one to protect me, I'm scared and I can't take it anymore." Suicide note left by Rita Atria

On the 26th of July 1992, one week after the assassination of Paolo Borsellino, Rita was overcome by despair and jumped from the fourth floor of the apartment building in Rome where she was living in hiding with her sister-in-law. She was only seventeen years old.

On the day of Rita Atria's funeral in Partanna the locals closed their shutters and pretended that nothing was happening. When The Fasting Women arrived in the village they approached the parish priest, Don Calogero Russo to find out what time the funeral would be held. His reply shocked them. It had been decided that there would be no funeral Mass. [166]

Furious that the girl had been abandoned in death, as she had been in life, the women of the Association of Sicilian Women against the Mafia and The Fasting Women stepped in to fill the breach. At five o'clock they carried the coffin themselves, past a crowd of journalists, to pay homage to the young girl who had the courage to tell the truth. Letizia Battaglia, a photographer who had spent two years photographing the victims of the Mafia to highlight the bloodthirsty nature of Cosa Nostra, led the mourners, while Michela Buscemi, who had also testified against the Mafia after her brothers were killed, walked behind the coffin.

At the very last moment, after seeing the crowd of journalists who had descended on the small town, the mayor decided to attend, with three carabinieri in tow. When everyone arrived in the cemetery the mayor gave a long speech about Rita, without once mentioning the Mafia and the fear that had led to the teenager's death.

Father Russo prayed – *"Pardon your servant for her sins ..."* but the Fasting Women were not having it, shouting that Rita had not sinned, she had merely told the truth and paid the ultimate price for it. At first there was a shocked silence at their angry response, but then some of the mourners clapped to signify that they agreed. [167]

Giovanna never forgave Rita and Piera. She did not attend Rita's funeral and after the ceremony she destroyed the tombstone put up by the antimafia women's associations to honour her daughter, attacking it with a hammer.

Piera Aiello was elected to Italian Parliament in 2018, campaigning on an antimafia platform without revealing her identity and her face. After becoming a Member of Parliament, she emerged from anonymity, twenty-seven years after becoming a witness for justice and going into hiding. The following year she was honoured by the BBC as one of the 100 most inspiring women from around the world in 2019.

11.6 The Reaction of the Italian State

The public outcry and massive protests in the streets finally galvanised the State to pass laws that Falcone and Borsellino had been insisting were required for years. This had been the case time and time again, with the State only acting when presented with an excellent cadaver, the human sacrifice of a patriot who had taken on Cosa Nostra without adequate support from the State.

The passing of the crucial Rognoni-La Torre Law only came about because of the assassination of Pio La Torre. The creation of the post of high commissioner for mafia investigations in Sicily only came to be after the murder of General Dalla Chiesa. The approval of Falcone's proposals would probably not have happened had it not been for the killing of Libero Grassi.

Once again, the brutal assassinations of Giovanni Falcone and Paolo Borsellino forced parliament's hand to take real action against the Mafia.

The death of Judge Falcone led to Article 41-bis of the Penitentiary Act being modified to impose *carcere duro* (hard prison regime) in cases of *"serious concern over the maintenance of order and security"* on the 8th of June. This imposed harsh living conditions for imprisoned *mafiosi*, severely curtailing their contact with the outside world. Some of the measures in the law included restrictions on the use of telephones and communication with other inmates in the prison, strict limits on money transfers both to and from the prisoner, controls on parcels and mail received and sent by prisoners, and limited visits from family, who could only see the *mafiosi* once a month and then only to communicate via intercom, seeing the prisoners through bulletproof glass.

After the assassination of Paolo Borsellino on the 19th of July, the State immediately swung into action. Within a few days, 7000 soldiers armed with automatic weapons were sent to Palermo in a massive show of force by the State.[168] The soldiers patrolled the city and protected the judiciary and politicians as helicopters and military transport aircraft were used to transfer 400 senior *mafiosi* from Palermo's Ucciardone prison to top security prisons at Ascoli Piceno, Cuneo, and to the island prisons of Pianosa and Asinara. In this way they not only curtailed communication but also imposed geographic distance between the imprisoned men and their *cosche* and families.

New laws were also passed in relation to the protection offered to *pentiti*. The State established Italy's first witness protection programme and officially instituted mechanisms for the reduction of sentences for *mafiosi* collaborating with the forces of justice.

In addition, several officials in key positions in Palermo were replaced, while those who had proven committed to the antimafia cause were given roles where they could finally make a real difference in the fight against the Mafia. The chief prosecutor of Palermo, Pietro Giammanco, who had been a thorn in the side of Giovanni Falcone and Paolo Borsellino, was transferred to Rome and replaced by Giancarlo Caselli, a fierce supporter of the late judges and the Antimafia Pool. Gianni De Gennaro, a police investigator who had worked closely with Falcone to painstakingly check Buscetta's testimony, was appointed the head of the *Direzione Investigativa Antimafia* (Antimafia Investigative Division), more commonly known as the DIA. Antonio Manganelli, who had investigated the allegations made by Antonino Calderone, was appointed the head of the *Servizio Centrale Operativo* – the national office coordinating organised crime investigations that had been proposed by Giovanni Falcone. And finally, Colonel Mario Mori was put in charge of the antimafia unit of the *carabinieri.*

Falcone and Borsellino had called for these laws and the creation of these entities for over a decade. Unfortunately, it was their deaths that finally made them materialise.

The new laws and the additional human resources committed to the antimafia effort soon bore fruit, both in Sicily and in other mafia-infested cities in southern Italy. Giuseppe Madonia, the second-in-command to Totò Riina on the Sicilian Mafia Commission, was captured in September, as was Carmine Alfieri, the top boss of the Camorra in Naples. That very same month the Italian and American authorities issued 201 arrest warrants, finally breaking up the drug trafficking and money laundering network operated by Cosa Nostra in Sicily and the United States, and the Medellin drug cartel in Columbia. Two months later a further 200 arrest warrants were issued for *mafiosi* in Sicily.

On the 24th of December the police arrested Bruno Contrada, a corrupt police officer and secret service agent who had kept Cosa Nostra apprised of any progress made in the search for the fugitive boss of bosses. This paved the way for the biggest victory of all - on the 15th of January 1993 the police arrested Totò Riina, who had been on the run for twenty-three years.

11.7 The Response of the Catholic Church
In October 1992 the ecclesiastical authorities published an official document entitled *Mafia and Evangelisation*, written by Archbishop

Giuseppe Agostino, which declared that *mafiosi* could not receive the sacraments unless they had repented and changed their ways. *Mafiosi* were also not allowed to become godparents through baptism, and Communion was not to be offered during the funerals of *mafiosi*.

The Mafia and Evangelisation doctrinal document was followed by a statement issued by the Sicilian Episcopal Conference, tracing the root of Sicily's problems to *"a mafia frame of mind, of behaviour and of structure; a spider's web of personal vested interests; a lack of timely and appropriate intervention by state authorities; a situation of cultural and economic underdevelopment; a deeply flawed and corrupt approach to the management of public resources."*

Four months later, on the 9th of May 1993, Pope John Paul II celebrated a mass at the archaeological site of the Valley of Temples in Agrigento. At the end of the mass the Pope intervened before the ushers could take away his microphone, making an unscripted and emotional speech condemning the Mafia.

"May there be harmony in this land of yours! Unity without deaths, without murder, without fear, without threats, without victims! May there be unity! This harmony, this peace to which every people and every human person and every family aspire! After so much suffering, you have a right to finally live in peace.

Those who are guilty of disturbing this peace, those who bear so many human victims on their consciences, must understand that they're not allowed to kill innocent people!

This community, the Sicilian people, so attached to life, people who love life, who give life, cannot always live under the pressure of an opposing civilisation, a civilisation of death. We need a civilisation of life! In the name of Christ, I say to those responsible, convert! One day you will face the judgment of God!"

Footage of the condemnation can be found on Youtube and is well worth watching. It is clear how strongly Pope John Paul felt about what he was saying. At one point he raised his hand to emphasise his words. What is also clear is the reaction of the priest standing behind him, who brings his hands up to his face in consternation as soon as he realises what the Pope is saying.

This denunciation was a major turning point in the relationship between the Catholic Church and the Mafia, creating an existential crisis in the minds of *mafiosi* who had convinced themselves that they were on the side of the righteous.

The mask was starting to slip.

11.8 The Retaliation of Cosa Nostra

The sunset
The afternoon is ending
The sunset is coming
A stupendous moment
The sun is leaving (to go to bed)
It is already night. All is finished.
A poem by Nadia Nencini (1984 – 1993). Nine-year-old victim of Cosa Nostra[169]

Infuriated about the arrest of Riina and Article 41-bis, Cosa Nostra launched a series of terrorist attacks on the Italian mainland. These were meant as retaliation against the Church and State, who had finally taken a firm position against Cosa Nostra, and also as a political manoeuvre designed to pressure the government to revoke *carcere duro*. In addition, the attacks served as a warning to all *mafiosi* who were considering defecting and becoming *pentiti*.

The attacks were the brainchild of Matteo Messina Denaro, the son of Francesco Messina Denaro, also known as Don Ciccio, who started his career as a *campiere* and ended it as the boss of the Castelvetrano *cosca* and the head of the Mafia Commission of Trapani. Don Ciccio groomed his son for the mafia from a young age. In the second mafia war the Castelvetrani forged an alliance with the Corleonesi, and Messina Denaro became a protegee of *la belva* (the beast) Totò Riina. He is accused of

THE BATTLE FOR SICILY'S SOUL

having killed more than fifty people. *"I could fill a cemetery with all the people I have killed,"* he often boasted in his youth.

By 1992, Messina Denaro, who at the time was just over thirty years old, had succeeded his father as boss of the Castelvetrano clan and head of the Trapani Commission. When he heard that the Police Commissioner of Mazara del Vallo, Rino Germanà, had initiated an investigation into his affairs, he decided to assassinate him. On the 14th of September 1992, Messina Denaro, Leoluca Bagarella and Giuseppe Graviano ambushed Germanà as he drove along the coast towards his rented holiday home. The Police Commissioner returned fire and dove into the sea. In a fortunate turn of events, Bagarella's Kalashnikov jammed and Germanà escaped alive.[170]

When Riina was captured on the 15th of January 1993, Messina Denaro came up with the retaliatory attack strategy. He travelled to Rome to scout the area and sort out the logistics for the attacks. The first ambush occurred on the 14th of May 1993, with a bomb targeting Maurizio Costanzo, a popular Italian presenter who had publicly rejoiced when Riina was arrested. Fortunately, Maurizio Costanzo and his wife Maria De Filippi survived, but he and another twenty-three innocent bystanders were injured by the blast.

A few days later, on the 27th of May, a stolen white Fiat Fiorino van packed with 280 kilograms of Pentrite and T4 mixed with TNT was parked under Torre dei Pulci in Via dei Georgofili in Florence. It detonated at one o'clock in the morning, blasting a crater three metres wide and two metres deep and scattering dangerous fragments of metal debris all over the street.

The explosion was so powerful that the entire inner city lost power and went dark. It killed five people, including an entire family - municipal police inspector Fabrizio Nencini, his wife Angelamaria, live-in custodian at the Accademia dei Georgofili, and their two daughters, nine-year-old daughter Nadia and two-month-old Caterina. A 20-year-old architecture student called Dario Capolicchio also lost his life. In addition, a further thirty-three people were injured and needed to be hospitalised.

The placing of the bomb, the massive quantity of explosives, and the time of day the bomb was set to detonate indicated clearly that the main target had been the Uffizi gallery and the fifteenth-century Torre dei Pulci. It was an attack on the culture and heritage of northern Italy. The Uffizi gallery had recently installed bulletproof glass, so although there was serious structural damage, the great majority of artworks survived intact. The Torre dei Pulci, on the other hand, was destroyed, and with it the Nencini family who lived there.

On the 27th of July, in a clear message to the Pope, two separate bombs hit the Basilica of San Giorgio (St George) and the Basilica of San Giovanni Laterano (St. John Lateran) in Rome. A third bomb was also detonated in Milan, with explosives packed in a car parked near a modern art gallery in via Palestro, killing five people.

The attack on San Giovanni Laterano was symbolic, as the church was the Pope's cathedral in his function as Bishop of Rome. However, the more serious damage occurred to the church of San Giorgio, which was left with a massive gaping hole. It was so damaged there was a serious possibility of it totally collapsing. However, the people of Rome were determined to save it and dozens of experts and volunteers rallied to collect the scattered fragments of the building, packing them away safely in over one thousand plastic boxes. It took over three years and two million euros to repair the damage.

11.9 The Assassination of Fr Pino Puglisi
"And what if somebody did something?"
Fr Pino Puglisi

In 1960 Cardinal Ruffini ordained Giuseppe "Pino" Puglisi, a man who was raised in Brancaccio, a district in Palermo. His father was a shoemaker, and his mother earned some money with occasional jobs as a seamstress, so Pino Puglisi understood the hardship experienced by working-class Sicilians and the lure of criminal organisations for youth who felt they had no way of bettering themselves, trapped in the same life of penury as their parents.

Bishop Salvatore Cuttitta was one of Fr Puglisi's altar boys in the 1970s when the priest was posted to Godrano, a small community 25 miles away from Palermo. Reminiscing about those days, he described Father Puglisi as having a natural talent for connecting with young people, encouraging them to look beyond the confines of their small town.[171]

By this time Cardinal Ernesto Ruffini was dead, but the Palermo Archdiocese was still adamant that the Mafia did not exist. The official position of the Catholic Church in Sicily was that the Mafia was a myth created and exaggerated by the enemies of Sicily. The truth on the ground was of course different. When Fr Puglisi arrived in Godrano, he found a town embroiled in a bitter war between rival Mafia clans. Fifteen people had just been killed – and this in a community of only one hundred people.[172] The town people were terrified, locking their doors and not leaving their homes at night out of fear of being caught in the crossfire.

Archbishop Salvatore Di Cristina was still a priest at the time, and he was good friends with Fr Puglisi. Speaking to The National Catholic Register, he described the impact Fr Puglisi had on the town, transforming the way that Godrano residents interacted with one another and fostering a community spirit that had died because of the multiple traumas that his parishioners had endured.[173]

Fr Puglisi worked quietly and tirelessly in Godrano, creating hope for a better way of life – one that was not based on criminality. He knocked on doors and prayed with his parishioners, encouraging them to come together to pray and read the Bible. He also advocated for forgiveness and reconciliation – in one particularly poignant case bringing together two mothers, one of whose sons had killed the son of the other.

"Peace is like bread -- it must be shared, or it loses its flavour." Fr Puglisi

This was problematic for the Mafia, who depended on fear and the acquiescence of the locals to continue their operations unmolested, so when Fr Puglisi was appointed the parish priest of St Gaetan in Brancaccio in 1990, the Graviano Mafia family, who controlled the neighbourhood, took notice.

Fr Puglisi had returned home to the working-class neighbourhood he knew so well. He was aware that he would not get any support from his superiors, but nonetheless he was determined to help his parishioners escape the yoke of criminality. He opened a social centre where children could gather in a safe and welcoming environment, but he knew that if he wanted to reach older youths he would have to venture out into the neighbourhood.

Every day, Fr Puglisi drove around the neighbourhood in his Fiat Uno, stopping to chat and joke with groups of youngsters he saw loitering on the street. He knew that these disadvantaged youngsters were at serious risk of being pulled into a life of mafia criminality, so he encouraged them to study and pointed out the danger of getting involved in delinquency and organised crime. This created an inconvenience for the Gravianos, who were now finding it harder to recruit foot soldiers.

Unlike other priests at the time, Fr Puglisi did not accept donations from the local Mafia clan. More importantly, he did not allow them to join religious processions in the streets of the town. At one point he even refused to award a contract to restore his church to a company that was affiliated with Cosa Nostra. Gradually, he built a relationship of trust with his parishioners, who were inspired by his courage and integrity. This made it possible for him to support and encourage them to collaborate with the police to bring *mafiosi* to justice.

The Gravianos were infuriated. Fr Puglisi was hampering their recruitment efforts and the locals were no longer as compliant and willing to turn a blind eye to the atrocities they perpetrated in the town. They tried to intimidate the priest by sending him death threats, but Fr Puglisi did not back down. Things escalated on the 29th of June 1993, when *mafiosi* set fire to the door of the church. However, Fr Puglisi kept on denouncing the Mafia and preaching about hope and a life free from criminality. He often said, *"I'm not afraid of the words of the violent, but the silence of the lambs."*

On the 15th of September 1993, as Fr Puglisi was unlocking the door to the apartment building where he lived in Piazza Anita Garibaldi, he was surrounded by a murder squad sent by the Gravianos. One of them was Salvatore Grigoli, who later testified that when the priest saw them, he smiled and said, *"I've been expecting you."*

The *mafiosi* shot Fr Puglisi in the head with a 7.65 mm pistol fitted with a silencer. The neighbours found the good priest a few minutes later, clutching the cross he always wore around his neck as he lay in a pool of blood. Desperate attempts were made to save his life, but his injuries were too serious. He died on his fifty-sixth birthday.

"We weren't supposed to kill Don Puglisi that evening, but then we saw him out on his own. He was making a phone call from a phone box near his church on Via Brancaccio. We went and got the gun fitted with the silencer, but when we returned, he was gone, so we went and waited for him by his house.

It was about 8:40 pm when we saw him. He parked his car, the Fiat Uno, and walked to the building. When he started to open the door, Gaspare (Spatuzza) grabbed his bag to make it look like a robbery by an addict or something like that. That's why we took the bag and used a small calibre pistol. When he looked at me he smiled. It was a smile full of light.

Don Pino Puglisi's smile. I will never forget it." Salvatore Grigoli[174]

CHAPTER 12

THE RISORGIMENTO

"Palermo è nostra e non di Cosa Nostra"

In 1992, Sicily was left reeling after the massacres in Capaci and Via D'Amelio. However, this time, instead of closing the shutters and cowering indoors, Sicilians took to the streets, raising their voices against the Mafia and the State, which they accused of doing nothing to prevent these atrocities. It was no longer possible to ignore the call of the people to stop the criminality and impunity of Cosa Nostra.

Leoluca Orlando, who had been the mayor of Palermo in the 1980s when he was still a member of Democrazia Cristiana, had built a reputation as being committed to counteract the corruption and immorality of the Mafia and had won respect for being willing to reveal ties and connections between his own political party and Cosa Nostra. Disillusioned by the corruption in Democrazia Cristiana, in January 1991 Leoluca Orlando was one of the founders of a new political party with a left-wing Catholic ideology called La Rete (The Network). In 1993 he ran for the local elections on an antimafia platform with the slogan "Palermo liberates Palermo," campaigning under heavy police protection. In November he was elected with 75 percent of the vote.

Orlando launched the Palermo Renaissance, hosting and sponsoring intellectuals, writers, and artists, and promoting a programme of cultural events ranging from theatre productions to art exhibitions and literary festivals with the aim of fostering a new antimafia culture in the city. In a spirit of fighting fire with fire, this new culture had strong religious undertones, using Catholic terminology and symbols.[175]

12.1 Reclaiming the City

One of the main goals of the Palermo Renaissance was to reclaim and beautify the city, which had been ravaged by neglect and the architecture left behind after the Sack of Palermo, when the Mafia, acting in conjunction with corrupt politicians and state officials, had disfigured the city with tons of concrete, destroying the city's historical and aesthetic legacy. Magnificent nineteenth-century villas had been demolished and construction debris was dumped by the coast, damaging the ecosystem and destroying beautiful beaches.

The city turned into a ghost town at night because people were afraid of walking outside after 8pm. It was clear that urgent action was needed to resuscitate Palermo, renovating and restoring the buildings that were still standing and rehabilitating entire neighbourhoods.

Land and buildings that belonged to *mafiosi* were seized by the State and repurposed. Property after property was brought back to life. A field in Capaci became a playground for special needs children. A large tract of land on the outskirts of the city became the Giardino della Memoria (Garden of Remembrance) - twenty-five thousand square metres of citrus trees under which plaques were laid to honour victims of Cosa Nostra. A large countryside villa became the headquarters of the Palermo Scouts.

Palermo was being returned to the people.

One of the renovations most emblematic of the Palermo Renaissance was that of Teatro Massimo. Designed by Giovan Battista Filippo Basile, a well-known architect from Palermo, its first stone was laid on the 12th of January 1875 in Piazza Giuseppe Verdi, with the participation of all the major city authorities and a speech by Baron Nicolò Turrisi Colonna. It was subsequently inaugurated on the 16th of May 1897 with a performance of Falstaff, an opera by Giuseppe Verdi. At the time it was the third largest theatre in Europe, totalling 7730 square metres in area.

In 1974 the theatre was closed for renovations, kicking off a saga of corruption and delays that would take twenty-three years to resolve. It was finally re-opened on the 12th of May 1997, just in time for its centenary.

The newly renovated Teatro Massimo became an important venue for ballet and opera, but it also evolved into a focal point in the community, helping to bring cultures together. In 2014 the theatre launched the Rainbow Choir in collaboration with the Consulta delle Culture, an elected body representing migrants' interests. The project targets young migrants, bringing them together to foster a spirit of belonging and community. This initiative highlights the fact that Palermo has once again become a melting pot of cultures, harking back to the days of Count Roger and the Normans. People from 127 countries live in the city, with an immigrant population of around 24,000.[176]

12.2 A New Antimafia Catholic Tradition
In 1994, as part of the Palermo Renaissance, the City Council revived the local festivities in honour of Santa Rosalia, the patron saint of Palermo. In a cleverly orchestrated campaign, the Council appropriated the legend of Santa Rosalia and repurposed it as part of their antimafia cultural revolution.[177]

Rosalia was a young Norman noblewoman who was devoutly religious and who chose to dedicate her life to prayer and contemplation. She lived as a hermit in a cave on Mount Pellegrino, where she died alone in 1166.

The legend of Santa Rosalia takes us back to 1624, when a plague ravaged Palermo and the dead piled up in the streets. According to the myth, Santa Rosalia first appeared to a sick woman and then to a hunter, explaining where her remains were to be found. She asked the hunter to bring her bones to Palermo and have them carried in procession through the city. The hunter climbed the mountain as instructed and found her bones in a cave. When he returned to Palermo with the relics, in an act of veneration and hope, the citizens carried them around the streets of the town three times, praying to be delivered from the terrible epidemic. Santa Rosalia intervened on their behalf and the plague miraculously disappeared. From that day onwards Santa Rosalia became known as the patron saint of Palermo and the saviour of its inhabitants. A sanctuary was built in the cave where her remains were discovered.

This story was ripe for re-interpretation, with Santa Rosalia once more saving the people of Palermo from a plague, but this time of *mafiosi*. Acting in coordinated synchrony, the mayor, priests, and archbishop of Palermo all recounted the legend during their speeches and sermons, calling on Santa Rosalia to save Sicilians from the scourge of the Mafia, inculcating this parallel into the public's consciousness. The message was also reinforced by the images and statues of the saint, with Santa Rosalia portrayed with a garland of roses in her hair, signifying Spring and a new beginning.[178]

The legend of Santa Rosalia was clearly eminently suited to spearhead the campaign to wrest Catholic symbols, feasts, and saints from the clutches of the Mafia. This was because apart from the legend, there was also a strong parallel between the story of Santa Rosalia, who chose to live a solitary life as a hermit, and the lives of men such as Judge Giovanni Falcone, Judge Paolo Borsellino and of course Leoluca Orlando himself, who knew that taking on the Mafia meant that they would lose their personal freedom and have to retreat from living a normal life for safety reasons. Celebrating Santa Rosalia thus also meant honouring those who had made this extreme sacrifice for law and justice.[179]

The feast of Santa Rosalia is celebrated on the 15th of July. Taking a leaf out of the handbook of the Mafia, the Mayor and the Archbishop of Palermo led the procession, as the statue of Santa Rosalia was carried in an imposing vessel-shaped chariot from the Cathedral to the Foro Italico, ending with a loud, colourful display of fireworks lighting up the Palermitan sky.

In 1994 the feast of Santa Rosalia was attended by around thirty thousand Palermitans, but it has since grown into a massive feast attended by over half a million devotees.

12.3 Education
One of the ways Cosa Nostra maintained its iron grip on Sicilians was through education, or rather the manipulation thereof. The Mafia

infiltrated the decision-making structures within the local administration, manoeuvring so that funds earmarked for the building of schools would instead be diverted towards paying astronomical rents for buildings which in the great majority of cases belonged to *mafiosi*, and which, to top it all, were often not even suitable to be used as schools.

In addition, the Mafia also made sure to have *mafiosi* or their associates employed within the education system, in positions such as janitors. This obviously had a chilling effect on students and educators and created an atmosphere of fear within schools, acting as a muzzle on teachers, who were only too aware that if they said anything untoward about the Mafia it was likely to reach the ears of the local mafia boss.

In the early 1980s, as the second mafia war raged, it became clear to educators in Palermo that something needed to be done to save future generations from the depredations of Cosa Nostra, and to instil in them an appreciation of morality and civic responsibility. Thus, in 1983 an Antimafia School and Culture Committee, commonly referred to as the Legality Group, came into being, with the mission of creating educational strategies to help break the hold that Mafia culture had on the population of the island. [180]

Part of the exercise included soul searching by educators who realised that even they had become caught up in the sense of hopelessness that permeated society and the belief that the Mafia was so strong and so enmeshed in the administration and all aspects of society that it did not make sense to even try to break free. The movement grew and more and more educators joined forces to transform the educational system and create tools specifically suited for influencing students' mental attitudes and assisting them in learning and internalizing the fundamental values of civil coexistence, including adherence to the law, respect for institutions and other people, a sense of solidarity and cooperation, a sense of belonging to a community, and a personal commitment to the rule of law.

By 1988 the Legality Group had matured into a legally constituted association called the Antimafia School and Culture Association. It was clear that several issues needed to be addressed – these included a prevailing lack of motivation and engagement by many students which resulted in rampant absenteeism, little to no involvement of parents in their children's education, and the total failure of the schools to inculcate any respect for civic responsibility in students.

Based on the Association's recommendations, the Superintendency of Schools for the Province of Palermo launched several initiatives. A team was set up to work specifically on the problem of student motivation and truancy, while a series of seminars, workshops and conferences were organised to bring together educators to discuss the problems they encountered and solutions to improve the education system within the city.

In 1992 a report was published outlining concrete plans for the delivery of an effective antimafia educational programme. The plan focused on interaction with the territory and the understanding that anti-criminality teaching should not be taught as a standalone lesson but had to be integrated in all subjects of the curriculum.

This was the year the situation in Sicily escalated to previously unimaginable proportions. The assassinations of Giovanni Falcone and Paolo Borsellino finally galvanised the State, the Church, the media, and civil society to work together for real change on the island, setting the scene for the cultural revolution that emerged from the ashes of the massacres in Capaci and Via d'Amelio.

When Leoluca Orlando was re-elected as mayor in 1993, education was one of the top priorities for the new administration. Orlando appointed Alessandra Siragusa as Commissioner of Education, tasking her with reforming the school system in collaboration with the Church, the media and civil society.

At the time there were only 200 classrooms available in Palermo. This was not enough to accommodate all students, so the schools were running on a double shift system. Since there weren't enough buildings for everyone to attend school in the morning, half the children attended school in the afternoon.

The great majority of these classrooms were in private buildings such as apartments, not schools, and the buildings were in the main owned by the Mafia. Of course, this meant that the classrooms were not properly set up for the children's education, and there was no such thing as transportation, libraries, or a school canteen. [181]

The newly elected city council immediately started building schools, with the very first one in Brancaccio, to honour Fr Puglisi who had advocated for a proper school in the area, rather than the makeshift arrangements that were in place at the time. By the year 2000, seven years later, the council had forty new schools – some of them were newly built while others used buildings the authorities had confiscated from *mafiosi*. Properties were also being rented, but the council was now conducting due diligence to make sure the landlords were not connected in any way to the Mafia.

The new capacity meant there was sufficient space for all children to attend school during normal school hours, consigning the afternoon shift system to the annals of history.

The Council also addressed the problems faced by disadvantaged families as regards schooling, allocating a budget to help those who could not afford uniforms, books or other equipment required for school. Funds were made available to cover the cost of school trips outside Palermo, with the primary aim of widening the children's horizons and opening their eyes to all the opportunities available to them beyond the strict confines of their neighbourhood.

These investments were obviously seen in a very negative light by *mafiosi*, who had not only lost a lucrative revenue stream when the rents stopped but were also concerned about the sense of solidarity and civic engagement these projects were creating in Sicilian communities. Determined to nip this energy and enthusiasm in the bud, they started a campaign of intimidation which rapidly escalated into actual violence.

In Croceverde-Giardina, the domain of the Grecos, the Mafia did everything in their power to prevent the construction of a school. They burnt the cars of construction workers and regularly threatened the engineers. However, works continued, and when the school opened many students wore sandwich posters. On the front the poster said - *"Everyone said that this school is not possible."* – but on the back it said - *"But we made it."*[182]

Once the investment in infrastructure was under way, the Commission for Education launched three projects. The first targeted the reclamation of Palermitan monuments, the second related to caring for the environment, and the third fostered multiculturalism and community.

Initially, the focus was on re-educating teachers about local history to empower them to teach the children about the history of Palermo and Sicily. This set the stage for the City Department of Education to launch a programme called *Palermo apre le porte. La scuola adotta un monumento* (Palermo opens its doors. Schools adopt a monument) also known as the Adopt a Monument project.

Every school was assigned a monument and the children studied its history and worked to restore it and re-open it to the public. They also created brochures and audio-visual materials about the monument and the locality and acted as guides for tours organised by the city council, where the children explained the significance and history of the landmark to adults and other students.

The Adopt a Monument project taught students that they had the power to change their circumstances and their surroundings, instilling in them a sense of civic pride which slowly influenced their parents, who then started getting involved in the projects with their children. Step by step, monument by monument, the people of Palermo reclaimed the buildings, parks, squares, theatres and even the streets of the city from the neglect and decay resulting from the corruption and maladministration engendered by Cosa Nostra.

Some of the monuments adopted by schools were privately owned by noble families and the rich upper classes. The project sought to bring together the different social classes in the city to heal the rift that had formed over centuries of exploitation and violence.

It became clear that the schools were a conduit not only to the children, but also to their entire families, so it made sense to embark on yet another project relating to the environment. Garbage collection was and still is a major issue in Palermo. The Mafia had won multiple rigged tenders for the collection and disposal of rubbish, but of course they were not doing the job properly and Palermo was getting buried under a mountain of garbage. So the children became involved in recycling, ultimately winning an award for the best environmental project in Italy, further reinforcing the children's sense of achievement and pride.

The third major initiative related to the building of community and solidarity. Courses were launched to teach Italian as a second language to immigrants and their children to help them integrate into Palermitan society.

"The only way to eliminate the Mafia is to make the kids who live among the Mafia aware that outside there is another world made up of simple, but beautiful, pure things, a world where you are treated for who you are, not because you are a child of this or that person, or because you paid pizzo for a favour." Rita Atria[183]

12.4 The Contribution of the Press

In 1996 the *Giornale di Sicilia* and the education department launched a project called Cronaca in Classe (City News Reporting from the Classroom). This project was created to enable schoolchildren all over Sicily to act as journalists, reporting on what they saw around them, and getting their articles published in a real newspaper distributed all over the island. In addition, every week groups of children met leaders such as the Prime Minister of Italy, or one of the Ministers of the cabinet, or the Mayor of Palermo, amongst many others. Every promise made by the politicians and leaders was noted and reported by the *Giornale di Sicilia*, to promote a culture of accountability. Discussions included the building of theatres, libraries, parks, facilities for the disabled, drug rehabilitation centres – the children showed a strong sense of civic engagement in their requests and the politicians sat down and listened, and when they made promises the *Giornale di Sicilia* held them to them.

The main aim of the project was to give children a voice and empower them to advocate for change. The students looked at the world around them with eyes that had not yet been jaded by experience – this led to them shining a light on issues that adults took for granted. Such was the case in October 1998 when two elementary school children published an article with the title *Exploitation of child labour. At Ballarò a boy sells salt*.[184] The following is an extract from the article in question.

"Making the rounds of Ballarò market, we saw lots of children, our age, who were working on a school day. Almost every day, we saw an eight-year-old boy who was selling salt, cigarettes, lemons, and other things. And we saw lots of other children like him working in bakeries, markets, food shops, carrying loads that were often very heavy. How is it that these people who exploit child labour don't get fined or arrested?"[185]

The article hit a nerve. It was picked up by national newspapers and finally even reached the BBC, who sent cameramen to Sicily to interview the children who wrote the article and to film the market. Educators started looking at their students with fresh eyes, noting those who fell asleep exhausted at their desks halfway through the school day. These exhausted children were obviously prime targets for the Mafia, who could lure them in by promising them more money for jobs that were at face value much less strenuous than their current employment. The article written by the school children even reached the ears of policy makers in Palermo and finally put the topic on the agenda.

Every year, the *Giornale di Sicilia* printed two books. One included all the articles written by children attending school in Palermo, while the second included the articles written by children from the eight other provinces on the island. These articles told the story of what was truly happening in Sicily, seen from the eyes of children. They included stories about the conversion of properties confiscated from the Mafia into facilities such as centres of assistance for Alzheimer patients or drug rehabilitation centres, complaints about access to school facilities for the disabled and discussions regarding the dangers of drugs. [186]

The children of Sicily had finally found their voice.

12.5 Spazi Capaci

Spazi Capaci is a three-year project launched in Palermo on the 23rd of May 2021, commemorating the 29th anniversary of the Capaci and via D'Amelio massacres. It aims to create solidarity within the local community and unite them in their collective opposition to the Mafia.

In addition to a solemn remembrance ceremony in the Ucciardone bunker, huge banners with images of Paolo Borsellino and Giovanni Falcone were unfurled in 19 Italian cities on well-known landmarks such as the Colosseum in Rome and the Museo del Novecento in Milan. In addition, the #unlenzuolocontrolamafia (a sheet against the mafia) campaign encouraged citizens all over the country to hang a sheet on their balcony in remembrance of all the victims of the Mafia.

The project is the brainchild of the Falcone Foundation, supported by the Italian Ministry of Education and private donors. It was created to counter the potential resurgence of the Mafia, aiming to recapture cityscapes and public spaces hijacked by the Mafia for generations and renewing the relationship between the city and its inhabitants, which had been disrupted by the Covid lockdowns.

The Foundation asked some of the most renowned Italian artists to create works of art to be displayed and incorporated into the landscape of key locations of civil redemption against the mafias. The artwork is also a testament to a city that is still visibly scarred by building speculation and the sack of Palermo. Speaking about the project, Maria Falcone explained that culture is crucial for the renewal of communities and the Foundation wanted beauty to be used as a weapon to combat crime's ugliness and to mark the town as belonging to the people, not the Mafia.[187]

According to Alessandro De Lisi, the General Curator of Spazi Capaci, over one thousand five hundred citizens of Palermo were involved in the project. This includes school children who met the artists to discuss their work and all the people who gave permission for murals to be painted on the side of their building.

The first phase of the project includes four major artworks commissioned by the Foundation.

The first is a contemporary art exhibition in the high-security bunker that had been built in 1985 next to Ucciardone prison to house the Maxi Trial. Velasco Vitali was commissioned to create *Branco* (The Pack), which consists of 54 life-sized statues of dogs. 53 of the dogs are made of iron, sheet metal and concrete and were displayed in the courtroom and in the outside carpark. The 54th and final sculpture is a golden dog made of bronze and wax, displayed inside the prison's high-security document archive. According to the curator of the exhibition, the dogs represent the *mafiosi*'s desire for power and the exploitation of society. The golden dog, on the other hand, is the protector of memories and justice.[188]

The second commission is *The Door of the Giants* by artist Andrea Buglisi - two gigantic 30m-tall murals. The first mural depicts Giovanni Falcone on the facade of an 11-storey building in via Duca Della Verdura, while the second is Paolo Borsellino in via Sampolo. Both murals are just a few metres away from the Ucciardone bunker.

The third commission is *The Wait* by Peter Demetz, a sculpture of a woman lost in thought gazing up at the Falcone tree, symbolising society waiting for justice, as well as the eternal wait for the judge and his wife to return home.

The fourth and final commission is *Burning Bush* by Igor Scalisi Palminteri. It consists of three murals in Piazza Anita Garibaldi in Brancaccio, with the middle mural depicting Fr Pino Puglisi. One side mural is the burning match that was extinguished when the priest was killed, and on the other side is an electrical substation consumed by the eternal fire lit by Fr Pino's courage. Enel, the owners of the substation, said that they welcomed the request of the Falcone Foundation, in the process turning the small building into a symbol of the fight against the Mafia and helping to beautify the neighbourhood.[189]

Commemorative projects such as *Spazi Capaci* are crucial to keep alive the memory of the brave men and women who lost their lives in the battle to save Sicily from Cosa Nostra. It has been thirty years since the traumatic events that finally shocked Sicilians out of their passive stupor and there is a danger that the new generation will forget exactly how depraved and bloodthirsty Cosa Nostra truly is, giving the Mafia an opportunity to establish *convivenza* once again and regain some of the impunity it lost after the Capaci and Via d'Amelio massacres. This would be a tragedy of immeasurable proportions and it is our responsibility to make sure that it never happens.

CHAPTER 13

THE HOLY SEE JOINS
THE BATTLE

"Pray for these mafiosi, so that they convert."
Pope Francis

In November 1994, the Archbishop of Catania, Luigi Bommarito, published an open letter to Pope John Paul II, who was about to visit Sicily to honour Fr Puglisi – *"The open, painful and bloody plague of the Mafia is carved in our social fabric and in our flesh, burning with the bitterness of its arrogance, its tentacles and its recurrent works of death."*

The time for dissembling was over. Addressing a huge crowd in Catania, the Pope called Fr Puglisi a *"courageous advocate of the Gospel."* He appealed to the people - *"Catania, rise up and cloak yourself in light and justice. At this point in history, there is no room for cowardice or inertia."* In a clear reference to Cosa Nostra, he exhorted the faithful to stand up to *"those arrogant, overbearing people who are destroying our lives."* During mass, later that day, he told the congregation - *"One must do what is right, no matter the cost to oneself."*

"I address the men of the Mafia to say to them: In the name of God, put an end to violence! Put an end to injustice! It is time to open your hearts to the true God, who is both just and merciful, and who asks of you a sincere change of heart!" Pope John Paul II

In November 1995 the Sicilian Episcopate published an important document outlining the Church's stand against the Mafia.

"We have no doubt at all in denouncing the Mafia phenomenon as one of the realities that are most sadly indicative of the socio-cultural and, in certain respects, also religious degradation of our land. As far as the Mafia is concerned, it is our duty to confirm the denunciation expressed on other occasions regarding its absolute incompatibility with the Gospel. Though this judgment stands out in all its clarity when referred to the savagery of the murders and the massacres the Mafia has perpetrated - crimes for which the Sicilian Episcopate has on several occasions imposed and renewed the censure of excommunication - it must not be considered as in any way less true when referred to the phenomenon as such. The Mafia is intrinsically incompatible with the Gospel for its own sake, its motivations and its ends, as also on account of the means and the methods it employs. Without possibility of exception, the Mafia forms part of the kingdom of sin and turns its operators into sure servants of the Evil One.

For this reason, all those who in any manner deliberately form part of the Mafia, or sustain it and commit acts of connivance with it, should know that they are and live in unhealable opposition to the Gospel of Jesus Christ and, consequently, also his Church. Likewise in total contrast with the Gospel are the presumed, alleged and distorted values peculiar of the Mafia, among them the keeping of silence, which should rather go under the name of complicity; Mafia honour, which should rather be described as infamous solidarity with dishonour; the prestige of the so-called man of honour, who can get himself "respected" only by the use of a violence that would be unworthy even of beasts; and the Mafia family, whose interest (most of the time a purely economic one) is put first and foremost at the cost of tears and blood.

We Bishops of Sicily intend to oppose this Mafia mentality and the violence of the Mafia with the unarmed but irreducible force of the Gospel, a force that for its own sake aims at the persuasion, promotion and conversion of people, but at the same time is intransigent in not authorising discounts or ingenuous transactions as far as evil is concerned, or whoever commits it or draws profit from it. Don Giuseppe Puglisi fully incarnated this twofold strength of the Gospel and represents an indication for all of us: the model that derives therefrom for the whole of Sicily's clergy and every true Christian is the challenge that we launch to everybody on the Mafia side.[190]

The Catholic Church in Sicily committed itself to fight the Mafia by disentangling itself from the fake religiosity of *mafiosi* who were using devotion and charity to camouflage their criminality. It finally made a conscious decision to take an active role in the battle for Sicily's soul, engaging with civil society and local administration with the aim of eradicating the culture of *mafiosità*, thereby instilling in parishioners a sense of civic responsibility and banishing the conspiracy of *omertà* and clientelism that infected Sicilian society.

13.1 Martyrs of the Mafia

On the 25th of May 2013, twenty years after his assassination, Father Puglisi was beatified during a mass in Palermo which was attended by more than 80,000 people. He has been recognised as the first martyr of the Mafia, who died *in odium virtutis et veritatis*, meaning hatred of virtue and truth.

Designating Fr Puglisi as a martyr is significant, because up to 2013 the Catholic Church defined martyrs as being killed *in odium fidei*, meaning hatred of the faith. In this case, however, the assassins were ostentatiously Catholic, and their motives had nothing to do with religion. However, there is no doubt that Puglisi's behaviour was dictated by his strong faith, and that is what ultimately led to him being killed.[191]

Cardinal Paolo Romeo, who was the Archbishop of Palermo from 2006 to 2015, presided over the beatification Mass, while Cardinal Salvatore De Giorgi, who was the Archbishop of Palermo from 1996 to 2006, formally represented Pope Francis at the beatification ceremony.

The day after the beatification, Pope Francis mentioned Fr Puglisi after reciting the Angelus to the crowd in St. Peter's Square. *"Don Puglisi was an exemplary priest, devoted especially to youth ministry. He taught children according to the Gospel and was taking them away from the Mafia, so they tried to defeat him and killed him. In truth, however, it is he who won, with Christ risen."*

Pope Francis went on to condemn the Mafia, which causes *"so much pain to men, women and even to children,"* highlighting prostitution as a type of slavery used by the Mafia to profit from the suffering of the innocent.

The beatification of Fr Puglisi opened the door for the recognition of other martyrs who stood up to the Mafia as an expression of their faith, and who were subsequently assassinated by *mafiosi*.

In December 2020 the Vatican's Congregation for the Causes of Saints issued a decree of martyrdom approved by Pope Francis to beatify Rosario Livatino, a young antimafia prosecutor who had been killed in 1990 by members of la Stidda (The Star), a criminal group founded by *mafiosi* who defected during the second mafia war in the 1980s. Livatino was the victim of a drive by the *stiddari* to flex their muscles and claim an excellent cadaver of their own.

Rosario Livatino was a devout Catholic who was aware of the dangers of prosecuting the Mafia. When taking notes, he always wrote "s.t.d.," the Latin acronym for *sub tutela dei* (in the hands of God). On the 21st of September 1990, as he drove along the Agrigento highway with no police protection, his Ford Fiesta was rammed by another car and forced off the road. Livatino tried to escape, running through the fields, but the killers caught up with him and shot him in the head at point blank range.[192]

Pope Francis called Rosario Livatino an example to all those who worked in the fields of law and justice because of the consistency of his faith and his selfless dedication to his profession. He also declared that the judge's assassination was a hate crime against Catholicism and those who believed in the values of Christianity.

13.2 Excommunication of Mafiosi
The Catechism of the Catholic Church describes excommunication as the most severe ecclesiastical penalty available, resulting in the exclusion of the person from the sacraments and other ecclesiastical acts. The main aim of excommunication is to encourage the excommunicated to convert and return to the light of God. An excommunicated Catholic can only be

absolved by the Pope, the bishop of the locality or priests who have been granted special authorisation to do so.

On the 22nd of June 2014, Pope Francis excommunicated all *mafiosi*, accusing them of practicing '*worship of evil and contempt for the common good*.'

"*Those who follow this path of evil, as mafiosi do, can never be in communion with God. They are excommunicated. This evil must be fought against, it must be expelled. We must say no to it. ... Our children are asking us to do so, our young people are asking us to do so. They need hope, and faith can help respond to this need.*"

In 2017, Pope Francis met the Italian Parliamentary Commission against Mafias and presented them with a programme to fight the various Italian mafias. He was blunt in his remarks to the lawmakers, emphasising the need to oppose politics based on party or personal interests, which stifle the call of conscience, confound truth with lies, and abuse one's position of public responsibility. He affirmed the importance of resolutely combating the serious issue of corruption, which disregarded the true interest of the public and served as the ideal environment for the growth and development of organised crime.[193]

The following year, in September 2018, during a sermon in Palermo commemorating the Blessed Fr Puglisi, Pope Francis made an appeal to *mafiosi,* who he called "*dear brothers and sisters*," to abandon their life of criminality and violence. He emphasised that Sicily needed "*men and women of love, not men and women 'of honour.'*" It was not possible to "*believe in God and be mafiosi*" at the same time.

"*A person who is a mafioso does not live as a Christian because his life and actions blaspheme against the name of God. I say to mafiosi: Change, brothers and sisters! Stop thinking about yourselves and money. ... Convert to the real God, Jesus Christ, dear brothers and sisters! I say to you, mafiosi, if you don't do this, your very life will be lost and you will suffer your greatest defeat.*"

On the 8th of May 2021, the day of the beatification of Blessed Rosario Livatino, the Vatican announced the creation of a working group focused on the excommunication of mafias. The group, working under the auspices of the Dicastery for Promoting Integral Human Development, has as its main aim the creation of an international network against organised crime and corruption.

Vittorio V. Alberti, the coordinator of the working group, explained that while the Pope has said *mafiosi* are excommunicated and many bishops in Italy and other countries have denied public funerals to notorious members of organised crime syndicates, it was essential to formally include the excommunication of *mafiosi* in the church's social doctrine, canon law and catechism. This is why the dicastery felt the need to establish a group to help bishops around the world apply the teaching of the Pope. In addition, the working group will also prioritise education of the public, to ensure that all Catholics understand that there can never be any compromise between the church and organised crime. [194]

13.3 Liberating the Blessed Virgin Mary

Over the years many mafia bosses financed the acquisition of splendidly adorned statues of the Madonna, as well as expensive religious events such as village feasts and processions. They leveraged their financial contributions to walk alongside the statue of Mary through the towns and villages of their territory, inveigling the mother of God into a twisted celebrity endorsement of the mafia *cosca* and the boss.

In September 2020 the Vatican announced that the Pontifical International Marian Academy (PAMI) had created a new department dedicated to *Freeing Mary from the mafia and from criminal powers.* The goal is to fight the exploitation by various mafias of the popular veneration of Mary to gain legitimacy and authority through association with one of the most powerful religious symbols in Catholicism.

The president of PAMI, Fr Stefano Cecchin, explained that the aim of the new department was to teach and evangelise a *"true theology of Mary,"* disentangling acts of veneration towards the Blessed Virgin from organised crime and mafia influence. This enmeshment had come into being when the Madonna was put on the vanguard of the battle against communism by the Catholic Church, as described in chapter 8 of this

THE BATTLE FOR SICILY'S SOUL

book. When the ecclesiastical authorities subsequently turned a blind eye towards the atrocities perpetuated by Cosa Nostra, this enabled the criminal organisation to co-opt the mother of God as their patron and advocate, a takeover which they cemented by sponsoring and dominating processions and feasts held in her honour.

Pope Francis showed his support for the initiative in a letter to Fr Cecchin, excerpts of which were released to the media. *"I am very pleased to hear that the Pontifical Academy has promoted a conference to launch the Department of Analysis and Study of Criminal and Mafia Phenomena. I wish to express my appreciation for the crucial initiative. Marian devotion is a religious-cultural heritage to be safeguarded in its original purity, freeing it from superstructures, powers or conditioning that do not meet the evangelical criteria of justice, freedom, honesty and solidarity. May the many devotees of the Virgin reject a misguided religiosity and embrace instead a devotion that is based on truth and honesty. It is necessary that the style of Marian displays conform to the message of the Gospel and the teachings of the Church."*

13.4 Ending the Abuse of the Sacraments

As has been shown in previous chapters, the Mafia has very effectively colonised the Catholic religion, abusing it and its rituals for its own nefarious purposes. In order to push back against this cultural and spiritual misappropriation, the Catholic Church not only put a stop to the Mafia financing of statues and processions, but also followed through on the excommunication of *mafiosi* by refusing them access to the sacraments.

13.4.1 Baptism

In 2017 the 73-year-old priest in the town of Corleone, Vincenzo Pizzitola, conducted a baptism where Salvatore Riina, the son of one of Sicily's most ruthless and bloodthirsty *mafiosi*, Totò Riina, became the godfather of his sister Lucia's child.

Salvatore Riina was a known *mafioso* who had served eight and a half years in prison for mafia association. This meant that he was excommunicated, as per the decree issued by the Pope in 2014 expelling all *mafiosi* from the Catholic Church. Return to the church was indeed possible but required repentance.

The Bishop of Monreale, Michele Pennisi, was infuriated when he found out that the parish priest had ignored the excommunication, issuing an angry statement to the press stating that the mafioso had not repented and could thus not participate in the sacraments. In order to press his point home he publicly chastised Pizzitola and issued a decree banning known *mafiosi* from acting as godfathers at baptisms in churches in his diocese, with includes Corleone. He also issued a decree banning religious funerals for known *mafiosi*.

13.4.2 Funerals

On the 20th of August 2015, a helicopter flew over the Basilica of San Giovanni Bosco in the outskirts of Rome, showering rose petals on a crowd of mourners who had gathered for the funeral of Vittorio Casamonica, the boss of the Casamonica mafia clan.

Enormous banners affixed to the entrance of the basilica featured images of Vittorio Casamonica, superimposed over Roman landmarks such as the Coliseum and St Peter's Basilica. One of the banners announced that Casamonica was the King of Rome, while others declared, "You conquered Rome, now you'll conquer paradise."

The coffin containing the dead mafia boss arrived outside the church in an antique black and gold carriage pulled by six black-plumed horses. As it was carried into the church, a live band played the theme music from *The Godfather* movie, drowning out the chorus of weeping mourners, and the petals from the helicopter hovering above added the final touch to what had clearly become a horrifying circus of impunity.

When news about the funeral hit the airwaves, a wave of condemnation swept over Italy, with several state officials, including Rosy Bindi, the president of the parliamentary antimafia commission, and Matteo Orfini, president of the ruling Democratic Party, condemning the ostentatious display of mafia power that had been allowed to deface the streets of Rome.

Questioned by journalists about the pomp and circumstance surrounding the funeral, the parish priest, Reverend Giancarlo Manieri, stated that he had no control over what happened outside the church.

Two years later, in November 2017, Totò Riina, the Mafia boss of bosses, died in prison after a battle with cancer. It was just a few months after the infamous baptism of his grandchild, and weeks after he had been caught on a wiretap saying that he had no regrets.

"They'll never break me, even if they jail me for 3,000 years." Totò Riina

This time the Catholic Church was determined not to get pulled into a mafia carnival.

"Totò Riina is to be considered a manifest sinner who didn't show the necessary public and true repentance for his crimes," declared Archbishop Michele Pennisi of Monreale.

Pennisi explained that since Totò Riina had been excommunicated, it was not possible for him to have a religious funeral in church, but he clarified that if the family requested, a priest could lead them in private prayer at the cemetery.

On the day of the funeral the coffin was taken straight to the cemetery, driving in through a side entrance to avoid the media. The only mourners were his widow and three of his four children. The fourth was in prison and could not attend.

Timeline of events mentioned in this Section

1960   Ordination of Giuseppe "Pino" Puglisi

1974   The Teatro Massimo is closed for renovations, kicking off a saga of corruption and delays.

1983   Formation of the Anti-Mafia School and Culture Committee that came to be known as the Legality Group.

1987   On the 16th of December the Maxi Trial ends. Of the 475 accused, 338 are convicted and 114 are absolved.

1988   The Legality Group becomes a legally constituted association, called the Anti-Mafia School and Culture Association.

1989   In June one of Giovanni Falcone's bodyguards finds a sports bag with 58 sticks of dynamite and a detonator below a beach house that the judge had rented for a vacation.

1990   Fr Pino Puglisi is appointed the parish priest of St Gaetan in Brancaccio.

On the 21st of September, Rosario Angelo Livatino, an assistant judge, is murdered as he travelled alone along the Agrigento highway.

On the 10th of December the Palermo Appeals Court overturns 86 Maxi Trial convictions.

1991   Disillusioned by the corruption in Democrazia Cristiana, Leoluca Orlando becomes one of the founders of a new political party with a left-wing, Catholic ideology called La Rete.

In March the new Minister of Justice Claudio Martelli appoints Giovanni Falcone to the post of Director-General of Criminal Affairs.

On the 9th of August, Antonio Scopelliti, an incorruptible judge presiding over the final appeal of the Maxi Trial, was ambushed and killed.

In November, Rita Atria turns state's witness and talks to Paolo Borsellino.

1992   On the 30th of January the Supreme Court confirms the convictions of the Maxi Trial, overturning the acquittals of the Appeals Court.

A report is published outlining concrete plans for the delivery of an effective antimafia educational programme in Palermo.

On the 23rd of May Giovanni Falcone is assassinated in a massive explosion after Cosa Nostra detonates 13 barrels of TNT and plastic explosives under Highway A29. In total, five people were killed - Giovanni Falcone, his wife Francesca Morvillo, and three police escort agents, Vito Schifani, Rocco Dicillo and Antonio Montinaro.

On the 25th of May thousands of Sicilians stand in the pouring rain to honour Falcone. As government dignitaries leave the Basilica at the end of the funeral mass, the crowd scream "Assassins" and call for "Justice."

On the 8th of June Article 41-bis of the Penitentiary Act is modified to impose *carcere duro* (hard prison regime) in cases of *"serious concern over the maintenance of order and security."*

On the 23rd of June a human chain made up of one thousand people holding hands winds around the streets of Palermo from the Palace of Justice to via Notarbartolo where Giovanni Falcone and Francesca Morvillo lived. This kicks off a week of events held to commemorate and honour the people killed in the Capaci massacre, culminating in a national demonstration in Palermo on the 27th of June, attended by one hundred thousand people from all over Italy.

On the 19th of July 1992 a car bomb explodes as Judge Paolo Borsellino arrives at his mother's house in Via D'Amelio. Five members of his police escort also die in the blast - Agostino Catalano, Emanuela Loi, Vincenzo Li Muli, Walter Eddie Cosina and Claudio Traina.

The state funeral for the five security guards killed in the Via d'Amelio massacre is held on the 21st of July. Judge Paolo Borsellino is buried a few days later in a private ceremony.

On the 23rd of July the Fasting Women announce a three-day vigil and fast.

7000 soldiers armed with automatic weapons are posted on every corner in Palermo in a massive show of force by the State. Helicopters and military transport aircraft transfer 400 imprisoned senior *mafiosi* from Palermo's Ucciardone prison to top security prisons at Ascoli Piceno, Cuneo, and to the island prisons of Pianosa and Asinara.

On the 26th of July Rita Atria is overcome by despair and dies by suicide.

On the 1st of August the Italian Employers' Association publishes a hard-hitting open letter pressuring the government to take appropriate action against the Mafia.

On the 8th of September five Sicilian bands give a concert in the Palermo football stadium, with all proceeds going towards the building of a new school named for the two slain judges.

On the 14th of September, Matteo Messina Denaro ambushes Police Commissioner Rino Germanà, who after exchanging fire manages to escape and survives the attack.

On the 29th of September the three trade union confederations present a document to the government with concrete proposals for meaningful antimafia reforms.

In October the ecclesiastical authorities publish a document entitled *Mafia and Evangelisation*, stating that *mafiosi* could not receive the sacraments unless they had repented.

1993   On the 15th of January, Totò Riina is arrested after 23 years on the run. He is replaced by Bernardo Provenzano.

On the 9th of May Pope John Paul II celebrates a mass in Agrigento. At the end of the mass, the Pope makes an unscripted and emotional speech condemning the Mafia.

On the 14th of May, a bomb targeting Maurizio Costanzo, a popular Italian presenter who had publicly rejoiced when Riina was arrested, explodes in a street in Rome. The presenter survives, but he and another twenty-three innocent bystanders are injured in the blast.

On the 27th of May, Cosa Nostra detonates a car bomb in Via dei Georgofili in Florence. Five people lose their lives, including an entire family who were killed when the Torre dei Pulci collapsed after the explosion.

On the 29th of June the Mafia sets fire to the door of Fr Puglisi's church.

On the 27th of July Cosa Nostra detonates three bombs almost simultaneously. The first is in Milan at the Pavilion of Contemporary Art, killing five people and the other two are in Rome, at the cathedral of San Giovanni Laterano and at the church of San Giorgio in Velabro.

On the 15th of September Fr Puglisi is killed. It was his fifty-sixth birthday.

Local elections in Palermo - in October Leoluca Orlando is re-elected as mayor with 75 percent of the vote. He appoints Alessandra Siragusa as Commissioner of Education, with a remit to reform the school system.

In November the Archbishop of Catania, Luigi Bommarito, publishes an open letter to Pope John Paul II.
During a sermon in Catania the Pope appeals to *mafiosi* – *"In the name of God, put an end to violence, put an end to injustice!"*

1994   The Palermo City Council revives the local festivities in honour of Santa Rosalia, the patron saint of Palermo.

Several projects are launched to reclaim the city of Palermo from the Mafia and to foster a sense of community and civic responsibility in its inhabitants.

The local administration launches a concerted effort to build more educational facilities to be able to accommodate all students during normal school hours and abolish the shift system that saw thousands of children going to school in the afternoon.

The Sicilian Episcopate condemns the Mafia using very strong terms.

1996   The *Giornale di Sicilia* and the education department launch a project called Cronaca in Classe (City News Reporting from the Classroom).

1997   The Teatro Massimo is re-opened on the 12th of May, a few days before its centenary.

2012   Alessandro D'Ambrogio, mafia boss of the Porta Nuova mafia faction of Palermo, is given the highly coveted role of carrying the statue of Our Lady of Mount Carmel in Ballarò.

2013   Leoluca Orlando launches the Consulta delle Culture, an initiative to promote harmony and a sense of community between people of different cultures in Palermo.

On the 25th of May Father Puglisi is beatified during a mass held in Palermo, attended by more than 80,000 people. He is hailed as the first martyr of the Mafia who died *in odium virtutis et veritatis*, meaning hatred of virtue and truth.

2014   On the 22nd of June Pope Francis excommunicates all *mafiosi*, accusing them of practicing '*worship of evil and contempt for the common good.*'

The Teatro Massimo and the Consulta delle Culture together launch The Rainbow Choir, a project targeting the migrant population of Palermo.

2017   In February 2017, Bishop Michele Pennisi publicly chastises Vincenzo Pizzitola, the 73-year-old priest in the town of Corleone, for conducting a baptism where Salvatore Riina, a known *mafioso*, is made the godfather of his sister Lucia's child. Bishop Pennisi issues a decree banning known *mafiosi* from acting as godfathers at baptisms in churches in his diocese, which includes Corleone

Pope Francis meets the Italian Parliamentary Commission against Mafias and presents a programme to fight organised crime.

In November 2017 Totò Riina dies in prison after a battle with cancer. The Church refuses to give him a religious funeral.

2018   In September 2018, during a sermon in Palermo commemorating the Blessed Fr Puglisi, Pope Francis makes an appeal to *mafiosi* to abandon their life of criminality and violence.

Piera Aiello is elected to Italian Parliament after running on an antimafia platform without revealing her identity. She then emerges from witness protection and the following year is honoured by the BBC as one of the 100 most inspiring women in the world.

2020   In September 2020 the Vatican announces that the Pontifical International Marian Academy has created a new department dedicated to Freeing Mary from the Mafia and from criminal powers.

The Vatican's Congregation for the Order of Saints issues a decree of martyrdom to beatify Judge Rosario Livatino.

2021   On the 8th of May 2021, the day of the beatification of Blessed Rosario Livatino, the Vatican announces the creation of a working group focused on the excommunication of mafias.

On the 23rd of May the Falcone Foundation launches Spazi Capaci, a three-year project commemorating the 29th anniversary of the Capaci and via D'Amelio massacres.

SECTION VI
THE TWENTY-FIRST CENTURY

"The reduction of the power of Cosa Nostra can only be achieved by the restoration of faith in public administration. No influx of financial resources, however massive, will improve the situation if the State and the institutions are not trusted to ensure the free and orderly progression of civil life. Otherwise, the recourse to alternative organisations that ensure materialistic advantages will continue and they will continue to enjoy the support of the public, whether expressed or passive."
Paolo Borsellino

CHAPTER 14

THE SWINGING PENDULUM

"... *even though the Mafia has been dealt really devastating blows, it has not yet been defeated once and for all. Its remaining parts are still active and dangerous.*" Leoluca Orlando[195]

One of the fundamental strengths of Cosa Nostra is the way its economic model and the focus of its criminality morphed according to the realities and changing circumstances in its environment, enabling it to always remain relevant.

As discussed in previous chapters, the Mafia survived in the shadows while holding Sicilian society in an iron-clad fist for over a hundred years. Its colonisation of Sicilian folklore, such as the legend of the Beati Paoli, and misappropriation of traditional Sicilian values, such as the importance of honour and love for the family, made them appear to be a timeless and inevitable reality of Sicilian life.

A very important part of this strategy was the takeover of Catholic symbols, rituals and performative events that are beloved by Sicilians. Sitting in privileged pews during mass, walking ostentatiously with the Madonna's statue during processions, flamboyant funerals featuring obsequiousness for the deceased by religious and administrative grandees – all these reinforced and burnished the image of a criminal organisation that presented itself as honourable and devout, while in fact it was anything but.

In essence, the Sicilian Mafia's slogan was – So it has always been and so it will always be.

Cosa Nostra's master plan worked like a charm, and it probably would have continued to do so were it not for the devastating second mafia war in the 1980s, when hundreds of people were killed. The carnage made it impossible for Sicilians to keep pretending that Cosa Nostra was a benevolent organisation using violence only to avenge injustice. The subsequent waves of *pentiti* and their damning revelations about the true nature of the Mafia, and the resulting Maxi Trial, where hundreds of homicides and crimes were laid bare for all to see, shattered the mask Cosa Nostra had hidden behind.

Any shred of doubt as to what the Mafia stood for was then smashed to smithereens in 1992 by the bomb attacks that killed Giovanni Falcone and Paolo Borsellino, along with Falcone's wife and several police officers, followed by the spate of terrorist attacks the following year that left many innocent bystanders injured or dead. Clearly the decision makers in the Mafia had not considered the possibility that Sicilians would react by rising against them as they did after the Capaci and Via d'Amelio bombings. They also did not envision the fact that the shockwaves of the bombings would reverberate all over the world, adding to the immense pressure that civil society in Sicily and the rest of Italy were putting on the State and the Church to finally take a firm stand against organised crime. The whole world was watching, and there was nowhere the Mafia could hide in the glare that replaced the shadows it was used to lurking in.

14.1 From Tractors to Accountants

Decisive action was required to salvage what was left of Cosa Nostra, which was considerably weakened after the Maxi Trial and the clampdown by the Italian authorities. An opportunity arose when Totò Riina was arrested, something that most likely only happened because *mafiosi* tipped off the police about the location of his hideout.

Riina's incarceration opened the way for Bernardo Provenzano to take over the leadership of Cosa Nostra. The new boss was very aware that to survive, the Mafia had to change modus operandi, presenting itself as a less overtly bloodthirsty organisation. He took Cosa Nostra underground in what became known as a submersion strategy and focused on building the legal side of the business to stabilise the financial side of operations. During this period, the man who had previously been known as *Binnu u tratturi* (Binnu the tractor) because of the vicious way he mowed down his victims in his youth, earned a new nickname – *il ragioniere* (the accountant).

Provenzano focused on creating networks of collusion and complicity with people in positions of influence, creating what came to be known as a grey zone between legality and illegality.[196] These networks included politicians, civil servants, police officers, judges, mayors, engineers, financial advisors, doctors, lawyers, businessmen, and anyone else who could bring something to the table that could prove useful to Cosa Nostra. As discussed in previous chapters the Mafia has long invested in building these networks of friendship and obligation, however now the focus was not on gaining social consensus, authority and *rispetto* in the eyes of the people living in their territory, but rather to infiltrate legitimate business opportunities using nonviolent illegitimate means, with a particular focus on highly lucrative government projects financed by public funds.

An excellent example of this strategy in practice is the infiltration of the Mafia into the private healthcare system in Sicily. An alliance was formed with a number of important actors in the sector, including Michele Aiello, a businessman who started his career in construction but then diversified into private health services; Domenico Miceli, a surgeon and municipal councillor responsible for Palermo's public health system; Salvatore Cuffaro, the Christian Democrat governor of Sicily; Giuseppe Ciuro, Marshal of the Guardia di Finanza in the Direzione Investigativa Antimafia (Antimafia Investigation Directorate); Giorgio Riolo, a Marshal of the Carabinieri with expertise in espionage technology; and Giuseppe Guttadauro, the boss of the Brancaccio *cosca,* who was also a surgeon.

According to *pentito* Antonino Giuffrè, Michele Aiello had a close relationship with Bernardo Provenzano and was involved in a convoluted network that included members of the police and representatives of the State, which enabled him to operate with considerable impunity.[197]

Aiello had invested in several state-of-the-art clinics in Bagheria, financed in part using mafia funds. He was heavily involved in laundering mafia money, and he leveraged his close relationship with Cosa Nostra to win several lucrative public contracts for his supposedly legitimate businesses. Domenico Miceli, who was indebted to Giuseppe Guttadaura for his election as municipal councillor, used his position to ensure that Aiello's clinics were accredited to be used by the State for several medical procedures at highly inflated prices. In this he also had the support of Salvatore Cuffaro, the governor of Sicily.

When the *pentito* Giuffrè exposed the alliance between Aiello, Guttadaura and Miceli, the Carabinieri Special Operations Group (ROS) launched an investigation into the allegations. As part of the operation, Giorgio Riolo was tasked with planting transmitters in Aiello's clinics, while Giuseppe Ciuro had access to all the evidence painstakingly put together by the ROS. Unfortunately, the two men were also part of the grey zone assiduously nurtured by Provenzano, so they kept Aiello and Guttadaura informed regarding the investigation, including the listening devices that had been placed in their properties, as did Salvatore Cuffaro, the governor, who also had access to highly confidential information about the progress made by the ROS and how they were planning to take the investigation forward.

Notwithstanding the leaks, the carabinieri succeeded in exposing the ring of collusion and in 2005 the participants were indicted on charges of mafia association, corruption, fraud and revealing investigative secrets. Michele Aiello was sentenced to fifteen years in prison, Salvatore Cuffaro and Giorgio Riolo were sentenced to seven, while Ciuro was sentenced to four years in prison.

"Rarely have we seen evidence of such relationships between a defendant accused of mafia association (Michele Aiello) and one convicted of the same crime (Giuseppe Guttadauro) with top ranked politicians, businessmen, professionals, with employees and directors of the public administration,

with people who work in the prosecutors' office and with police officials from the force." Palermo Public Prosecutor's Office[198]

When the appeals process was exhausted and the sentences confirmed by the Court of Cessation in 2011, Aiello's properties and financial holdings, in total worth 80 million euro, were confiscated by the State. This included the private oncology clinic, Villa Santa Teresa, in which Provenzano was a silent partner, and where the boss of bosses had secretly received treatment for bladder cancer while on the run.

Giorgio Riolo was part of the team working to capture Bernardo Provenzano, a fact which likely explains why the fugitive always seemed to be one step ahead of the authorities. This was soon to change. One year after Riolo was arraigned, Provenzano was finally arrested after 43 years on the run. Surveillance had noted that Provenzano's wife regularly sent out bulky parcels from her home in an apartment above a car dealership. The police followed the parcel, which each time was delivered to a different location. However, by arranging surveillance at these locations it then emerged that the parcel was in fact travelling on a route from one house to the next in seemingly haphazard fashion. Finally, the police succeeded in following the parcel from Provenzano's apartment, step by step from one location to the next, until the parcel had travelled to ten different locations over a period of three days, all the way to a rundown farmhouse just outside Corleone, where the boss of bosses was finally captured.

Provenzano was incarcerated in a maximum-security prison, subject to the regime of Article 41-bis. He received a total of twenty life sentences and solitary confinement for thirty-three and a half years.[199] In July 2016 he died from bladder cancer. The Church refused to give him a religious funeral, so he was cremated and his ashes were buried in the family grave in Corleone.

14.2 The Rise of Diabolik

It is widely believed that after Provenzano's capture, Matteo Messina Denaro (aka Diabolik) became the most powerful boss in Cosa Nostra, although it is not certain whether he is the acknowledged boss of bosses. He has been convicted in absentia for several crimes, including the kidnapping and torture of the eleven-year-old son of Santino Di Matteo, a *pentito* who had turned state's witness. When Di Matteo did not retract his testimony, Giovanni Brusca, acting on Messina Denaro's orders, killed the child and dissolved his body in acid.

As discussed earlier in the book, Messina Denaro had been the brains behind the terrorist attacks in Rome, Milan and Florence in May 1993. After the attacks Diabolik went into hiding and he was a fugitive on the most wanted list since June 1993. It is ironic that a man who started his career as a *mafioso* flaunting his wealth for all to see and conspicuously living the high life, driving a Ferrari and wearing expensive and tailored Armani suits accessorised with top-of-the-range Rolexes, managed to remain hidden for thirty years. In 1998 the police came close to capturing him by following his girlfriend, Maria Mesi, to a safehouse in Bagheria. When the police raided the place, the fugitive had flown, leaving behind a jar of Nutella, a jar of caviar, an unfinished puzzle, and a carton of cigarettes – a clear indication of how far the once flamboyant playboy had fallen.[200]

By now Casa Nostra was no longer the international powerhouse it had once been, and the 'Ndrangheta in Calabria had taken over the international narcotics trade, while the Mafia was relegated to trafficking in Sicily. However, Messina Denaro continued to develop the grey zone and operate in the intersection between legality and illegality, as per the original strategy of Provenzano. The revenue kept coming in, especially from construction, where Cosa Nostra had a firm grip on every stage of the construction process, from the provision of construction materials to the labour and machinery required to build hundreds of illegal houses all along the coast of Castelvetrano and Mazara del Vallo. The money was then laundered through a complicated network of shell companies set up in places such as South America and Africa.

In 2021 details emerged about Operation Xydi, a police investigation that focused on the Agrigento mafia. The *capo provincia* of the Agrigento *cosche* is Giuseppe Falsone, who is known to be fiercely loyal to Messina Denaro. Falsone is currently serving a life sentence in a maximum-security prison, as provided for by the 41-bis law.

In January 2022, Palermo Judge Paolo Magro ordered the indictment of nine of the thirty initial defendants arrested as a result of Xydi. Amongst the accused are three lawyers, an assistant chief of police and a penitentiary officer, proving that the tentacles of Cosa Nostra reach deep within the justice system of Italy.[201]

One of the lawyers is Angela Porcello, who has since been disbarred. She is accused of acting as a conduit for messages between Giuseppe Falsone and Matteo Messina Denaro, using her position as legal counsel to meet Falsone in the maximum-security prison and enabling the bosses to bypass the communication restrictions imposed by Article 41-bis. She is also accused of making her legal office available to regional mafia bosses for their meetings, thus abusing the protection offered by the law for lawyer-client privilege by giving the top echelons of the Mafia a safe place to talk which could not be bugged by the police.[202]

The indictments shed light on how Messina Denaro was able to control the Mafia while on the run. Using corrupt lawyers such as Angela Porcello, and her colleagues Annalisa Lentini and Calogero Lo Giudice, who also stand accused of having forged court documents, he communicated orders and instructions down the mafia hierarchy. In addition, by corrupting police officers in different police stations and investigative units, he was always a step ahead of the authorities.

One of the intercepted conversations between Angela Porcello and Giuseppe Falsone reveals the worldview of *mafiosi*, in what is clearly an attempt to rationalise the terror that they have unleashed for nearly two hundred years in Sicily. Harking back to the origins of the organisation, he describes Cosa Nostra as a bastion protecting Sicilians from chaos. The Mafia had done much good for society, he told her.[203]

Falsone is not the only *mafioso* misrepresenting his true nature as a criminal. Notwithstanding his bragging about the number of people he has killed, Messina Denaro follows in his predecessors' footsteps, making himself out to be a fair and just man who has simply done what needed to be done, and suffered for it. In a letter found in 2005 in an abandoned hideout, he calls himself a humble man who was at peace with himself, supported by his strong faith.[204]

After thirty years on the run, Messina Denaro was captured on the 16th of January 2023.

14.3 A Return to Agriculture

In an ironic turn of events, organised crime in Sicily has returned to its roots as tyrants and enforcers in the agricultural sector, through a system of *caporalato*. This is a gangmaster arrangement with strong parallels to the days of the feudi, where absentee landlords, amministratori, gabellotti and campieri exploited powerless peasants.

In the first chapter of this book, I described the feudal system and the feudal charters that were in force in sixteenth-century Sicily. Workers were brought in from impoverished areas across the island, as well as from other countries, and installed in hamlets in remote locations, forced to travel great distances to the different plots of land they cultivated. They were terrorised and exploited by gabellotti and campieri who extracted several payments from them and loaned them money at usurious rates of interest, thereby creating a defacto system of indentured slavery.

Nowadays the terminology is different, but the mechanics remain the same. Immigrants, both regular and irregular, are housed in isolated settlements, ferried around in lorries by *caporali* (gangmasters) to different agricultural estates to harvest crops such as oranges or tomatoes. Just like the feudal lords (and subsequently the landowners) only dealt with intermediaries, the farmers of today deal directly with the *caporali*, negotiating the lowest labour costs possible without ever interacting directly with the workers, thus enabling them to stay one step removed from the uncomfortable reality that these rates are only possible because of the exploitation of the weak and the vulnerable. The asylum seekers are paid a total of around twenty euros for ten to twelve hours of backbreaking labour in the fields.[205]

The Mafia has secured a steady stream of men and women desperate for any form of employment by getting involved in the provision of board and lodging for the irregular migrants who are flooding into Italy, a lucrative arrangement which enables them to siphon money from the State through massive public contracts, while exploiting the people they are supposed to be caring for.

The *Centri di Accoglienza per Richiedenti Asilo (CARA* - welcome centres for asylum-seekers) accommodate thousands of migrants, charging the State a daily rate of €35 for adults and €45 for minors. The centres controlled by the Mafia inflate the numbers, charging the State for more residents than they actually have. In 2017 an investigation in the CARA Sant'Anna in Calabria concluded that the Arena mafia has embezzled over €33M from the State, while feeding residents very little food, a lot of which was expired. The resulting indictment described the centre as "*a cashpoint for the Mafia.*"[206]

Once the workers enter the *caporalato* system they are moved to isolated worker ghettos, creating another opportunity for profit for the *caporali,* who charge ridiculous rates for transportation and other essential items such as food or water, just like the *gabellotti* of old charged inflated prices for seed or other necessities. Typical charges are €3.00 to get on a dangerously overloaded lorry, €3 to €4 euro for sandwiches or a drink, and €20 to be taken to hospital if injured or sick.[207] The result is that workers end up owing the *caporali* money and are caught in a never-ending cycle of exploitation and abuse.

Workers are not only sourced from the CARA centres but are also imported from Eastern European countries such as Romania, where salaries are low and unemployment is rife. They are lured to Italy with the promise of work and decent salaries that would enable them to send remittances back home. Instead, they find themselves isolated in encampments, enslaved by *mafiosi.* Many of the workers are women, who in addition to suffering from the backbreaking labour on the farm also end up the target of sexual predators.[208]

As is always the case with the Mafia, the threat of violence is never far away. If any of the workers rebel or speak up for better conditions for themselves and other workers, retribution swiftly follows. This is what happened to Adnan Siddique, a Pakistani migrant who was stabbed to death in 2020 after acting as a translator to help other migrant workers report the abuse they were suffering at the hands of the *caporali*.[209]

14.4 The Covid Era

The Covid-19 pandemic gave Cosa Nostra an opportunity to re-establish its image in Sicilian society. Italian Police report that in 2020 and 2021, as Covid brought Italy to its knees, *mafiosi* jumped at the opportunity to curry favour with locals in their neighbourhood and build networks of obligation by distributing food parcels to the needy. Once again, the *mafiosi* were claiming the mantle of protectors of the weak, helping Sicilians who were being ignored or had been abandoned by the Italian State. In Palermo, for example, the brother of a Cosa Nostra boss distributed food packs to poverty-stricken families in the Zen neighbourhood, where the Mafia has a strong presence.

Of even greater concern is the report published in February 2021 by the Italian Government's Antimafia Investigation Directorate (DIA). According to the findings of the report, several small and medium-sized enterprises on the verge of financial ruin because of the sharp contraction in economic activity resulting from Covid lockdowns and the collapse of tourism, were taking out loans from criminal organisations such as Cosa Nostra at usurious rates of interest. The DIA highlighted the risk that the Mafia would initially present itself as a helping hand, offering loans to struggling companies, only to then use these financial commitments as leverage to force the owners out of the business, enabling Cosa Nostra to take them over and turn them into money laundering operations and a new smokescreen for their activities. [210]

This situation is causing serious concern in many circles, including the Vatican. In March 2021 Pope Francis warned that criminal organisations were using the pain and misery brought by Covid for criminal ends. He called for states and societies worldwide to remember the victims of the mafias and to commit to stopping the spread of these criminal organisations.[211]

14.5 The Shadow Justice System
"The solution to the problem of the Mafia is to make the state work."
Paolo Borsellino

Covid is not the only opportunity being leveraged by the Mafia to reconstruct its image. The failure of the Italian State to offer an efficient and timely legal and justice system has created a golden opportunity for Cosa Nostra to reclaim its role as provider of security and avenger of injustice.

In Italy, simple civil disputes take two to three years to resolve, while more complex ones, such as a labour dispute in Calabria, took 12 years. A similar dispute in Sabaudia, a town in Lazio, central Italy, took 11 years to resolve. Entrepreneurs who want a fast resolution are left with no choice other than to take matters into their own hands, or rather, put the matter in the hands of their local *cosca*.[212]

In April 2021 investigators released a *Public Order of the Territory* report about the Pagliarelli mafia clan, whose territory includes Palermo's main prison, hospital and several university buildings. The report states that while the Palermitan Cosa Nostra is no longer the powerful force it was forty years earlier, the Mafia has slowly managed to rebuild its bonds of *convivenza* with the locals. In a return to their initial raison d'être, *mafiosi* are once again operating as entrepreneurs of violence, a shadow justice system operating in a town where local law and order are not able to maintain full control of the situation.[213]

The report details several cases where otherwise law-abiding, respectable local business owners called in Cosa Nostra instead of the police to sort out situations such as robberies. In one case an owner of a local bar called the mafia boss to ask for his intervention after a car was stolen, and the car was duly returned five days later. In another case a shop owner gave CCTV footage of robbers to the Mafia. The culprits were apprehended and tortured, and the stolen goods were returned. The assistance of the Mafia is not only requested in the case of robberies or to right injustices. The local bosses are also involved when businessmen want to create an unfair competitive advantage by intimidating a competitor, or even to strongarm debtors to settle their dues.[214]

It is thus clear that the pendulum has swung and the scene is now set for a comeback of the men of honour. The Sicilian Mafia is going through yet another transformation to adapt to the new realities of the twenty-first century. This time it is focusing on changing its image and reclaiming the position in Sicilian society that it lost thirty years ago, while returning to its roots when it comes to the services it provides.

This ability to adapt has enabled it to survive over the last two hundred years, and unfortunately, this same agility and resilience will ensure that it survives for many more.

Timeline of events mentioned in this section

1992   On the 23rd of May, Giovanni Falcone is assassinated in a massive explosion.

On the 8th of June Article 41-bis of the Penitentiary Act is modified to impose *carcere duro* (hard prison regime) in cases of *"serious concern over the maintenance of order and security."*

On the 19th of July 1992 a car bomb explodes as Judge Paolo Borsellino arrives at his mother's house in Via D'Amelio.

On the 14th of September, Matteo Messina Denaro ambushes Police Commissioner Rino Germanà, who after exchanging fire manages to escape and survives the attack.

1993   On the 15th of January Totò Riina is arrested after 23 years on the run. He is replaced by Bernardo Provenzano.

On the 14th of May a bomb targeting Maurizio Costanzo explodes in a street in Rome. Costanzo survives, but he and another twenty-three innocent bystanders are injured in the blast.

On the 27th of May, Cosa Nostra detonates a car bomb in Via dei Georgofili in Florence. Five people lose their lives, including an entire family who were killed when the Torre dei Pulci collapsed after the explosion.

Matteo Messina Denaro goes into hiding and is put on Italy's most wanted list.

On the 27th of July, Cosa Nostra detonates three bombs almost simultaneously. The first is in Milan at the Pavilion of Contemporary Art, killing five people and the other two are in Rome, at the cathedral of San Giovanni Laterano and at the church of San Giorgio in Velabro.

1998   The police come close to capturing Matteo Messina Denaro in a safehouse in Bagheria, but he escapes just before the raid.

2005   Indictment of a network of politicians, carabinieri and businessmen accused of collaborating with the Mafia to defraud the State through the private healthcare system. Charges include mafia association, corruption, fraud and revealing investigative secrets.

2006   Bernardo Provenzano is captured after 43 years on the run.

2016   Bernardo Provenzano dies on the 13th of July.

2017   An investigation in the CARA Sant'Anna (a centre for asylum-seekers) in Calabria, concludes that the Arena mafia had embezzled over €33M from the State.

2020   Adnan Siddique is stabbed to death after helping other migrant workers report the abuse they were suffering at the hands of the *caporali*.

        The Mafia uses Covid to foster *convivenza* by giving food and loans to poverty-stricken Sicilians unable to work because of the pandemic.

2021   A report published in February by the Italian Government's Antimafia Investigation Directorate (DIA) reveals that Cosa Nostra is lending money to small businesses in a move likely orchestrated to grow the Mafia's money laundering network.

        In February the police arrest 23 associates of Matteo Messina Denaro after concluding an investigation into the Agrigento mafia, code named Operation Xydi.

        In March, Pope Francis warns that criminal organisations are using the pain and misery brought by Covid for criminal ends.

        In April 2021 investigators release at *Public Order of the Territory* report about the Pagliarelli mafia clan, showing that they are acting as a shadow justice system with the full collaboration of local entrepreneurs.

2023   Matteo Messina Denaro is captured on the 16th of January.

BIBLIOGRAPHY

Acemoglu, D., De Feo, G. & De Luca, G.D. (2019) "Weak States: Causes and Consequences of the Sicilian Mafia," *Review of Economic Studies,* no. 87, pp. 537-581.

Allan, P. (2021) "Finding the Cure for Scurvy," *Naval History Magazine,* vol. 35, Number 1.

Allum, F., Merlino, R. & Colletti, A. (2019) "Facilitating the Italian Mafia: The Grey Zone of Complicity and Collusion," *South European Society & Politics,* vol. 24, no. 1, pp. 79-101.

Anderson, R.T. (1965) "From Mafia to Cosa Nostra," *The American Journal of Sociology,* vol. 71, no. 3, pp. 302-310.

Bandiera, O. (2003) "Land Reform, the Market for Protection, and the Origins of the Sicilian Mafia: Theory and Evidence," *Journal of Law, Economics, & Organization,* vol. 19, no. 1, pp. 218-244.

Barreca, M. (2000) "Education for Lawfulness in Palermo schools," *Trends in Organized Crime,* vol. 5, no. 3, pp. 45-51.

Benigno, F. (2018) "Rethinking the Origins of the Sicilian Mafia. A New Interpretation," *Crime, Histoire & Sociétés,* vol. 22, pp. 107-130.

Blok, A. (1974) *The Mafia of a Sicilian village, 1860-1960: A Study of Violent Peasant Entrepreneurs,* Basil Blackwell & Mott, Oxford.

Borsellino, R. (2000) "In Spite of Everything, The Popular Anti-Mafia Commitment in Sicily," *Trends in Organized Crime,* vol. 5, no. 3, pp. 58-63.

Buonanno, P., Durante, R., Prarolo, G. & Vanin, P. (2015) "Poor Institutions, Rich Mines: Resource Curse in the Origins of the Sicilian Mafia," *The Economic Journal (London),* vol. 125, no. 586, pp. F175-F202.

Carrillo, E.A. (1991) "The Italian Catholic Church and Communism, 1943-1963," *The Catholic Historical Review,* vol. 77, no. 4, pp. 644-657.

Coluccello, R. (2015) *Challenging the Mafia Mystique: Cosa Nostra from Legitimisation to Denunciation,* Palgrave Macmillan UK, London.

Crawford, F. (1900) *The Rulers of the South, Vol. 1 of 2: Sicily, Calabria, Malta, Macmillan* UK, London.

Cristina, M.S.D. (2000) "The Church's Moral Condemnation of the Mafia and the Clergy's Role in the Parish," *Trends in Organized Crime,* vol. 5, no. 3, pp. 39-45.

Cutrera, A. (1900) *La Mala Vita di Palermo: Contributo di Sociologia Criminale* 2nd edn, Alberto Reber, Palermo.

Dickie, J. (2005) Cosa Nostra: *A History of the Sicilian Mafia,* St. Martin's Publishing Group UK, London

Dickinson, R.E. (1954) "Land Reform in Southern Italy," *Economic Geography,* vol. 30, no. 2, pp. 157-176.

Dimico, A., Isopi, A. & Olsson, O. (2017) "Origins of the Sicilian Mafia: The Market for Lemons," *The Journal of Economic History;* vol. 77, no. 4, pp. 1083-1115.

Ellwood, D.W. (1993) "The 1948 Elections in Italy: A Cold War Propaganda Battle," *Historical Journal of Film, Radio, and Television,* vol. 13, no. 1, pp. 19-33.

Ellwood, D. (2003) "The Propaganda of the Marshall Plan in Italy in a Cold War Context," *Intelligence and National Security,* vol. 18, no. 2, pp. 225-236.

Fana, M. (2019) "Communists Against the Mafia," *Jacobin.*

Franchetti, L. (1876) *Condizioni Politiche e Amministrative della Sicilia.*

Gambetta, D. (1993) *The Sicilian Mafia: The Business of Private Protection,* Harvard University Press.

Jamieson, A. (2000) *The Antimafia: Italy's Fight Against Organized Crime,* Macmillan.

Klimczuk, S. & Warner, G. (2009) *Secret Places, Hidden Sanctuaries,* Sterling Publishing Company.

LaGumina, S.J. (2016) *Operation Husky,* Springer International Publishing, Cham.

Lewis, N. (1967) *The Honoured Society: The Mafia Conspiracy Observed,* Penguin Books.

LiPuma, E. (1989) "Capitalism and the Crimes of Mythology: An Interpretation of the Mafia Mystique," *Journal of Ethnic Studies,* vol. 17, no. 2, pp. 1-21.

Lupo, S. (1993) *Storia Della Mafia: Dalle Origini ai Giorni Nostri,* Donzelli.

Lupo, S. (1997) "The Allies and the Mafia," *Journal of Modern Italian Studies,* vol. 2, no. 1, pp. 21-33.

Martinez, C.E. & Suchman, E.A. (1950) "Letters from America and the 1948 Elections in Italy," *Public Opinion Quarterly,* vol. 14, no. 1, pp. 111-125.

Merlino, R. (2013) "The Sacred Oath of a Secret Ritual: Performing Authority and Submission in the Mafia Initiation Ceremony," *Forum (Edinburgh),* no. 17, pp. np.

Merlino, R. (2014) "Tales of Trauma, Identity, and God: The Memoirs of Mafia Boss Michele Greco and Leonardo Vitale," *The European Review of Organised Crime,* vol. 1, no. 2, pp. 49-75.

Merlino, R. (2014) "Sicilian Mafia, Patron Saints, and Religious Processions: The Consistent Face of an Ever-Changing Criminal Organization," *California Italian Studies* 5.1 (2014): 21. Web.

Merlino, R. (2015) "Devotion and Identity in the History of the Sicilian Mafia. The Case of Provenzano," *Reset Dialogues Civilizations.*

Mori, C. (1933) *The Last Struggle with the Mafia,* Black House.

Murphy, F.J. (1981) "Don Sturzo and the Triumph of Christian Democracy," *Italian Americana,* vol. 7, no. 1, pp. 89-98.

Orlando, L. (2000) "From a Culture of Lawfulness to an Economy of Legality," *Trends in Organized Crime,* vol. 5, no. 3, pp. 7-10.

Orlando, Leoluca (2001), *Fighting the Mafia and Renewing Sicilian Culture,* Encounter Books, 2001, New York.

Pepi, G. (2000) "A Contribution by Local Press to Sicily's Civic Renewal," *Trends in Organized Crime,* vol. 5, no. 3, pp. 64-70.

Pospielovsky, D. (1987) *A History of Soviet Atheism in Theory and Practice, and the True Believer,* St. Martin's Press, New York.

Puccio-Den, D. (2008) "The Sicilian Mafia: Transformation to a Global Evil," *Etnográfica (Oeiras, Portugal),* vol. 12, no. vol. 12 (2), pp. 377-386.

Rakopoulos, T. (2020) "Two Kinds of Mafia Dependency: On Making and Unmaking Mafia Men," *Social Anthropology,* vol. 28, no. 3, pp. 686-699.

Riall, L. (2003) "Elites in Search of Authority: Political Power and Social Order in Nineteenth-Century Sicily," *History Workshop Journal,* vol. 55, no. 1, pp. 25-46.

Santino, U. (2001) "La Mafia è Male, Però...," *Narcomafie* July – August 2001, pp. 48-53.

Schneider, J. (2018) "Fifty Years of Mafia Corruption and Anti-Mafia Reform," *Current Anthropology,* vol. 59, no. S18, pp. S16-S27.

Schneider, J. & Schneider, P. (1976) *Culture and Political Economy in Western Sicily*, Academic.

Sergi, A. (2017) *From Mafia to Organised Crime - A Comparative Analysis of Policing Models,* Springer International Publishing.

Siebert, R. (1996) *Secrets of Life and Death: Women and the Mafia,* Verso.

Siragusa, A. (2000) "Educating for Citizenship, Reconstructing the Identity of Our City," *Trends in Organized Crime,* vol. 5, no. 3, pp. 52-58.

Sonnino, S. (1876) *La Sicilia nel 1876.*

Stille, A. (1996) *Excellent Cadavers: The Mafia and the Death of the First Italian Republic*, Vintage.

Sturzo, L. (1939) *Church and State,* Geoffrey Bles.

Ventresca, R.A. (2003) "The Virgin and the Bear: Religion, Society and the Cold War in Italy," *Journal of Social History,* vol. 37, no. 2, pp. 439-456.

Villari, P. (1878) *Le Lettere Meridionali ed Altri Scritti Sulla Questione Sociale in Italia,* Successori Le Monnier, Firenze.

ACKNOWLEDGEMENTS

My greatest thanks go to my husband, Andrew, who was more confident in my ability to write this book than I was myself. He did not just provide moral support but was actively involved in the process, reading drafts and giving me sound advice. This book is much better than it would have been, thanks to him.

I also want to thank my daughter, Jade, who patiently proofread the book, leaving lots of little comments and suggestions in the margins. My darling, I am so proud of you.

Finally, I would like to thank those people in my life who encouraged me every step of the way. Becky, Monica, Lisa – I am referring to you. Thank you.

NOTES

Chapter 1

1 Vittorio Emanuele Orlando was the Prime Minister of Italy from the 30th of October 1917 to the 23rd of June 1919. Extract from a speech he made in 1925, my translation.

2 Anton Blok, *The Mafia of a Sicilian village, 1860-1960: A Study of Violent Peasant Entrepreneurs,* Basil Blackwell & Mott, Oxford 1974, pp. 30, 31.

3 Leopoldo Franchetti, *Condizioni Politiche e Amministrative della Sicilia,* 1876 – p. 80 my translation.

4 Franchetti 1876 – p. 80 my translation.

5 Franchetti 1876 – p. 80 my translation.

6 Diego Gambetta, *The Sicilian Mafia: the Business of Private Protection,* Harvard University Press 1993, p. 80.

Chapter 2

7 Nicolò Turrisi Colonna (Baron of Buonvicino), *Public Security in Sicily,* my translation.

8 Franchetti 1876, p. 79 – my translation.

9 Sidney Sonnino, *La Sicilia nel 1876,* p. 286 – my translation.

10 Translating the Italian word "questione" as "question" is technically incorrect and a more accurate translation would be the word "issue." However, the common usage of the term 'question' in this particular

case is widely accepted, both in daily life and in academia. For this reason, "la questione romana" will be referred to as "the roman question" in this book.

11 Mack Smith as cited in Blok 1974, p. 39.
12 Lucy Riall, "Elites in Search of Authority: Political Power and Social Order in Nineteenth-Century Sicily," *History Workshop Journal,* 55(1), pp. 36.
13 Blok 1974, p. 61.
14 Blok 1974, p. 66.
15 As in point 4 above, 'la questione meridionale' will be referred to as 'the southern question' in this book.
16 Darren Acemoglu, Giuseppe De Feo and Giacomo Davide De Luca, "Weak States: Causes and Consequences of the Sicilian Mafia," Review of Economic Studies, (87) 2019, p. 541.
17 Pasquale Villari, *Le Lettere Meridionali ed Altri Scritte sulla Questione Sociale in Italia,* Successori Le Monnier, Firenze 1878, p. 20 – my translation.
18 Villari 1878, p. 21 – my translation.
19 Villari 1878, pp. 22, 23 - my translation.
20 Villari 1878, p. 24 - my translation.
21 Villari 1878, p. 25 - my translation.
22 Villari 1878, p. 27 - my translation.
23 Villari 1878, p. 27 - my translation.
24 Villari 1878, pp. 36, 37 - my translation.
25 Villari 1878, p. 39 - my translation.
26 Villari 1878, p. 117 - my translation.
27 Franchetti 1876 p. 33 – my translation.
28 Franchetti 1876, p. 31 – my translation.
29 Philip Allan, "Finding the Cure for Scurvy," *Naval History Magazine* 2015, Volume 35, number 1.
30 Arcangelo Dimico, Alessia Isopi and Ola Olsson, "Origins of the Sicilian Mafia: The Market for Lemons," *The Journal of Economic History 2017* vol. 77, no. 4, p. 1092.
31 Dimico, Isopi, and Olsson 2017, p. 1092.
32 John Dickie, *Cosa Nostra: A History of the Sicilian Mafia,* Sceptre 2005, p. 39.

33 Salvatore Lupo, *Storia della Mafia: Dalle Origini ai Giorni Nostri,* Donzelli 1993.

34 Gambetta 1993, p. 53.

35 Oriana Bandiera, "Land Reform, the Market for Protection, and the Origins of the Sicilian Mafia: Theory and Evidence," *Journal of Law, Economics, & Organisation 2003;* 19(1), pp. 218-244.

36 Dickie 2005.

37 Francis Crawford, *The Rulers of the South,* New York and London: MacMillan & Co. 1900, chapter 5.

38 Franchetti 1876 p. 80 – my translation.

39 Crawford 1900, chapter 5.

40 Dimico, Isopi, and Olsson 2017, p. 1105.

41 Paolo Buonanno, Ruben Durante, Giovanni Prarolo and Paolo Vanin, "Poor Institutions, Rich Mines: Resource Curse in the Origins of the Sicilian Mafia," *The Economic Journal, London 2015,* 125(586), pp. F175-F202.

42 Dickie 2005.

43 Robert T. Anderson, "From Mafia to Cosa Nostra," *The American Journal of Sociology* 71(3) 1965, p. 308.

44 Acemoglu, De Feo et al. 2019, p. 546.

45 My translation.

46 Acemoglu, De Feo et al. 2019, p. 544.

47 My translation.

48 My translation.

Chapter 3

49 The interrogation of Tommaso Buscetta.

50 Gambetta 1993, p. 137.

51 Franchetti 1876 p. 81 – my translation.

52 Crawford 1900, chapter 5.

53 Giuseppe Pitrè 1889, Vol. II, p. 292.

54 The interrogation of Tommaso Buscetta.

55 The interrogation of Antonino Calderone.

56 Villari 1878, p. 23 - my translation.

57 Francesco Benigno "Rethinking the Origins of the Sicilian Mafia. A New Interpretation," *Crime, Histoire & Sociétés,* vol. 22 2018, p. 120.

58 Luigi Natoli, *I Beati Paoli*, 1921 – my translation.

59 Natoli 1921 – my translation.

60 The interrogation of Tommaso Buscetta.

61 Extract from the police report drafted by the officer who took the witness' statement.

62 Giovanni Alfredo Cesareo Cesareo 1920 – my translation.

63 Rino Coluccello, *Challenging the Mafia Mystique: Cosa Nostra from Legitimisation to Denunciation,* Palgrave Macmillan UK, London 2015, p. 109.

64 The interrogation of Leonardo Vitale.

65 The interrogation of Salvatore Contorno.

66 The interrogation of Tommaso Buscetta.

67 The interrogation of Antonino Calderone.

68 The interrogation of Antonino Calderone.

69 The interrogation of Tommaso Buscetta.

70 Gambetta, p. 135.

71 Time, 19 April 2019.

72 Alexander Stille, *Excellent Cadavers: The Mafia and the Death of the First Italian Republic,* Vintage 1996, p. 95.

Chapter 4

73 Anderson 1965, p. 308.

74 The interrogation of Antonino Calderone.

75 The interrogation of Leonardo Messina.

76 The interrogation of Antonino Calderone.

77 The interrogation of Tommaso Buscetta.

78 Rossella Merlino, "The Sacred Oath of a Secret Ritual: Performing Authority and Submission in the Mafia Initiation Ceremony," *Forum (Edinburgh) 2013,* no. 17.

79 Anderson 1965, p. 302.

80 The interrogation of Antonino Calderone.

81 The interrogation of Tommaso Buscetta.

82 The interrogation of Gaspare Mutolo.

83 Dickie 2005.

84 Merlino 2013, pp. np.

85 Dickie 2005.

86 Rossella Merlino, "Sicilian Mafia, Patron Saints, and Religious Processions: The Consistent Face of an Ever-Changing Criminal Organisation," California Italian Studies 2014, 5(1), pp. 109 - 129.

87 Merlino 2014, pp. 116, 117.

88 Merlino 2014, p. 112, 113.

89 Merlino 2014, p. 115.

90 The interrogation of Leonardo Messina.

91 Merlino 2014, p. 124.

92 Merlino 2014, p. 117.

This is a play on words, changing the surname Bontade to Bontà, which signifies kindness.

93 Merlino 2014, p. 114. "See how human judgement is often wrong!"

94 Merlino 2014, p. 114.

95 Norman Lewis, The Honoured Society: the Mafia Conspiracy Observed, Penguin Books 1964, p. 17.

96 Anderson 1965, p. 305.

97 Discovery News, 17 April 2006.

98 Rossella Merlino, "Devotion and Identity in the History of the Sicilian Mafia. The Case of Provenzano," Reset Dialogues 2015, pp. np.

99 Merlino 2015, pp. np.

100 Merlino 2015, pp. np.

Chapter 5

101 Umberto Santino, "La Mafia è Male, Però...," Narcomafie July – August 2001, pp. 48-53.

102 Santino 2001.

Chapter 6

103 Salvatore LaGumina, Operation Husky, Springer International Publishing 2016, p. 29.

104 Antimafia Commission 1976 .

Chapter 8

105 National Catholic Reporter, 30 May 2017.

106 Dmitry V. Pospielovsky, *A History of Soviet Atheism in Theory and Practice, and the True Believer,* St. Martin's Press, New York 1987, p. 65.

107 National Catholic Reporter, 30 May 2017.

108 National Catholic Reporter, 30 May 2017.

109 Merlino 2014, p. 117.

110 Santino 2001.

111 Collettiva, 13 February 2021.

112 Dickie 2005, p. 214.

113 Marta Fana, *Communists Against the Mafia*, Jacobin 2019, pp. np.

114 Stille 1996, p. 19.

115 D. W. Ellwood "The Propaganda of the Marshall Plan in Italy in a Cold War Context," *Intelligence and National Security 2003,* vol. 18, no. 2, p. 21.

116 C. E. Martinez and E. A. Suchman, "Letters from America and the 1948 Elections in Italy," *Public Opinion Quarterly* 1950, vol. 14, no. 1, p. 113.

117 Congressman Anfuso's 1948 letter regarding the Italian election provided by the Center for Migration Studies (New York) – my translation

118 Martinez and Suchman 1950, p. 115.

119 Martinez and Suchman 1950, p. 118.

120 Ellwood 2003, p. 21.

121 Robert A. Ventresca, "The Virgin and the Bear: Religion, Society and the Cold War in Italy," *Journal of Social History,* 37(2) 2003, p. 445.

122 Ventresca 2003, p. 444.

123 Ventresca 2003, p. 445.

124 Ventresca 2003, p. 445.

125 Ellwood 2003, p. 24.

126 Ellwood 2003, p. 29.

127 Santino 2001.

128 Santino 2001.

129 Merlino 2014, p. 110.

130 The Christian Science Monitor 1995.

Chapter 9

131 Antimafia Commission 1972, Vol. 1, p. 114.

132 Pezzino as cited in Acemoglu, De Feo and De Luca 2019, p. 547.

133 New York Times, 25 February 1987.

134 The interrogation of Salvatore Allegra.

135 Antimafia Commission 1972, Vol. 1: 873-952; Antimafia Commission 1976.

Chapter 10

136 Jane Schneider, "Fifty Years of Mafia Corruption and Anti-Mafia Reform," *Current Anthropology* 2018, vol. 59, no. S18 pp. S16-S27.

137 Schneider 2018, pp. S16-S27.

138 Antimafia Duemila, 26 January 2014.

139 Stille 1996, p. 391.

140 The Christian Science Monitor, 17 *February 1983.*

141 La Repubblica, 1982.

142 Lodato as cited in Jamieson 2000, p. 137.

143 Santino 2001.

144 Jamieson 2000, p. 138.

145 The Christian Science Monitor, 17 *February 1983.*

146 Stille 1996, p. 124.

147 Stille 1996, p. 124.

148 Theodoros Rakopoulos, "Two Kinds of Mafia Dependency: On Making and Unmaking Mafia Men," *Social Anthropology* **28**(3) 2020, pp. 686-699.

149 A. Sergi, *From Mafia to Organised Crime A Comparative Analysis of Policing Models, 2017.*

150 The interrogation of Salvatore Contorno.

151 The Chicago Tribune, 13 August 1985.

152 Stille 1996, p. 171.

153 Jamieson 2000, p. 31.

154 Stille 1996, p. 174.

155 Stille 1996, p. 174.

Chapter 11

156 Stille 1996, p. 383.

157 The interrogation of Leonardo Messina.

158 Stille 1996, p. 363.

159 Stille 1996, p. 364.

160 La Repubblica, 23 June 1992.

161 La Repubblica, 23 June 1992.
162 Siebert 1996, p. 291.
163 Jamieson 2000, pp. 131, 132.
164 Stille 1996, p. 367.
165 Redazione La Pressa 2017.
166 The Independent, 21 September 1992.
167 Siebert 1996, p. 95, 96.
168 Stille 1996, p. 325.
169 The Florentine, 24 May 2012.
170 Castelvetrano Prima Pagina, 14 September 2021.
171 National Catholic Register, 27 May 2013.
172 National Catholic Register, 10 May 2013.
173 National Catholic Register, 27 May 2013.
174 The interrogation of Salvatore Grigoli.

Chapter 12
175 Deborah Puccio-Den, *The Sicilian Mafia: transformation to a global evil, Etnográfica (Oeiras, Portugal),* 12(vol. 12 (2)) 2008, pp. 377-386.
176 Deutsche Welle, 13 September 2021.
177 Puccio-Den 2008, pp. 377-386.
178 Puccio-Den 2008, pp. 377-386.
179 Puccio-Den 2008, pp. 377-386.
180 Mario Barreca, "Education for Lawfulness in Palermo schools," *Trends in Organized Crime* 2000, vol. 5, no. 3, p. 46.
181 Rushda Majeed and Laura Bacon, *Innovations for Successful Societies Innovations for Successful Societies,* Woodrow Wilson School of Public and International Affairs and the Bobst Center for Peace and Justice *Series,* p. 2.
182 Majeed and Bacon 2012, p. 4.
183 I Siciliani Giovani, Associazione Antimafie Rita Atria - Luglio 2012.
184 Giovanni Pepi, "A Contribution by Local Press to Sicily's Civic Renewal," *Trends in Organized Crime* 2000, vol. 5, no. 3, p. 65.
185 Pepi 2000, p. 65.
186 Pepi 2000, p. 67.
187 The Art Newspaper, 28 May 2021.

188 The Art Newspaper, 28 May 2021.
189 BlogSicilia.it 22 May 2021.

Chapter 13
190 Mons. Salvatore Di Cristina 2000, pp. 41, 42.
191 National Catholic Register, 10 May 2013.
192 The Guardian, 22 December 2020.
193 Crux, 22 September 2017.
194 Catholic News Service, 5 October 2021.

Chapter 14
195 Orlando 2000, p.9.
196 Felia Allum, Rossella Merlino & Alessandro Colletti, "Facilitating the Italian Mafia: The Grey Zone of Complicity and Collusion," *South European Society & Politics* 2019, vol. 24, no. 1, pp. 86, 87.
197 Corriere Della Sera, 5 November 2003.
198 Procura della Repubblica presso il Tribunale di Palermo, Direzione Distrettuale Antimafia, N. 12790/02 R.G. D.D.A. Notizie di Reato, Memoria del Pubblico Ministero – my translation.
199 La Repubblica, 25 March 2014.
200 Il Post, 15 September 2021.
201 Agrigento Notizie, 17 January 2022.
202 Agrigento Notizie, 17 January 2022.
203 MeridioNews Edizione Sicilia, 2 February 2021.
204 Il Post, 15 September 2021.
205 Vice, 11 August 2020.
206 The Guardian, 20 June 2019.
207 The Guardian, 20 June 2019.
208 The Guardian, 12 March 2017.
209 Vice, 11 August 2020.
210 The Financial Times, 24 February 2021.
211 Reuters, 21 March 2021.
212 BBC News, 6 June 2021.
213 BBC News, 6 June 2021.
214 BBC News, 6 June 2021.

Printed in Great Britain
by Amazon

20855773R00169